Tanya

Anya Hursh

© 2024 by CAM Books, a wholly owned, for-profit subsidiary of Christian Aid Ministries, Berlin, Ohio.

All rights reserved. No part of this book may be reproduced or stored in any retrieval system, in any form or by any means, electronic or mechanical, without written permission from the publisher except for brief quotations embodied in critical articles and reviews.

ISBN: 978-1-63813-355-1

Cover and interior design: Kristi Yoder

Printed in the USA

Published by:
CAM Books
P.O. Box 355
Berlin, Ohio 44610 USA
Phone: 330.893.4828
Fax: 330.893.4893
cambooks.org

Tanya

A story of God's redeeming grace—
of triumph over circumstances.

Anya Hursh

Dedication

Dedicated to Marina, Bogdonna, and Anechka.
May the redeeming grace that radiated from your
mother's life be yours as well.
I see her inner beauty and faithfulness reflected in you.

Acknowledgments

I am indebted to so many people who have invested in my life and in this book.

Tanya, without you this book would never have existed. Thank you for allowing me to be a part of your life, for sharing stories when it would have been easier to be silent, and for reflecting God's redeeming grace to the rest of us.

Valentine, thank you for being willing to let your wife's story be told, even though there are things you wish you had done differently. While you can't rewrite the past, I see you striving, by the grace of God, to grow in your relationship with Him and to be the father your children need.

Marina and Bogdonna, thank you for your interest and encouragement in this book. Your courage in spite of deep grief blesses me. You remind me of your mother in so many beautiful ways. You will always be so special to me!

Anechka, I wish you knew your mother as well as I did. She loved you so much and wished with all her heart to be able to care for you. In those dark days of grief following your mother's death, you filled my life with sunshine. You are still my sunshine.

The ladies in the InkCourage writers' group—Amy Schlabach, Rachel Zimmerman, Mary Derstine, and Karissa Horst—I don't know where this book would be if it weren't for you. Thank you for critiquing and commenting and coaching me through the writing of this book. You and your words have left a great impact on me and my writing.

Aunt Verna Hahn, thank you for believing even when I doubted—for encouraging me on even when I trembled. Your coaching and prayer support have made a profound difference in my life. I will ever be indebted to you.

Alisa Mast, you did so much for me during this whole project. Thank you for your willingness to listen, encourage, and support. Every writer needs a friend like you.

My school students, you are my favorite fans. Thank you for your interest in my writing projects. I love to see your talent developing. It won't be long until you pass me up in the writers' world. Keep it up!

The CAM Books team. Thank you for your patience and perseverance, even when I failed to meet deadlines. You have taken this manuscript and created a book. I owe so much to you. A special thank you to Dennis Kline for his thorough editing—for polishing and perfecting and making this book easier to read.

Most of all, I am grateful to God. He is the Author of Tanya's story. As I ponder Tanya's life, I am grateful to know that the redeeming grace that laced her life is available to all the rest of us. To God be all the glory and honor. He alone is worthy!

Tanya

Contents

	Prologue	13
1.	Boarding School	15
2.	Hit by a Brick	21
3.	A Bad Start to a New Year	29
4.	Worrying Won't Help	35
5.	From Student to Slave	41
6.	The Nightmare	49
7.	The Funeral	57
8.	Valley of Grief	63
9.	Life in Kyiv	73
10.	Uncle Yuri	83
11.	More Changes	93

12. Adjustments	101
13. The Landlady's Son	107
14. Is This Love?	113
15. A Renter No Longer	121
16. Mama's Story	127
17. The Wedding	135
18. Motherhood	143
19. Answered Through Lilacs	149
20. Growing Pains	153
21. Daycare Daze	159
22. The Reflection in the Mirror	165
23. God's Gift	173
24. The Mysterious Magazine	183
25. Buried in the Barn	189
26. The Murderer's Daughter	195
27. "Save the House!"	203
28. Bartender Again	209
29. A New Job	215
30. From Slacks to Skirts	219
31. The Strange Believers	227
32. Resurrection Morning	235
33. God's Smile of Approval	243
34. Tough Love	249
35. Part of the Family	253
36. The School of God	259
37. Answered Through Pumpkin Seeds	267
38. Oh, Happy Day	271
39. The Resurrection Power	277
40. War!	281
41. The Smoking Battle	287

42. Released	295
43. A Lost Battle	301
44. A Gift of Grace	305
45. The Shock	313
46. Abortion?	319
47. "You Know the Way"	325
48. Now Where?	331
49. "Lord, Lead Us"	339
50. "What Next, Lord?"	345
51. Solomia	351
52. Safe in the Arms of Jesus	359
53. Pain Is Never Wasted	367
54. Limitless Love	373
55. Death's Door	377
56. The Missionary in the Hospital	385
57. "I Will Lift Up My Eyes"	393
58. Trials and Temptations	401
59. The Pilot	407
60. "I Want to Go to Jesus"	411
61. Faithful to the End	415
Epilogue	421
Author's Note	423
About the Author	427

Prologue

I climbed into Lina's van, looking forward to shopping with my friend. As I slid into the seat, I noticed the smell of alcohol and cigarettes. I glanced at the seat behind me and saw a man and a lady. They looked like villagers, but I did not recognize them. I looked questioningly at Lina.

"This is Valentine and Tanya," she said, introducing the couple to me. "They needed a ride to town, and I said they could ride along with us."

"Of course!" I said, nodding my head. "There's plenty of room!" Hitchhiking was a normal part of life in Ukraine.

There was something about the deep sadness in Tanya's eyes that caught my attention. I wondered who she was and why I had not seen her before.

After Lina had dropped off her passengers, I voiced my questions. "Who are those people? Are they from our village?"

Lina smiled. "It's a long story. Yes, they are from our village, and Valentine is working for my dad. Do you remember the man who buried a boy in his barn?"

I nodded. Of course I did. The whole village knew about that. It was something we would never forget.

"Well, Tanya is his daughter."

Little did I realize that these strangers would one day become an important part of my life, and that Tanya would become one of my dearest friends. But God was writing a story—a story of redemption. Of bringing beauty from ashes.

chapter 1

Boarding School

1997

Clutching her backpack tightly, Tanya stepped off the bus. As it roared away, she stood still, soaking up the beauty of the familiar scenery. It was wonderful to be back in the quiet village. She smiled, watching a stork glide overhead. *Before I left, I never realized how beautiful Kryvoshyintsi is. And who would have guessed I would even miss the storks? City life just can't compare to the peaceful beauty of the country!* She slung her backpack over her shoulder and strode toward home.

Tanya's younger sister Svetta was sweeping the walk when she neared the gate. With a cry of delight, Svetta threw down the broom. "Welcome home!" she cried, wrapping her arms around Tanya's waist.

Tanya dropped a kiss on her sister's upturned face. "It's good to be home. I missed you." She looked around. "Where are Papa and Mama? In the garden?"

"Mama is in the garden, but Papa is at work."

"At work? He's usually home by now."

"He came home at six like usual. But there was a fire at the other end of the village, so he had to go help fight it. He should be back soon."

Tanya set her backpack inside the enclosed veranda and hurried out to the garden. "Mama, I'm home!" she called.

"Welcome back, Tanya. It's good to see you." Natasha gave her daughter a welcoming smile. "I missed you."

"I missed you too, Mama. Here, let me take that pumpkin." She took the pumpkin Natasha was carrying.

"Thank you!" Natasha said. "I'll grab some other vegetables, then I'll be right in. I want to hear all about your first week at boarding school."

How good it felt to be at home! Tanya set the pumpkin on the table and peered into the kettle on the stove. Ah, Mama's *borsch!*[1] Her favorite! She didn't mind that it was no longer hot. She filled a bowl and sat at the kitchen table, savoring each bite.

Had it really been only a week since she had left home? It seemed longer than that. When she had graduated from high school, she had never dreamed how hard it would be to go to boarding school. Being sixteen years old was bringing challenges she had not anticipated.

Tanya looked up as her mother entered the house with an armful of fresh vegetables. "Mama, it's so good to be home! Your borsch never tasted better."

A pleased look crossed Natasha's face. "Thanks, Tanya. It's no different than usual. You're just extra hungry. Are you getting enough to eat at the boarding school?"

"Yes, I'm doing fine." Tanya's eyes twinkled. "Actually, I made an agreement with the other girls in my room. I do the cooking for the

---

[1] A favorite vegetable soup including red beets and cabbage.

four of us if they buy the groceries. I call it a fair trade."

"That's nice." Natasha filled a cup with *compote*[2] and sat down across from her daughter. "But when do you find time to do all that cooking? It seems to me the other girls are making you work too hard."

"No, Mama," Tanya laughed. "It's not a problem. I'd get lonely in the evenings if I didn't have the cooking to do."

"How do the other girls spend their evenings?" Natasha asked as she began sawing the pumpkin in half. "Are you making friends with them?"

"We get along all right, but we don't have much in common. They're city girls, and I'm just a poor village girl. They spend their evenings hanging out with boys, going to movies, or relaxing in the parks."

Natasha looked up from where she was spreading the pumpkin seeds out to dry. "Tanya, I want you to have friends, but you need to be careful."

Tanya nodded. "I know, Mama. And our dormitory is in a dangerous part of the city. I don't like the looks of the men who hang around the area." She shuddered. "I'm too scared to be out late at night. Besides, there's a strict curfew. We have to be in by ten o'clock, or we'll be locked outside for the night."

"Oh, please be careful." Concern filled Natasha's eyes as she looked at her daughter. "I never imagined how hard it would be to see you go off and study. I worry about you. May the guardian angels keep you from harm."

"Don't worry, Mama. I'll be all right. Policemen guard the dormitories every night."

Just then the door burst open and Tanya's father, Mikoli, entered, bringing the smell of smoke with him. "Well, well, look who's here. I believe it's the young lady who's studying in Bila Tserkva!" He gave his daughter a slight smile. "It seems like a long time since I've seen you."

---

[2] A sweetened fruit drink.

Boarding School

Eleven-year-old Svetta, who had followed her father into the house, giggled. "Papa, she was just gone for a week!"

"I know," Mikoli chuckled. "But I missed her."

"It's good to see you too, Papa." Tanya's heart warmed at her father's words. Papa was a nice man when he wasn't drunk, but compliments like this were a rare treat. "Did you get the fire out?"

"Yes, the fire is out, and we can sleep in peace." Mikoli sighed as he sat down on a chair. "If only people would think! An old *babushka*[3] who lives at the other end of the village was burning trash, and the wind blew a spark onto her barn roof. Before she realized what was happening, the straw in the hayloft started burning. Thankfully, we got there in time to save the lower part of the barn. The animals all survived—except maybe the mice in the loft." Mikoli chuckled as he reached for a cup. "Could you get me a drink? The smoke still tickles my throat."

Tanya jumped up and filled his mug with compote. It felt wonderful to be sitting at home with her family. Much better than living with a bunch of strangers in a dormitory! If only she wouldn't have to go back.

The weekend at home passed too quickly. Early Monday morning, Tanya caught the bus back to Bila Tserkva. She smiled as she peered into the bag of food her mother had sent along. *Ah, pumpkin seeds!* How she would enjoy that healthy snack!

Each morning Tanya woke early enough to drink a cup of tea and eat a *butterbrod*[4] before walking the few kilometers to school. It would have been faster to take the bus, but Tanya didn't like to spend her hard-earned *hryvnia*[5] on bus fare every day. Besides, she was used to walking and enjoyed the time alone.

Tanya poured her heart into her studies. Her teachers were strict,

---

[3] An elderly lady or grandmother.

[4] A slice of bread often topped with meat or cheese.

[5] The basic Ukrainian monetary unit.

but she respected them. They learned to love this quiet, studious girl.

Tanya soon joined an evening school, taking additional classes. These classes helped fill the empty hours after school. However, as winter drew near, the days became shorter and darkness came early. With the streetlights shedding only feeble rays onto the dark streets, Tanya dreaded the walk back to her dormitory after classes. Fear stalked her every step of the way.

Finally she could no longer handle it. She dropped out of evening school and spent long evenings at the dormitory. Books became her constant companions, and she borrowed them from anyone she could. Hours became minutes when she was immersed in a book.

She got along fine with the girls in her dorm, but they usually spent their evenings partying with their boyfriends. Occasionally they would invite Tanya to join them. She usually declined, but one evening, after much persuading, she agreed.

It felt good to hang out with them. They walked through the city park and then headed for the theater. Tanya didn't like to spend her precious money on a ticket, but she didn't want to look poorer than the other students. Reluctantly she bought a ticket, determined to enjoy every minute of the show.

As the movie dragged on, Tanya became nervous. It grew later and later. Would the movie never end? What if they didn't get back to the dorm before curfew? Finally she could stand it no longer. She slipped through the crowd and ran down the back streets to the dormitory.

Tanya was out of breath by the time she reached the dormitory. To her relief, the door was still unlocked.

A few minutes later her friends came barging in. They were laughing and talking. "Tanya, you should have stayed. You missed the most exciting part."

Tanya didn't care that she had missed the ending. She decided she would never again go to the theater. It cost too much money and wasn't that interesting anyway. Most of all, it wasn't worth the risk of missing curfew.

One night a few weeks later, Tanya awoke with a start. What was that noise? She lay rigid in bed, her ears straining. There it was again. It sounded like someone at the window! She turned toward the window, and her heart chilled. A man was trying to pry open the window, his face contorted with evil. Fear tingled through Tanya's body. *What if he breaks in? Where can I hide?* Tanya covered her face with her blanket, shivering in terror.

The seconds seemed like hours as the man fumbled with the window. Suddenly there was a shout, and the blue lights of a police car flashed in the night. Tanya quivered with relief. Help had come; someone had alerted the police. They would take care of the villain.

Gradually Tanya's racing heart slowed, but the terror of the night lingered. Wide awake, she turned restlessly on her bed. When she finally drifted off to sleep, horrible nightmares tormented her.

Would city life never be safe?

chapter 2

Hit by a Brick

1998

Sunlight filtered through the lace curtains as a rooster gave his morning call. Tanya rubbed the sleep from her eyes. The shout of a cow herder and the lowing of a cow told her the village cows were already on their way to graze in the pasture. Although Tanya had enjoyed the boarding school, she had not liked the city. At the end of the school year, she had joyfully moved home for the summer.

Svetta, who shared the bed with Tanya, stirred. "It's fun to sleep with my big sister again," she murmured with a yawn.

"Well, I'm no longer sleeping, so you shouldn't be either!" Tanya gave her sister a playful swat as she pulled off the covers. "Come on, sis. It's time to get up. What are you going to do today? Will Mama make us hoe weeds in the garden?"

Svetta giggled. "Maybe. But it's much more fun when you are here to help."

Suddenly Svetta sat up straight. "Oh, Tanya! I had the most amazing dream last night!"

"Really? What was it?"

Svetta's face shone with excitement. "I dreamed you were married!"

"You silly girl!" Tanya exclaimed. "Are you making this up?"

"No! I really had a dream about you. And it seemed so true. I dreamed you were married to a nice man, and you were holding the sweetest baby. She looked just like me when I was little. Her name was Marina!"

"You funny girl! I still think you are making this up! Anyway, who says I'll ever get married? You'll probably get married before I do."

Svetta shook her head. "No, I won't. This dream was so real. I think it's going to happen!"

"I guess we'll just have to wait and see," Tanya said. "Come on. Let's go eat breakfast."

Papa had already gone to work, and Mama was milking the goats. Tanya decided to cook some *kasha*[1] for breakfast. It felt good to make food for her family again.

After breakfast, Svetta took the goats out to graze. She staked them in the pasture next to the pond, alongside a few other goats and cows. Tanya joined her mother in the potato patch. The potatoes were barely peeking through the ground, but the garden was already carpeted with weeds.

"Mama," Svetta called when she came back, "may I go play with Olya? I told her I would come over to play with her today."

Natasha thought a bit before replying. "I'd like you to hoe a row of potatoes first. It's not good for you to play all the time."

---

[1] A traditional Ukrainian porridge made with oatmeal, buckwheat, or cream of wheat.

A pout crossed Svetta's face. "But I don't want to hoe potatoes. It's too hot."

"Svetta, stop complaining, or…" Mama didn't finish the sentence, but Svetta could guess what she meant. Sullenly she took a hoe and began to work.

Tanya, an ever-observant big sister, remarked, "Hey, Svetta. You're doing a great job! I can't believe how fast you can work for an eleven-year-old."

Svetta's cheerful disposition soon returned, and the trio laughed and talked as their hoes flew back and forth.

Summer days brought plenty of activity for the Dmitruk family. Mikoli was busy at the collective farm where he worked as a driver, and Tanya and her mother spent many hours working in the garden. Svetta also helped, but she was always eager to play with the neighbor children.

The cherries turned from green to pink, and finally they were ready to pick. Tanya was delighted to spend the morning hiding in the cherry tree. As she climbed from branch to branch picking the ruby fruit, her bucket slowly filled with cherries. It brought back fond memories of when she was a little girl.

The laughter of children floated across the summer breeze. From her vantage point high in the tree, Tanya could see Svetta and the neighbor children playing down the street. It looked like they were having a lively game of tag.

Suddenly a shriek of pain rang through the air. Startled, Tanya gripped the tree branch as she peered down the street to where the children were playing. Svetta was running toward home, screaming. Tanya slid down the tree and dashed to meet her sister. "What happened,

Svetta?" she panted. "Are you all right? Your head is bloody!"

"Where's Mama?" Svetta cried. "I need Mama!"

Tanya led Svetta to the house, then ran to the garden to find her mother.

"Whatever happened, child?" Natasha wondered as she dipped a washcloth in the bucket of water. Gently she wiped away the blood and cleaned the gash on the back of Svetta's head.

"He threw a brick at me!" Svetta sobbed. Her words were laced with anger and pain.

"Who did?" Natasha demanded. "Why would anyone throw a brick at you?"

"Vasya did."

"Vasya? But he's just a little boy. He's only about six years old. How could he have hurt you?" Natasha squeezed ointment onto the gash and began wrapping gauze around Svetta's head.

"We were playing tag," explained Svetta. Her sobs subsided as she continued her story. "Every time I got caught, I would chase Vasya and tag him. He was the easiest one to catch. But he could never catch me." A hint of a smile sparkled through her tears. "He tried so hard to catch me, but I always got away. He was mad at me, so when I wasn't looking, he picked up a brick and flung it at me." Tears welled up in her eyes again. "It hit me right on my head. Oh, it hurts!"

"Well, I guess you learned your lesson the hard way. It doesn't pay to be unkind to little children. Why don't you lie down until lunchtime? That might help you feel better."

Natasha turned to Tanya. "You should get back to your cherry picking. I'd like to can some compote this afternoon."

By the time twilight cloaked the village, the cherries were picked and many jars of compote were filled and sealed. Svetta was her cheerful self again, though her head still ached. When her father came home from work, she told him in great detail what had happened.

Mikoli laughed heartily. "Well, I guess you got what you deserved. Vasya is a feisty little fellow. But you are too big to be playing with him." He looked at Natasha. "I think you should keep this young lady busy in the garden so she doesn't have time to play on the streets. We don't want this to happen again."

Svetta's wound healed nicely, and a week or two later the scar was barely visible. However, headaches began to plague her.

"You just need more time to recover from your injury," her mother said. "It can take a long time for something like that to heal. Besides, this heat is enough to give anyone a headache."

It was true. The summer sun beat down mercilessly. And though an occasional cloudy day brought a little relief, no rain fell.

One day Svetta ran out to the garden where Mama and Tanya were working. "Mama, what is the priest doing by our well?"

"The priest? I don't know. Maybe their well is dry, and he came for some water."

The well the Dmitruk family used was a village well shared among the neighbors. The priest, who lived farther down the road, had his own well.

"No, Mama. I don't think so. He's at the well with the two ladies that sing with him. I think they are having a ceremony of some kind."

"Oh, now I understand." Natasha glanced up at the cloudless sky. "They came to bless the water and ask God to send rain."

"God sends us rain? How does He do that?" Svetta wondered. "I thought the rain just falls from the clouds. You mean God sends it?"

"I don't understand it all," her mother said. "The rain does come from the clouds, but they say God sends the clouds. I don't know if I believe it."

"I wonder if their ceremony will work. I'll watch and see if God sends rain."

Hit by a Brick

Sure enough. The next day storm clouds filled the sky, and the family waited eagerly for the rain that would refresh their parched crops. But before the clouds produced any rain, strong winds came and blew them away.

"But, Mama!" Svetta cried out in dismay. "I thought God would hear their prayers!"

"I'm sorry, child. I don't know what to believe. In school they taught us that there is no God. Now they say maybe there is. It's all confusing to me. If there is a God, I don't think He sees us or cares about us."

All too soon summer vacation was over, and it was time for Tanya to return to Bila Tserkva for her studies. As always, the peer pressure that came from living and studying with so many young people overwhelmed her. She was often embarrassed about her clothing. Though she wanted to fit in, she found it impossible.

Tanya enjoyed her studies, especially the sewing course. She learned how to cut, serge, sew, and transform a piece of cloth into something practical or beautiful. She dreamed of someday getting a job in a sewing factory.

Pani[2] Pavilevna was the head teacher and the director of the school. Most of the students avoided her, but there was something about her that Tanya liked. Behind her rough exterior was an attractive gentleness.

Although Tanya went home most weekends, the poor potato crop affected how often she could make the trip. It had been discouraging to dig the little potato marbles from the dry clumps of dirt. Potatoes were a staple part of Ukrainian cuisine, and the Dmitruks always planted plenty, hoping they would have enough to sell some. But this year they

---

[2] A feminine term of respect.

barely had enough for themselves. Others in the village also suffered from the dry summer.

"If only you would have come when we needed you," Tanya muttered under her breath as she hurried to school one rainy morning. Her umbrella did little to keep the pouring rain from soaking her clothes. "Rain, rain, rain. You are too late to help us now." Tanya scowled at the gray sky.

By the time the long, dry summer had ended, it was clear the crops were a failure. The sun that had beat down day after day now remained hidden behind a sheet of gray. Rain drizzled almost daily, and the sidewalks oozed with mud. *Is this what the priest was praying for? He should have prayed sooner if it takes God this long to answer.*

The gray weather dampened her spirits, and something else also gnawed at her heart. On her last visit home, Tanya had noticed that something seemed wrong with Svetta. She seemed listless and irritable.

And she still has those headaches, Tanya fretted. *If anything, they are getting worse.*

A Bad Start to a New Year

1998-1999

As the end of the year drew near, Tanya traveled home for her long-awaited two-week vacation. The village was cloaked in a blanket of white. Smoke curled from the chimneys, and a warm glow of light spilled from the windows and into the quiet evening. Tanya's heart rejoiced as she ran and slid on the snow-packed path leading toward home. The holidays had arrived, bringing cheer and festivity.

The day before New Year's Eve was a flurry of activity. Tanya helped her mother cook and clean to prepare for the big holiday. Tanya deftly plucked the feathers off an old hen they were butchering. What a treat it would be to have gelled chicken broth again. After the hen was cooked and tender, Tanya deboned it and arranged the meat in shallow bowls. Tanya knew the secret in making the delicious gel was to cook the broth with the chicken feet. Carefully she strained the hot broth into bowls and carried them out to the porch to cool.

By New Year's Eve, the enclosed porch had the rich smell of tasty foods. The house shone clean, and excitement filled the air. Uncle Sergei and his family had arrived to celebrate the coming of the new year. Aunt Elena brought cabbage rolls, cakes, and sweets. What a feast they would have.

A shadow crossed Tanya's face when her father entered the house carrying several bottles of beer. "You can't celebrate New Year's without this stuff," he joked as he put the bottles on the table. This was the part of the holidays that Tanya dreaded the most. Hopefully Papa would not drink too much—just enough to make him happy.

The party began. Smoke from the cigarettes hung in the air, mingling with the savory smells of food. In the corner of the room stood a small pine tree that Svetta had helped Papa cut in the forest. Tanya looked at it longingly. Unlike the trees in other homes in the village, their tree had no lights or gifts gracing it. But she knew better than to complain. And anyway, she was too grown up to need gifts and lights to make her happy. Being poor was just a part of their family's life.

As usual, her cousins shoveled food onto their plates in an unspoken competition to see who could get the most. Music from the old radio blared in the background. As the clock neared midnight, everyone was in good spirits. Mikoli continued to guzzle down beer, but Uncle Sergei sipped only a little.

"Hey, Mikoli," Uncle Sergei chided, "are you sure you want to drink that much?"

"It's New Year's, man! There's no better way to celebrate." Mikoli shook with laughter. "Come on. Let's toast for our health."

Uncle Sergei added a little more to his cup and toasted with Mikoli. "Yes, we need health. Especially little Svetta here." He flashed his niece a sympathetic smile. "Are your headaches still bothering you?"

Svetta nodded. "But on a night like tonight, I try to forget about it." She giggled as she reached for another piece of candy. "New Year's Eve is too exciting to be sick!"

"You got that right!" Mikoli laughed.

As the night wore on, Tanya found herself too tired to party any longer. She crawled into bed beside her sister, who was already sleeping soundly. From the refuge of her bedroom, she could hear the noise of the party. She shivered as she heard her parents arguing and hollering at each other. *Is this really the way to start a new year?*

The winter sun was high in the sky when Svetta woke Tanya. "Come on, Tanya. Get up. Let's go caroling!"

Tanya felt groggy from her late night. Papa and Mama were still snoring as the girls crept through their room and out to the kitchen.

"Svetta, I'm too old to go caroling. No one would give me candy. It's just for children."

Disappointment crossed Svetta's face. "But I want to go!"

"You can go with the neighbor children," Tanya encouraged her sister. "Make sure you bring back some candy for me." She flashed Svetta a smile.

Svetta bundled up and headed out the door. Tanya watched as her sister tramped down the road. Even in her winter clothes, she looked frail. *What is causing her headaches?* Tanya wondered. *How sick will she have to be before Mama and Papa take her to the hospital?*

Tanya surveyed the messy kitchen and dining room. *Is this what holidays are all about?* Wearily she cleared the table and put away the leftovers from the night before. She heated water to wash the dishes, then tackled the bits of food stuck onto the crusty dishes. She scrubbed hard, venting her frustration on the dirty dishes.

Knock. Knock. Knock.

Tanya hurried to open the door. Three rosy-cheeked village children stepped inside. "May we carol for you?" one asked.

Before Tanya had a chance to reply, they were singing. Their childish voices rang through the house. While they sang, Tanya scurried to the kitchen to find a treat for them. She scooped up a few pieces of candy left from last night's party and returned to the carolers. She smiled as she listened to them sing. It was a familiar carol; one she had sung as a child. When the carolers were finished, Tanya added her candy to their already bulging bags. They beamed their thanks and hurried on to the next house.

Tanya returned to the waiting dishes. The carol the children had sung echoed in her memory. *"Rejoice, O earth, for today God's Son is born."* She was puzzled. *What does it mean? Why would the world rejoice at the birth of God's Son? Who really is Jesus?*

Tanya's thoughts were interrupted when Svetta clumped into the house. Snow stuck to her boots, and her face was flushed red.

"Back already, Svetta? Did you get a lot of candy?"

"Here it is." Svetta handed her the bag with candy. "I'm so tired I didn't know if I could make it home." She sank into a chair and rested her head on the table.

"Svetta, please take off your boots before the snow makes puddles on the floor. Then you can lie down and rest."

"I'm…so…tired…" Svetta's voice slurred as she slumped over on the chair.

Uneasiness gripped Tanya. Something was wrong. Hurrying to her sister, she gently shook her. Svetta only groaned. Tanya knelt and pulled off Svetta's boots. Then she pulled her sister to her feet and dragged her to the couch. Svetta groaned again, mumbling something about her head hurting.

Tanya hurried to her parents' room. She paused at the door. Should she wake them? She knew Papa would be out of sorts after his drinking spree the night before. But maybe Mama could help.

"Mama!" Tanya's soft voice carried a sense of urgency. "Mama! I need your help. Something is wrong with Svetta."

Natasha opened her bleary eyes. "Huh? What do you need?"

"Mama, please get up!" Tanya persisted. "Svetta needs you. She's not feeling well."

Natasha stumbled out of bed and into the dining room where Svetta lay on the couch. "What's wrong?" she asked groggily. "She looks fine to me."

"Mama, she's not fine. A few minutes ago she was outside caroling. Now she's lying here sound asleep—too tired to even take off her coat. Is that fine?" Exasperation laced Tanya's voice.

Natasha stepped into the kitchen and began heating water for tea. "Oh, that is just Svetta. She sleeps a lot these days. It has something to do with her headaches, I think."

Frustration welled up within Tanya. "Mama, something is wrong! Shouldn't we call the doctor?"

Natasha didn't answer. She just shrugged her shoulders.

The silence grew heavy. The only sound was Natasha slurping her tea and Svetta's deep breathing.

"Mama," Tanya asked again, "shouldn't we take her to the hospital and find out what's wrong?"

Natasha sighed. "Yes, we probably should. The problem is…" Her voice trailed off. "We don't have the money."

"But we can't just sit here." Tanya's eyes traveled to the empty beer bottles on the table. "Look at all those bottles, Mama." Tanya spat out the words with disgust. "I bet all the money spent on drinks last night would have been enough to get Svetta to the hospital."

"What about treatment?" her mother challenged. "What good would it do to take her to the hospital if we can't afford treatment?"

The two sat in silence, then Tanya spoke. "Don't you think we should at least try to find out what her problem is? Then maybe we can find someone to help us pay for it. Maybe Uncle Sergei would lend us some money."

"Maybe," Natasha sighed. "But oh, I hate begging for money. Maybe she'll soon feel better."

chapter 4

Worrying Won't Help

1999

Christmas vacation ended and Tanya returned to school. But a part of her remained at home. Worry for her sister gnawed at her heart, making it difficult to concentrate on her studies.

Natasha finally persuaded her husband that Svetta needed to see a doctor. They called Doctor Srudmillo out to the house. He didn't know what was causing her headaches and sent her to the Skvira hospital for further testing. Tanya had not yet heard the results. *Will the doctors be able to help her?*

Tanya was never outgoing, but now the worry about her sister caused her to distance herself from her classmates even more. One day as she trudged down the hall after a busy day of classes, Pani Pavilevna, the head teacher, stopped her. "Tanya, do you have a minute?"

Tanya stopped short. "Sure, I'm not in a hurry. What would you like?"

"Come with me to my office." The teacher turned and led the way.

What have I done wrong? Tanya wondered. *I know my grades haven't been very good lately. Has one of the teachers filed a complaint?*

Pani Pavilevna looked her straight in the eyes. "I'm worried about you, Tanya. Are the other students mistreating you?"

Tanya shook her head. "No, the students are great. We don't have any problems getting along."

"But something is wrong," the teacher probed. "You're not your usual cheerful self. What's bothering you?"

"I'm all right," Tanya said, attempting to smile. But the sympathy on Pani Pavilevna's face encouraged her to go on. "I guess I am worried about my sister Svetta."

"What's wrong with her?"

"She's been having severe headaches. Sometimes it's so bad that she passes out. She's losing weight and is very sick." Tanya blinked back a tear.

"Oh, I can see why you're worried. That sounds serious. Is she getting medical help?"

Tanya nodded. "She was at the hospital this week. When I go home for the weekend, I'll find out what they say."

"Keep me updated, and if there's anything I can do to help, let me know." The teacher gave her a sympathetic smile. "I know it's hard to be away from home at a time like this but do your best to put your heart into studying. Worrying won't help you or Svetta."

Tears blurred Tanya's eyes as she turned to go back to the dormitory for the evening. Pani Pavilevna's soothing words had given her new courage.

The sun had disappeared from the horizon and a cold wind blew as Tanya hurried home, the snow crunching beneath her boots. Eager to hear what the doctors had said about Svetta, she increased her pace as the little house came into view. But then she stopped short, a chill creeping through her body. No smoke curled from the chimney. No rays of light shone from the windows.

Tanya hurried to the door; it was locked. She found the key in its usual spot in one of the boots by the door. She hesitated a moment, then entered the house. In the gathering darkness, Tanya stumbled her way across the room to the light switch.

The single light bulb hanging from the ceiling cast an eerie glow over the room. Tanya's stomach knotted at the mess before her. Dirty dishes, beer bottles, and sunflower seed shells littered the table. Along with the familiar smell of cigarettes, the putrid odor of spoiled food hung in the air.

Tanya shivered, and her heart sank as she realized the whole house was frigid. She opened the little door of the wood stove and stirred the ashes, hoping to see the glow of a hot coal. Frustration rose as she gathered kindling to start a fire. *Where is everyone? Why is no one keeping the fire going?* Her numb fingers fumbled to strike a match. The little glow of flame sputtered and went out. Again she tried. Many matches later, a fire flickered in the stove and the sharp cold was being softened by the heat.

Tanya's heart was numb. *What should I do?* She looked out into the night. She could see lights glowing in the house down the street. *Maybe neighbor Galya would know.*

A few minutes later, Tanya knocked on Galya's door. Gathering courage, she opened the door and stepped inside. "Anyone home?" she called, stamping the snow off her boots.

Galya bustled into the entrance. "Why, Tanya! It's good to see you.

Come in. How can I help you? Will you stay for some tea?"

"Good evening, *Totya*[1] Galya. I just came from school. When I got home, the house was locked and there was no one around. Do you know where my family is?"

"Come on in, child. We need to talk. I will get you a cup of tea so you can warm up. You look chilled to the bone."

Tanya took off her boots and followed Galya into the sitting room. Soon a steaming cup of hot tea warmed her cold hands. Tanya could wait no longer. "Please, Totya Galya, tell me what's wrong. What do you know about my family?"

"Your mama is in the hospital with Svetta." Galya stirred a spoonful of sugar into her tea before continuing. "The doctors are very concerned about her condition. It seems there is a tumor growing near her brain."

"A brain tumor?" The lump in Tanya's throat threatened to choke her. "Does she have cancer?"

"Don't cry, Tanya dear," Galya comforted. "Everything will be all right; it's not cancer. The doctors think the tumor comes from the head injury Svetta had last summer."

"From the brick that hit her head?" Tanya asked, her eyes wide. "The one Vasya threw?"

Galya nodded sadly. "Yes, that's what they think. They would like to send her to the hospital in Kyiv. They're hoping the doctors there can help her."

Tanya stared into her teacup, lost in thought. Finally she said, "But what if we don't have enough money to send her to Kyiv?"

Galya reached over and squeezed Tanya's hand. "Remember, you are part of the village. We will work together. If your little sister needs to go to the hospital in Kyiv, we will do all we can to get her there. Don't

---

[1] A term meaning "aunt," but often used in a more general way as a term of respect.

worry, we'll help."

Suddenly Tanya straightened. "But where is Papa? Why isn't he at home? Is he at the hospital too?"

Galya shook her head. "No, he's not at the hospital. I saw him at the bar just an hour ago. He was quite drunk."

Tanya's eyes darkened. "Oh, why does Papa have to drink? I hate when he's drunk!" She stood to leave. "I must be going. Thanks for the tea." She pulled on her boots.

"You are welcome. Let me know if I can do anything more for you. I hope your papa makes it home from the bar without freezing. It's a cold night to be out."

Tanya nodded and stepped out into the winter night. The wind stung her face. As she neared home, her steps slowed. She dreaded entering the silent, empty house.

She was relieved to find the fire still glowing. Grabbing the last few pieces of wood from the wood box, she poked them into the fire. Then she headed out to the woodshed.

As Tanya added another piece of wood to her already full load, she heard the bleat of a goat. She glanced toward the barn and blinked back bitter tears. *Who is caring for the animals?* She threw the wood into the wood box and changed into old work clothes.

As she opened the barn door, the chickens stirred from their roosts and the goats bleated eagerly. It took a bit for her eyes to adjust to the dim light. She gritted her teeth and grabbed the empty water bucket. The frigid wind cut as she trudged to the well and cranked up a bucketful of water. She poured it for the goats, taking care not to splash her numb hands.

After scattering a few handfuls of grain for the chickens, Tanya climbed the ladder to the haymow to fork down hay for the goats. The goats chewed contentedly on the hay while she stripped the milk from their swollen teats. As frustration and despair clawed at her heart, salty tears trickled down her cheeks and joined the warm milk in the tin bucket.

Her father's loud snoring startled Tanya when she entered the house. She set the milk in the unheated veranda and tiptoed into the kitchen. *He must have stumbled in while I was out doing the chores. At least I won't have to go to the bar to help him home.*

Mikoli lay slumped over on the couch. Tanya stuffed a few more pieces of wood into the stove before slipping past him into her bedroom. The tiny bedroom that had always felt crowded now seemed empty without her little sister. Tanya buried her face in the pillow so her father couldn't hear her sobs. *Why, oh why, did Svetta have to get sick? Will the doctors be able to help her? Why does Papa get so drunk?*

Tanya's thoughts churned on as she tossed and turned. *Quit worrying,* she told herself. *It won't help anyway.*

chapter 5

From Student to Slave

1999

"Sorry, Tanya, but there's no other way. You have to stay home from school." Natasha's face looked haggard as she sat down across from Tanya. "The doctors are sending Svetta to Kyiv. I can't leave her there alone."

"But, Mama," Tanya interrupted, "what about my schoolwork? I hate to get behind the others in my class."

"Stop thinking about yourself. It's time you grow up." Natasha set her teacup on the table with an impatient bang. "Later there will be time for you to study. Right now we need your help at home. Papa is busy with his work at the collective farm, and I will be in Kyiv with Svetta." Grimly she looked at Tanya. "There is no other choice. You need to stay home and do the chores."

The other students would laugh if they could see me, Tanya thought bitterly as she split another piece of wood. Her slender arms ached from chopping wood, and her fingers were numb with cold. *I've become an old village woman, slaving away while the other young people are off studying. It's not fair.* Depressing thoughts clouded the feeble winter sunshine. *I don't like boarding school that well, but right now I would do anything to go back and just be a normal young girl.*

But Tanya's carefree days of girlhood seemed to be over. There was always work to do. There was wood to chop, water to carry, and animals to care for. As the days dragged by, Tanya became lonelier than she had ever imagined possible. She missed Mama and Svetta, and she rarely saw Papa. He spent his evenings at the bar, usually coming home only after he was drunk and irritable.

True to their word, the neighbors had done what they could to help get Svetta to the hospital in Kyiv. Neighbor Galya had gone through the village to collect money from the villagers. If her father had tried to gather money, no one would have given him any. And even now, rumors were going through the village that Mikoli was using the villagers' money to buy beer.

One evening Mikoli came home from work earlier than usual. His steps were steady, and he had a pleased look on his face. "I just got a call from the hospital in Kyiv. Mama said Svetta is scheduled for surgery on March 10. The doctors think they can get the tumor out. Hopefully we'll soon have our healthy girl back."

"March 10? That's only a week from today. Oh, I wish I could see Svetta before she has surgery," Tanya said wistfully.

Mikoli laughed. "Well, you can. Because of Women's Day on March 8, the doctor has allowed her to come home for a few days."

Tanya

"Oh, it will be so good to see Mama and Svetta!" Tanya's eyes shone with delight. "I can hardly wait!"

The next few days sped by as Tanya cleaned the house and prepared for the March 8 holiday. Women's Day was always a big holiday in their village, and Tanya smiled as she remembered Women's Day flowers and cards she had gotten from her classmates in bygone years. *But I'm not in school this year, so there will be no cards or flowers. They have probably forgotten all about me. But that's all right. Having Svetta come home is the best gift I could ask for!*

The kitchen smelled of freshly baked buns, and a pot of borsch bubbled merrily on the stove. *It's evening already,* Tanya thought, peering out the window for about the tenth time. *Surely they'll be here soon. Is that them?* In the distance she saw two forms moving slowly in her direction. The one leaned heavily on the other. *Is it Mama and Svetta?* Tanya strained her eyes. *Yes, it is!* She slipped into her rubber galoshes and dashed out through the puddles of melted snow to meet them.

"Mama! Svetta! Welcome home!" she cried as she embraced her sister. "It's so good to see you! I missed you!"

"We missed you too," Svetta smiled. Exhaustion and weariness etched her face. "I can hardly wait to be home again. I just want to lie down on my own bed. Hospital beds are so uncomfortable."

"Well, let's hurry to the house," Tanya urged. "We'll eat some supper, and then you can go to bed."

Tanya was startled to see how much her mother had aged in the last few weeks. "Here, let me carry your bag," Tanya offered. "You look tired." She grabbed the valise and hurried on ahead of them. "I'll dish out the borsch so it's ready when you come in," she called over her shoulder.

To Tanya's disappointment, Svetta didn't want to eat. "The bus ride wore me out," she apologized. "Maybe I'll feel better after I rest." She crawled into bed, and a few minutes later she was snoring softly.

"I'll be glad to eat the borsch you made," Natasha said as she hung her coat on the hook. "I'm hungry for homemade food again. Hospital food is so bland!" She looked around. "Where's Papa? Isn't he home from work yet?"

Tanya shook her head. "He rarely comes straight home from work. He's at the bar almost every evening."

Natasha's shoulders drooped. "But what else is there to do? That's the best way to forget your troubles. I just wish he wouldn't waste so much money doing it." She added a dollop of sour cream to her borsch. "Mmm, this tastes delicious!" she exclaimed as she took her first bite. "It's good and hot. Just what I need to warm up after our cold ride from Kyiv."

Tanya poured water into the teakettle and put it on the stove to heat. "Mama, how is Svetta really doing?" she asked. "She looks so pale and thin! Are the doctors doing anything to help her?" Tanya's eyes burned with unbidden tears.

"I think so," Natasha said. "At first I didn't know if we were getting much help, as we were sent from one doctor to the next. It really tired out Svetta."

"Poor girl," Tanya murmured. "She's too young to go through all this."

"That's for sure!" Natasha refilled her bowl with borsch before continuing. "But now the doctors think they know what they're working with. She has an aggressive brain tumor, and they want to do surgery on Friday." Worry lines creased her forehead. "They have been giving her IVs to strengthen her and build her immune system, and I think it's making a difference. She has really perked up in the last day or two."

"Good," Tanya said. "I'm so glad you could come home for Women's Day. It's good to be together again. I got so lonely while you were gone!"

Natasha sorted through her purse and found a little box of tablets. "I had better go check on Svetta. It's time she takes her painkiller pills. She is supposed to take them every two hours. It helps her endure the intense head pain."

Tanya was washing the dishes when her mother returned to the kitchen. Natasha cleared her throat. "I think I'll go for a walk and see if I can find Papa," she said. "I could use a good drink too. You stay here with Svetta." Natasha zipped up her coat and slung her purse over her shoulder.

"Please don't get drunk," Tanya pleaded. "I hate it when Papa is drunk, and it's even worse when both of you are drunk!"

"When will you grow up, child?" Natasha cast Tanya an impatient look. "It's high time I have a good drink. I haven't been able to party at the bar with my friends for a long time!"

"But, Mama, I thought you said we don't have any extra money for alcohol."

"Stop it, child!" Natasha snapped. "That's no way to talk to your mother." She slammed the door behind her and disappeared into the dark night.

Tears stung Tanya's eyes. *Stop crying,* she told herself. *You've got to be brave. Just be glad they aren't all coming here to drink. Then we'd have to hear all the hollering and laughing.*

Tanya masked her pain and put on a smile as she went to see how Svetta was feeling. "How are you?" she asked softly as she entered the room.

Svetta turned and gave her a sweet smile. "I'm feeling a little better now that I've rested."

"Can I get anything for you? Would you like some borsch or maybe a bun with cottage cheese?"

A smile twinkled in Svetta's eyes. "A cottage cheese bun? What a treat! Where did you get the cottage cheese?"

"I made it," Tanya laughed. "With you and Mama gone, we couldn't use all the milk from the goats, so I made cottage cheese. I baked the buns this morning, so they're still soft and fresh."

"They sound good; I'd like to eat one. And maybe I'll have a cup of tea. I'm always cold."

Tanya hurried to the kitchen and soon returned with a cup of tea and a bun. "Here, Svetta, let me get another pillow to prop you up." Tanya slid a large feather pillow under her sister's head. "There, that's better. Do you think you can drink your tea now?"

Svetta nodded and reached for the cup. Her hands trembled and the tea threatened to overflow. Tanya steadied the cup and gently guided it to Svetta's mouth.

After taking several sips of tea, Svetta reached for the bun. "Mmm, this is good!" she murmured as she took a bite. "So soft and tasty. You are a good baker!" But after several bites, Svetta pushed it away.

Again Tanya steadied the cup as Svetta sipped more tea. *This is so unlike Svetta! She's so thin and weak. Will she ever get better?*

"Svetta, tell me about your time in Kyiv. It's been so long since we were together." Tanya tried to think of something positive to say. "What was your favorite part of the trip? Were you able to go to the park or do anything fun?"

Svetta slowly nodded her head. "We didn't go to the park much. It was too cold, and I wasn't feeling well. But we went on a walk to the river." A sparkle lit her eyes. "What do you think I found growing there?"

Before Tanya could reply, Svetta answered her own question. "Pussy willows! That means spring is almost here!" She closed her eyes and rested a bit before continuing. "I picked some and made a bouquet for Mama. I gave it to her for an early Women's Day gift. When I gave it to her, she said I should have waited until March 8 to give it. But I wanted to give it while I could."

"That was kind of you!" Tanya said, but she was puzzling over Svetta's last words. *What did she mean—give it while she could?* An uneasy chill crept up her back.

"Tell me more, Svetta. Did you do anything else interesting?"

Svetta looked thoughtful for a moment. "Oh, yes, I almost forgot. We spent one weekend with Aunt Ira. We stayed in their apartment."

"Oh, interesting! Did you have fun with Bogdon and Zhenia?"

Svetta nodded her head.

"Good. That was nice. We don't see our cousins from Kyiv very often."

A soft smile crossed Svetta's face. "The best part about being there was going to church."

"Church?" Tanya couldn't keep the surprise from her voice. "You went to church?"

"Yes, we went to church with Zhenia." Svetta closed her eyes and rested.

Tanya knew she shouldn't bother her sister, but curiosity got the best of her. "Svetta, what was so great about going to church? You don't usually like to go to church."

"It was different." Although Svetta's eyes were closed, a smile played on her lips. "At this church, there were benches and we could sit down. And the people sang such beautiful songs…" Her voice trailed off.

A few minutes later Svetta opened her eyes. "Tanya, I wish you could have heard them sing. They sang about Jesus and how He loves us. And they sang about heaven. It was beautiful!"

Again Svetta's eyes closed, as though she was sleeping. The only sound in the room was her soft breathing.

Tanya studied her sister's face. There was something about it she couldn't quite define. Something almost angelic.

Church? Singing? Heaven? Maybe Mama can tell me more.

chapter 6

The Nightmare

1999

Tanya awoke with a start in the middle of the night. *What's wrong?* Suddenly it all came back. *Svetta is home from the hospital, and Mama and Papa are at the bar.*

A moan cut through the silence.

"Svetta, are you all right?" Tanya reached out and touched her sister's hand.

"My head! It hurts!" Svetta moaned again.

Tanya looked at the clock. "Oh, it's past time for you to take your pills." She hurried out to the kitchen where her mother had set her purse. *Oh, no, she took it with her. Now what do I do?*

Another moan came from the bedroom. Hurrying to Svetta's side, Tanya gripped her hand, trying to stay calm.

"Help! It hurts." Svetta's face twisted. "Pills! Give me my pills!"

Panic rose inside as Tanya watched her sister suffer. "Svetta dear, be brave. I'm going to run over to Galya's house to see if she has any pills you can take." Tanya squeezed her sister's hand and ran out of the room. Svetta's groans followed her, each one a spear into her heart.

"Totya Galya!" Tanya pounded on her neighbor's door. "Can you please help me?" Her voice rose in desperation as she pounded harder. "Totya Galya!"

Galya came to the door clad in her housecoat and rubbing the sleep from her eyes. "Tanya! What's wrong, child?"

"It's Svetta. She's in terrible pain."

At the startled look on Galya's face, Tanya rushed on. "She came home from the hospital for a visit. Mama and Papa are both at the bar, and Mama took Svetta's pain medicine with her."

"Step inside where it's warmer." Galya ran her fingers through her hair. "I wonder if I could talk to your mama if I called the bar. I'll try that."

Tanya leaned against the doorframe. The seconds stretched into eternity, but finally Galya returned.

"I talked with your mama. She's coming home soon, but she said I could give you this." Galya handed her a small bottle. "Give Svetta a spoonful of this, and it should help her pain."

"Thank you!" Tanya grabbed the bottle and turned to leave.

"Be strong, child, be strong," Galya called after her. "Everything will be all right."

Tanya brushed the tears from her eyes as she entered the house. *Svetta must not see how distressed I am.* Another groan cut through the silence.

Tanya grabbed a spoon from the kitchen and rushed to her sister's side. "I'm back, Svetta." She touched her sister's shoulder.

Svetta opened her eyes for a moment, then her face twisted in agony as another moan escaped her lips.

"I brought some medicine." Tanya lifted a spoonful to her sister's lips. "Open your mouth. This will help you feel better." She poured it into Svetta's mouth, catching the bit that trickled down her chin.

"Mama! I want Mama!" Svetta cried in distress.

"Mama will be here soon," Tanya soothed as she kissed her sister's forehead. "Be brave." A grim smile played on her lips as she realized she was comforting herself as well as her sister.

Again Svetta groaned, and Tanya stroked her hand. Each groan seemed to rip Tanya's heart into pieces. She was relieved when the rattle of the door announced her mother's arrival. Now she could take charge.

"You'll be all right, Svetta," Natasha said. She spoke briskly. "I have your pills here, and you should feel better soon." Although her mother spoke with confidence, Tanya noticed her forehead was creased with worry.

"Tanya, bring a head of cabbage from the cellar."

Tanya stared at her mother in bewilderment. "Cabbage? What for?"

"Just do as I say. Quick!"

Tanya knew from the tone of her mother's voice not to argue. She slipped into her galoshes and stumbled across the muddy courtyard. As she felt her way down the ladder, the darkness felt suffocating. She groped around until she found the sack of cabbages. Grabbing one, she hurried up the ladder. With its slimy outer leaves, the cabbage threatened to slip from her hands.

Tanya stepped into the bedroom. "Here's the cabbage, Mama. What should I do with it?"

"Peel off a few clean leaves and dip them into hot water to soften them," Natasha commanded. "I've heard that cabbage leaves can relieve pain."

Natasha placed the cabbage leaves on Svetta's head and firmly wrapped it in gauze. "That will help you feel better," she assured Svetta. "Doesn't the cabbage feel cool and refreshing?"

Svetta nodded, exhaustion and pain written on her face.

"The cabbage will help draw out the toxins and relieve the pressure," Natasha explained.

As the night hours dragged by, Natasha and Tanya stayed by Svetta's side, doing what they could to ease her discomfort.

A few hours before dawn, Svetta finally relaxed. "I think I can sleep now, Mama. You should go to bed. I will be all right."

Natasha kissed her daughter's forehead. "If you're sure, I think I will lie down for a while. Tanya will be here beside you if you need anything, and I'll be in the next room." She paused at the door. "Sleep well, my dear."

"I think I will," was the sleepy response.

A few minutes later, Svetta's even breathing told Tanya she was asleep. Tanya closed her eyes and tried to relax. Scenes from the previous hours flashed through her mind until she had a throbbing headache. Svetta's groans still echoed in her ears. *Oh, why does Svetta have to suffer so? Will she ever get better?* The pounding questions had no answers.

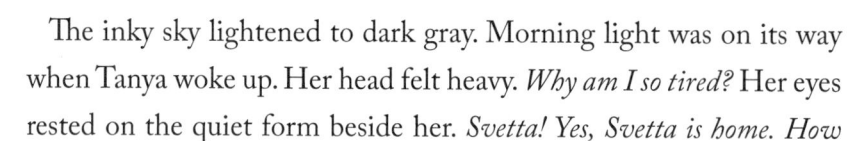

The inky sky lightened to dark gray. Morning light was on its way when Tanya woke up. Her head felt heavy. *Why am I so tired?* Her eyes rested on the quiet form beside her. *Svetta! Yes, Svetta is home. How could I have forgotten?*

Tanya reached over to tuck the covers around her sister. *Her lips are blue!* "Svetta, are you all right?" She reached for her sister's hand.

The cold fingers numbed Tanya's heart. Choking back a sob, she rushed into her mother's room. "Mama, come quickly!" she wailed. "Something is wrong! I'm afraid Svetta…" The words choked in her throat.

Natasha leaped out of bed and rushed to the girls' room. "Svetta, answer me!" she cried, grabbing her daughter's hand. "Svetta! Oh, Svetta, come back!" she sobbed. The form on the bed didn't move.

Tanya flipped on the light switch and stepped closer to her sister's side. "Mama, look!" she gasped. "She is smiling!" The blue lips were parted in a peaceful smile.

"But she's gone!" Natasha buried her head in her hands and sobbed.

Tanya watched mutely, numbed by the shock and pain.

Natasha looked up. "Run and tell Papa. He's on night duty."

Quickly Tanya donned her coat. The eerie quietness of the morning unnerved her. Tears blinded her eyes as she hurried down the road toward the collective farm. She fought to keep her footing. The mud threatened to suck off her galoshes, but still she ran. Finally, through the thick fog, she could see the outlines of the gray farm buildings.

She pounded at the gate. "Let me in!" she screamed. "Hurry! It's an emergency! I need to talk to my papa!"

The guard came out, rubbing sleep from his eyes. "What's the deal?"

"Open up!" she urged. "I need to talk to my papa, Mikoli Dmitruk, the firefighter!"

As soon as the gate was unlocked, she shoved it open, nearly knocking the guard off his feet. She sprinted past the startled man to the office next to the fire truck garage. "Papa! Oh, Papa! Please come!" she yelled as she ran inside.

In a moment, her father was at her side. "What's wrong, Tanya?" he demanded. "What's all the commotion about?"

"It's Svetta," Tanya choked, panting for breath. "She's—she's—I'm afraid she's…"

Before Tanya could finish her sentence, her father was out the door. "Come!" he hollered over his shoulder as he jumped into a truck and motioned for her to follow. The guard opened the large gate and the roar of the truck broke the stillness of the morning.

"What happened?" Mikoli asked as they bounced through the village.

"When I woke up this morning…" Tanya bit her lip to keep from

The Nightmare

crying. "Her lips were blue, and she didn't respond."

Mikoli looked straight ahead, his mouth pursed tightly.

A minute later they screeched to a stop. Mikoli leaped from the truck and dashed across the yard. *It's no wonder Papa makes a good firefighter,* Tanya thought as she followed him. She paused at the door, dreading to face the stark reality. *If only I could wake up and find out this is just a bad dream. Surely it's not true! Svetta can't be dead!*

Mikoli stood by the bedside holding Svetta's hand, despair and defeat written on his face. The moans from hours before still echoed in Tanya's ears. Surely Svetta would moan again. But the room was silent except for her mother's sobbing.

Finally Natasha got to her feet. "We might as well get busy. We have a lot of work to do before tomorrow." She brushed a strand of hair from her face. "Mikoli, can you go call the doctor?"

Mikoli nodded and slipped out of the house.

"Tanya, freshen up and get yourself ready. People will be here before we know it."

Methodically, Tanya brushed her hair. The mirror reflected her glazed and bloodshot eyes. The fears she had not dared to acknowledge were now a reality, and they threatened to choke every bit of life out of her.

"Bring water from the well," Natasha commanded, "and heat some on the stove."

Tanya was relieved to get out of the house. She grabbed two buckets and headed to the well. The morning was gray and damp, but she didn't notice. As she cranked the bucketful of water, she observed one of their neighbors heading her way, carrying flowers. *Oh! Word must have spread fast if the neighbors are already bringing flowers.*

But as the neighbor neared, he called out, "Happy holidays!" and continued down the road.

Tanya was so startled she let go of her bucket. It plummeted to the bottom of the well with a splash. *Happy holidays? What did he mean?* With a flash, she realized it was March 8, Women's Day. The neighbor was taking flowers home to his wife. *How could I have forgotten?*

Bitter tears blurred her vision. *How unfair life is!* Again she cranked the pulley to pull the bucket to the top. Water splashed on her feet, but she did not care. *Happy holidays indeed! My sister, my only sister, is dead!*

"I'll let you take care of the chores," Natasha instructed when Tanya brought in the buckets. "You know better than I do what's going on in the barn."

Alone in the refuge of the barn, Tanya's grief poured forth in a torrent of tears. The goats seemed to sense her sorrow and bleated softly. The hens clucked contentedly, as if to assure her she was not alone. Resting her head against the warm flank of a goat, she sobbed until no more tears could come.

chapter 7

The Funeral

1999

The rest of the day passed in a blur. Neighbors came to show their sympathy, and relatives arrived to share the grief and help prepare for the funeral. Uncle Sergei and Aunt Elena arrived first. They entered the bedroom where Svetta's body lay. "It seems like just yesterday she was enjoying the New Year's celebration," Uncle Sergei said huskily. "Now she's gone."

After the men went to buy a casket, Aunt Elena and Natasha began the job of preparing the body for the funeral. Tenderly they washed Svetta and combed her silky hair.

"What are you planning to dress her in for her burial?" Aunt Elena asked.

Natasha shrugged. "I don't know. I never planned for this!"

"Svetta has always been a special niece." A tear slid down Aunt Elena's cheek. "Maybe it's because I never had a daughter of my own. If it's all right with you, I'd like to give her my wedding dress."

Tanya and her mother gasped. "Are you sure?" Natasha asked in surprise. "You'll never be able to see the dress again!"

Aunt Elena nodded. "Yes, I want to give it to her. She'll never be a bride. This is the last chance she has to wear a wedding dress." A sob choked her.

Meanwhile, the kitchen teemed with activity. Ever efficient, Aunt Olya took charge of the kitchen and gave orders to anyone who would listen. Having cried out all her tears, Tanya walked numbly around the house, running errands for Aunt Olya. There was water to haul, food to bring from the cellar, and buckets of potatoes to be peeled. A few hens were caught and butchered. It would take a lot of food to feed everyone after the funeral.

The next day, neighbors and friends filled the muddy courtyard to pay their last respects. To Tanya's amazement, the school director and a crowd of school students joined the somber crowd. Children rarely attended funerals, but this time almost all the children in the village came to mourn the loss of their classmate.

Tanya tugged at the black veil covering her hair. She wasn't used to wearing a scarf, but this was the accepted way to express grief. Tanya wished she could see what she looked like. But all the mirrors in the house were covered with blankets, and she didn't dare pull them back. People said the spirit of the deceased roamed the house and could be seen in the mirrors. Just the thought gave her shivers.

People stepped out of the way as the long-robed priest arrived, carrying his prayer book. Three singers followed him. Slender candles were passed around. As Tanya held the lighted candle, she whispered a prayer that God would be merciful and accept Svetta into His kingdom.

The priest tucked a candle into Svetta's folded hands and placed a ticket to heaven on her forehead. Tanya was puzzled. *How can a little piece of paper determine someone's eternal destiny?*

"The kingdom of heaven. The kingdom of heaven. The kingdom of heaven…" Again and again the priest and his singers chanted the same phrase. The singsong voices sent chills up Tanya's back. "Be merciful. Be merciful, O God."

Will God be merciful? Tanya hoped so. *Svetta was not a great sinner. Not like I am sometimes.* Tanya shuddered.

A few of the neighbor men carried the open casket to the waiting truck. Uncle Sergei, carrying a cross to use as a grave marker, led the procession. Behind him, the women of the village walked in pairs, carrying large wreaths to put on the grave. The truck with the casket puttered along behind, followed by the family, the priest, and the rest of the mourners.

Tears burned Tanya's eyes as she plodded along behind the truck carrying her precious sister. The priest and his singers continued to chant as the procession made its way down the highway. Vehicles stopped by the side of the road, waiting respectfully for the procession to pass. *Each step is taking us closer to Svetta's grave,* Tanya thought as she put one foot in front of the other. Panic threatened to choke her. *Svetta! Oh, Svetta! Why did you die?*

At the graveyard, Maximovich, the village head, faced the crowd. "Dear family, relatives, and friends of Svetlana Mikolievna, we have gathered to walk the last mile with her. Our hearts are filled with sorrow at the untimely death of this young girl.

"We will always remember Svetta as a cheerful girl. She shone as a star student in school. She was an example to many and a friend to all. We will miss her greatly. I trust that in her absence, no evil will be remembered. If Svetta has ever offended you, I ask you now to forgive her."

Together the crowd chorused, "We will forgive her."

He turned to the casket. "Svetta, you are forgiven for anything you might have done. Rest in peace, and may God be with you."

The village head stepped back into the crowd and the priest again took charge. He chanted long portions from his little book. The Old Slavic words blurred together, making little sense to Tanya.

Villagers passed by the casket for one last look, kissing Svetta's forehead, her hands, and her feet.

Tanya thought her heart would rip with pain as she gazed at her sister for the last time. *She looks like an angel, dressed in Aunt Elena's wedding dress and veil. Is she with the angels in heaven?* Sobs choked her as she bent to kiss her sister for the last time.

Natasha's wails broke the hushed silence, and Aunt Elena had to pull her back from the casket. Mikoli turned away, his face twisted in unspoken anguish.

The harsh bang of the hammer jarred the air as the gravediggers nailed the lid to the casket. With each rhythmic thump, the nails of grief were pounded deeper into Tanya's heart.

Natasha's wails turned into panicked screams. "Don't take my daughter! Oh, Svetta! Don't let them bury you! Help! Somebody help!" Frantically she tried to stop the men from putting the casket into the ground.

Aunt Elena gripped Natasha's arm to subdue her as the doctor hurried to the scene. Pulling a bottle from his black satchel, he poured a dose of tranquilizer down Natasha's throat. She resisted, but the doctor forced it down.

Moments later, Natasha's wails subsided. Her eyes glazed as Aunt Elena led her to the edge of the grave, where they each threw a handful of dirt into the hole. Uncle Sergei, Mikoli, and other close relatives all threw a handful of dirt into the hole. Her father looked questioningly at Tanya when she didn't take her turn.

"I can't!" she mouthed, shaking her head. "I just can't do it!"

The gravediggers took their shovels and began filling the hole. As people began to leave, Mikoli cleared his throat and announced, "I thank you all for coming to share in our grief. You are all welcome to come to our house, where a meal will be served in memory of Svetta."

Aunt Olya and a few others had not joined the procession to the cemetery. By the time the burial was over and the mourners had walked back to the house, the tables were set with steaming food. The crowd had thinned out, but not everyone fit around the tables. Tanya sat wedged between her mother and Aunt Elena. The thought of food choked her. Cigarette smoke hung in the air. Again and again Mikoli filled his glass with vodka.

"Here, Tanya. You drink some too," he urged, filling her glass. "You need something to help you forget."

Numbly Tanya took a sip. It burned its way down her throat. She shook her head. "I don't want to forget!" She slammed her glass on the table. "I will never forget my dear sister Svetta!"

chapter 8

Valley of Grief

1999

One dark day after another slipped by. The weather hovered just above freezing. The stark trees, the gray sky, and the oozing mud matched Tanya's feelings. Life continued as usual, but not for Tanya. Her life had paused the day Svetta died.

Funeral expenses swallowed the small amount of money that hadn't been spent on Svetta's treatment. Mikoli again frequented the bar to drown his grief. And more often than not, Natasha joined him. Tanya couldn't help but wonder where the money came from to buy alcohol. She was afraid Papa was begging money off the neighbors.

One evening when her father was mostly sober, Tanya gathered up courage and asked the question burning in her mind. "When can I go back to boarding school? Now that Mama's home, I'm not needed here to take care of the chores anymore."

"Humph!" Mikoli snorted. "You just want to go back to school to get out of work!"

"Papa, that's not true! You know that!" Bitterness edged her words. "You're the one that's lazy! What is there for me to do here? If you let me finish boarding school, I could get a job at a sewing factory. If I stay here, I'll never be able to get a job anywhere."

Mikoli stared out the window.

"What do you want me to be, Papa? A bum like you and Mama?"

The instant the words were out of Tanya's mouth, she cringed, wishing she could retrieve them. She knew the danger of talking back to Papa.

Mikoli's face darkened. "How dare you talk to your father like that?" he bellowed. "You disrespectful brat! I'd send you packing if I could!" His eyes squinted in fury. "But there's no way for you to go back to school. There's no money for bus fare or for food. You're stuck here."

Tanya jumped up and grabbed her coat. Slamming the door behind her, she disappeared into the dark evening. She wasn't thinking about where she was going. She just needed to get out of the house, away from Papa. Her steps turned toward the village center.

Music blared from the clubhouse. *Ah, yes, it's Saturday evening. There will be young people there tonight.* The sound of laughter and joking drew her in. Soon she was singing and dancing with the others. She masked her pain with hilarity. To her surprise, she realized she actually enjoyed mingling with other village youth again. Many of them were childhood friends and classmates who were home for the weekend.

A few hours later, as Tanya walked down the dark village street toward home, an emptiness again gnawed at her heart. She had been able to forget the ache for a little, but now it returned full force. *Why did Svetta have to die? Why do Papa and Mama drink so much? Why can't I go back to school?* Unanswered questions pounded her mind, and a wave of bitterness burned away all traces of the evening's happiness.

A few days later, a little car pulled up to the Dmitruk home. Tanya looked out the window in surprise to see Pani Pavilevna, her teacher and director from the boarding school, picking her way up the path toward the house. *What does she want?* Panic flooded Tanya's mind. *I can't let her see me in these old clothes! She must be horrified at the way we live!*

Fighting the urge to run, Tanya answered the knock at the door.

"Tanya!" Pani Pavilevna wrapped her in a warm hug. "I'm so glad to find you! When you didn't return to school, I became quite worried about you!"

Tanya blinked back tears as her teacher's love and compassion washed over her aching heart. She stood at the door, unsure what to say.

Pani Pavilevna noticed her hesitation. "I came to see how you are doing. Could we visit a bit?"

Tanya nodded. "Come on in. I'll heat water for tea."

"Tanya, I'm so sorry. So your sister has died?" She nodded toward the black veil covering Tanya's hair.

Tanya nodded.

"I'm sorry. I can only imagine how hard this must be for you."

As the two sipped their tea, Tanya found herself pouring out her tale of woe. "I wish I could come back to school."

"Why don't you?"

Tanya avoided her teacher's eyes as she answered, "Papa doesn't want me to. He says…" She couldn't finish.

"Go on," Pani Pavilevna encouraged. "What's your papa's reason?"

"There's no money for bus fare or for food." Tanya's face flushed. "He and Mama spend every last hryvnia on drink. Ever since Svetta died, they drink all the time." The words came out in a bitter whisper.

"Hmm." The director studied the girl before her. Finally she spoke. "If the money part would be taken care of, do you think your papa would allow you to come back?"

Tanya shrugged her shoulders. "I suppose, but I don't know how that could happen."

"I have an idea," the director said. "If you go back with me today, you won't have to pay any bus fare. And it will soon be the end of the school year, so you won't need to come home before then. I could help you find a job for evenings and weekends to make enough money to pay for your food." She smiled cheerfully. "What do you think of that?"

A glimmer of hope fluttered in Tanya's heart. It sounded too good to be true. "Do you really think I could get a job? I don't have my certificate yet."

Pani Pavilevna chuckled. "Yes, I think you can get a job. I have connections. I'll find something for you."

Tanya soon adjusted to life at the boarding school again. To catch up with the studies she had missed and to drown her grief, she threw her heart into diligent study.

Tanya felt self-conscious in her black veil, but she was grateful for the protection it gave her. It gave her an unspoken license to avoid parties—to spend time alone and to grieve. The other students treated her with respect and silent sympathy.

When the forty days of mourning Svetta's death were over, Tanya took off her veil and tried to resume normal life. Makeup hid some of the sadness around her eyes, but her heart still ached with grief.

True to her word, Pani Pavilevna procured a job for Tanya on a city bus. The bus had its route through the city, with stops every kilometer.

Tanya's job was to collect payment from the passengers as they boarded.

Pani Pavilevna took Tanya to meet the bus driver and rode along on her first route. Tanya's hands trembled as she collected the passengers' money, and she hardly dared to look at them as they entered.

"Tanya, look at me," her teacher urged. "You need to be more confident. Greet the passengers with a welcoming smile as they come in. You have nothing to be afraid of."

It took more confidence than Tanya thought she possessed, but gradually she learned to look people in the eye and speak clearly.

Tanya found the busy schedule exhausting. She had to get up early and spend several hours on the bus before school started and then hurry back as soon as school was over, often working until nearly bedtime. The work was easy, but the schedule was tiresome. The minimal pay was just enough to provide Tanya with cash for personal needs and groceries. Sometimes her work schedule took her from school for a few hours, but Pani Pavilevna graciously excused her absences.

As spring warmed its way into the city, Tanya began saving money for a trip home. She knew she must return home for Provody, the holiday set aside to remember deceased relatives. As Tanya walked down the path toward her house, she was gripped with apprehension, dreading the reminder of Svetta's absence.

Her parents welcomed Tanya home, but she noticed the dark shadows under her mother's eyes and the pain etched on her father's face. How they had aged in the past few months!

Tanya and her mother spent a good part of Saturday in the cemetery. Many other villagers were also cleaning up the graves of their loved ones. Tanya had bought some primroses in the city, which she tenderly planted on the fresh dirt of Svetta's grave. Natasha added daffodils and tulips.

On Sunday morning the family joined the crowds of people gathered in the cemetery. Each family gathered around the graves of their loved ones. Uncle Sergei and his family joined Tanya and her parents at Svetta's grave. Aunt Olya came, bringing with her many tasty foods to add to the picnic lunch. The cloudy sky matched their somber mood. Sorrow etched their faces as they mourned the youngest member of the family.

Uncle Sergei broke the quietness. "We miss Svetta. If she were here with us, we wouldn't be sorrowing like this. But would she want us to sit here mourning?" Svetta had always enjoyed this day. To her, Provody had been an exciting time with relatives.

Natasha shook her head. "But how can we go on without her?"

"She will always be in our hearts," said Aunt Elena. "I remember how she used to recite poems. She had such a keen memory. Even as a four-year-old, she learned poems and liked to recite them to anyone who would listen."

"And if no one would listen, she'd recite them to the chicks," Tanya added with a giggle.

As they shared memories of Svetta, their hearts lightened. The sun peeked through the clouds, and the flowers danced in the breeze. Prayers ascended to God, asking Him to be merciful to the souls of the departed.

I wonder if Svetta's spirit really roams the world on Provody, Tanya thought as she studied the plate of food sitting by the tombstone. *Does God actually hear our prayers for her? What will happen if we don't keep praying for her?* Plates filled with food, cups of beer, and bags of candy were set by the gravestones. *Will the spirits really eat the food?* Questions haunted Tanya as she walked home that evening.

Tanya pushed the questions away as she returned to boarding school and immersed herself in studying for the end-of-the-year exams. As the test dates approached, her stomach churned in apprehension. Studying had always been hard for her, and missing so many days had only complicated matters. It would be a relief to have her years of education finished.

"Hey, Tanya," a classmate called one evening as Tanya hurried down the hall. "What do you think about the upcoming school trip? Won't it be awesome to go to the mountains? I can hardly wait!"

"Yeah, it sounds like fun," Tanya smiled awkwardly. "But I haven't given it much thought. I've been too busy preparing for the tests."

I told the truth, Tanya comforted herself that evening. *It does sound like fun. But there's no way I can go. Trips cost money, and I don't have any to spare. There's no use wasting energy wishing to go. It's just not possible.*

The tests were as hard as she had imagined, but Tanya did her best. To her great relief, she passed the exams and received her diploma and seamstress certificate.

"See you at the train station!" called a friend as Tanya toted her packed bags out of the dormitory.

"See you soon!" called another. "I can't wait till our trip to the mountains!"

Tanya forced a smile. "Goodbye, girls! I'll miss you."

Everyone else seemed to be in jolly spirits, but Tanya's heart felt heavy. A chapter of her life was closing; her years of studying were over. Now what was she supposed to do? Where should she go?

Returning to life at home was harder than Tanya had expected. Reminders of Svetta surrounded her. Even simple tasks triggered memories, wrapping her in grief.

Bitterness clawed at her heart, and depressing thoughts taunted her. *No one loves me. I am not good enough. Nothing will ever work out for me.* The harder she fought these thoughts, the fiercer they became. *No*

Valley of Grief

one cares about me. Why bother living? No one would miss me anyway.

One day when it seemed the sun would never shine again, Tanya heard a knock at the door. To her great astonishment, there stood Pani Pavilevna. Speechless, Tanya stared at her. What had brought her here?

Her teacher smiled and said, "I've missed you, Tanya." She reached out and gave Tanya a squeeze. "It's good to see you again."

Tears blurred Tanya's eyes, embarrassing her. "I've missed you too, Pavilevna, and I was afraid I would never see you again."

Her teacher's soft chuckle warmed Tanya's heart. "Oh, really? Why did you think that? Aren't you going along to the mountains with us?"

Tanya bit her lip and shook her head. "I can't," she whispered.

"Yes, you can. I've figured it all out. I have come to pick you up."

"But I can't. Don't do this to me," Tanya protested. "It's not even an option."

Pani Pavilevna reached into her purse and pulled out a paper. "Look at this," she urged.

Tanya took the paper and looked at it. "It's not for me," she said, confusion on her face. "This is a pass for Katya, not me."

"I know," her teacher replied. "But did you ever think about how much you and Katya look alike? You have the same blond hair and brown eyes. And both of you are slender with a long narrow face."

Tanya nodded slowly, not following what that had to do with going to the mountains.

"And Katya is a Chernobyl victim, so she gets to travel for free."

Again Tanya nodded, still puzzled.

"Well, it's like this. Katya can't go along because she has other plans, so her pass is not needed. And I'd like to give it to you!" Pani Pavilevna smiled triumphantly at Tanya. "For a few days you can pretend you are Katya. And it'll be free. The train ticket won't cost you a thing!"

A glimmer of hope shone in Tanya's eyes. "Are you serious?"

"Of course I'm serious! Now get your bags together. The train leaves at 9:00 this evening."

Tanya stood dumbfounded at the change of events. Slowly she shook her head. "But there's no way I can go. Even if the ticket is paid for, I don't have money for the other expenses."

"Don't worry, I'll make sure you have all you need!"

"But I can't pay you back," Tanya stammered.

"Dear, don't worry about that. Your effort in school this year more than covers any costs you will have on this trip. You have worked hard, and this is your reward."

That night as Tanya stretched out on the hard bunk on the train, she couldn't help but wonder if it was just a dream. The rhythmic click-clacking calmed her nerves. She shivered in delight as the lonely sound of the whistle echoed through the darkness. This was too good to be true.

The grandeur of the Carpathian Mountains took her breath away. For a village girl who had grown up on the flat, fertile plains, the mountains were a wonder. Tanya savored every moment. She filled her lungs with the fresh mountain air, inhaling the woodsy scent of pine mingled with fragrant violets. Mushrooms popped through the leaves on the ground, their little red parasols speckled in white.

Tanya enjoyed every part of the trip—the late-night parties with her classmates, the hikes up the mountain, and the evenings around the campfire. But most of all, she loved the quiet mornings.

While the other girls were still sleeping, Tanya would slip out of the cabin and follow the trail to the gurgling brook. From her perch on a moss-covered rock, she watched wildflowers nodding in the morning breeze and the sun's rays filtering through the treetops. She would close her eyes and rest in the music of the mountain morning. The singing of the birds and the murmuring of the water babbling over the rocks soothed her. As Tanya soaked up the beauty, the sharp ache and bitterness eased their grip on her weary heart.

The week flew by, and all too soon it was time to return home.

"Thank you, Pavilevna, for taking me along on the trip." Tears shone in Tanya's eyes. "The beauty of the mountains was just what I needed."

Pani Pavilevna nodded encouragingly. "I'm glad you are feeling better. You've been through a lot." She shook her head. "It's got to be tough. But you are a strong, brave girl. You can make something out of yourself. Put your knowledge to good use. Go to Kyiv and get a job. You can do it!"

Tanya tried to speak, but the lump in her throat made it hard. "Thank you. You've done so much for me. I'll never forget your kindness."

chapter 9

Life in Kyiv

1999-2000

*B*ack at home, Tanya found each day as empty and meaningless as the one before.

Her mother lived in a daze. She was no longer the diligent housekeeper who took pride in having her yard and house in order. She took no notice of the peeling paint on the doors, the dingy white of the house, or the leaking roof. Most of her evenings were spent at the bar.

Papa also drank away his evenings, being drunk more often than not.

What shall I do? Tanya wondered. *Is it worth trying to live a decent life? Would I be better off drowning my grief with drink?*

Some evenings she tried that, but the next morning her grief would be sharper than ever. *It's not worth it. I can't stay here.*

"Mama, I'm leaving for Kyiv next week," Tanya announced one evening. "It's time I get a job. I called Aunt Ira, and she said she would make arrangements. She knows of a sewing factory where I can find work."

Natasha sighed. "I wish you wouldn't leave, but it's probably best. You need the money."

As Tanya packed her bags and prepared to move, trepidation and excitement tickled her stomach. Although relieved to be leaving home, she dreaded living in the big city. *Will I be able to sew well enough to get a job? Where can I stay?* Again and again her teacher's parting words echoed in her mind. *"You are a strong, brave girl. You can make something out of yourself. Put your knowledge to good use. Go to Kyiv and get a job. You can do it!"*

She would prove her teacher right. She would make something out of herself.

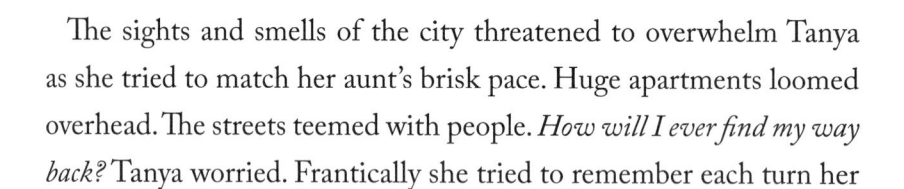

The sights and smells of the city threatened to overwhelm Tanya as she tried to match her aunt's brisk pace. Huge apartments loomed overhead. The streets teemed with people. *How will I ever find my way back?* Tanya worried. Frantically she tried to remember each turn her aunt made.

"Aunt Ira," she panted, catching up to her. "I don't think I can find my way out of here. How will I know how to get back to your place?"

Ira laughed. "Oh, it's not that hard. You'll soon get used to it. Once you understand the bus and metro system, you'll be able to go anywhere." They turned onto a narrow back street. "We're almost there, Tanya. Are you ready for your interview?"

Although the summer sun warmed her back, Tanya shivered. "I'm ready to have it over with!"

The interview went better than she had expected. She was relieved to find that the factory had living quarters for their workers—a little dormitory attached to the factory. Although she was disappointed with the small salary, she knew that as a new seamstress she couldn't expect more.

The novelty of her new job soon wore off, and Tanya realized one didn't need much sewing expertise to work at this factory. The workers worked in an assembly line. For the first few weeks, Tanya's job was to iron seams open. Standing at the ironing board for eight hours a day quickly became monotonous. The summer warmth and the heat from the iron made the factory about as comfortable as a poorly ventilated greenhouse. "I feel like a wilted flower," she complained to a coworker one day. "I don't know how much longer I can take this. Hoeing beets back in the village was easier than this!"

Her coworker laughed. "Enjoy the heat. Just wait until winter, then you'll know what torture is. Everyone wants the job of ironing!"

When winter arrived, Tanya realized her coworker was right. To cut back on costs, the dormitory and the factory were poorly heated. The cement building was damp and cold.

"My fingers are so numb I can barely sew," Tanya remarked ruefully to the seamstress next to her. By now Tanya had graduated from her ironing job, but putting pockets in slacks was almost as monotonous. Numbed fingers complicated the job.

Night after night Tanya shivered in bed, tossing and turning, trying to warm up. She could see her breath in the air like a cloud of steam. At work, her clumsy fingers did their best to sew neatly and keep up with the other seamstresses. At lunch break, she huddled close to the stove and wrapped her fingers around a cup of tea. The steam caressed her cold cheeks, and the soothing tea warmed her from the inside. But even the hot tea couldn't take the numbing ache from her toes.

The exposure to the cold gave her a deep-set cough. Though she still shivered with cold, her body soon burned with fever. Her head throbbed and every bone ached.

One day Tanya stumbled into the manager's office. "I'm sorry, but I'm sick. I can hardly work." She paused as another coughing fit attacked her. "May I take a few days off to recuperate?"

Permission granted, she traveled to her aunt's apartment on the other side of Kyiv. The bus routes and metro systems were no longer a tangled confusion, and soon she was climbing up the flights of stairs to Aunt Ira's apartment on the fifth floor.

Aunt Ira welcomed her warmly. "Tanya, child!" she exclaimed. "You're sick!" She led her to the couch. "Here, let me help you take off your coat. I'll bring you a cup of tea."

As Tanya collapsed onto the couch, another coughing fit racked her body. When she finally managed to stop coughing, she smiled wearily at Aunt Ira. "Yes, I am sick. I came here to warm up. The factory and the dormitory are so cold there's no chance of me ever getting better if I stay there!"

"Please lie down and rest," Aunt Ira said. "If you're not feeling better by morning, we're going to see the doctor."

Tanya nodded. "Whatever you say."

By morning, Tanya was sicker than ever. Aunt Ira wasted no time taking her to the doctor.

"How long have you been coughing like this?" the doctor asked, his face grave.

"Several weeks. I'm not sure when it started, but it got worse in the last week." Tanya's attempts to look perky were a miserable failure.

"You must go to the hospital immediately," the doctor said. "You are one sick woman! You have pneumonia." He looked at her medical book. "But I see you are from Kryvoshyintsi, so we can't admit you here. You need to go to your local hospital in Skvira."

Tanya's heart sank. She didn't want to return home. Especially not now.

"Are you sure there's no way she can be accepted at a hospital here in Kyiv?" Aunt Ira asked. "I don't think it will work for her to go back to Skvira."

"I'm sorry, but there's no way she can be admitted to a hospital here."

Aunt Ira took Tanya by the arm and led her out of the hospital. As they flagged a bus back to the apartment, tears burned Tanya's eyes and the ache in her chest almost smothered her. "I don't want to go back!" she whispered fiercely.

"I'm sorry, dear, but you must get help. If Skvira is the only hospital that will take you, then we must get you there as soon as possible." Aunt Ira handed her a cup of tea. "Drink this while I make plans. The sooner you get help, the better."

Tanya could hear Aunt Ira talking on the phone in the next room, but her head ached too badly to follow what she was saying. *If only I could feel better and go back to work!*

"I wish I could go with you," Aunt Ira said as she returned to the kitchen. "But I can't leave Zhenia and Bogdon for that long. I called your neighbor Galya and asked her to tell your mother that you're sick and will be coming home this afternoon. She is supposed to meet you at the bus stop and take you straight to the hospital."

The bus ride passed in a blur. Natasha met Tanya at the bus stop and helped her to the hospital. Although she scolded Tanya for getting so sick, Tanya was relieved to see her. When the doctor gave a list of medications and supplies, Natasha glared at Tanya. "Do you expect me to pay for this? Is that why you came home instead of going to the hospital in Kyiv?"

Tanya cringed as she pulled a few hryvnia from her wallet. "Of course not," she rasped. "The hospital in Kyiv wouldn't accept me because I'm not local. Take this money; it should be enough."

Natasha soon returned from the pharmacy with the needed supplies, and the doctor immediately started Tanya on IVs. Her mother stayed until Tanya was settled in her room, promising to return the next day to see how she was doing.

The Skvira hospital lacked the comforts of home, but it was much better than the cold dormitory at the sewing factory. The food was bland, but Tanya didn't mind. It provided nourishment for her weakened body.

For the first few days, Tanya could barely get out of bed. She tossed and turned, her body burning with fever. By the time her fever was under control, her strength was exhausted. She lay miserably, too weak to sit. Every few days her mother came to visit, and occasionally a neighbor would stop in with a snack or some fruit. Tanya appreciated their thoughtfulness, but she hated the pity she could see in their eyes. *I don't want to be pitied! I don't like to feel poor and needy.*

As days turned into weeks and Tanya still lay in the hospital, discouragement washed over her. Along with the cold wind that shrieked around the hospital came a harsh reality. City life was not what she had dreamed it would be. The sewing job was monotonous, the hours long, and the paycheck meager. With the arrival of winter, it had been torture.

Sometimes Tanya thought longingly of the little house in the village, of cozy winter evenings eating sunflower seeds with Svetta. She longed to return to those days, but she knew that even if she returned home, it would never be the same.

No, going home was not an option. With Svetta gone and Papa and Mama often drunk, she would never be happy there. But she also dreaded the thought of going back to work.

Tanya

One day Tanya summoned up her courage and asked to use the hospital telephone. Her fingers trembled as she dialed Aunt Ira's number. *Will she be willing to help?*

Desperate for help, Tanya poured out her discouragement to Aunt Ira. "I've used up all my money, and I don't know what to do. If I go back to the sewing factory, I'll probably get sick again. But I don't want to go home either!"

"Why don't you come and live with us for now," Aunt Ira suggested. "You aren't well enough for a job yet. You need time to regain your strength. While you recuperate, we'll look for another job."

Natasha agreed to the idea and grudgingly gave Tanya enough money for the bus fare to Kyiv. After being in the hospital for more than a month, Tanya felt like a bird released from prison. She toyed with the idea of going home for a few days before heading to Kyiv. After all, she had missed the winter festivities. New Year's and Christmas had come and gone while she lay ill in the hospital. But she pushed the thought aside. It would be better if she went to Kyiv and forgot the memories of last Christmas with Svetta.

Under Aunt Ira's care, Tanya's strength slowly returned. The apartment was cramped, but it was a welcome haven for Tanya. She enjoyed sharing a bed with her cousin Zhenia, a fun-loving fifteen-year-old. Tanya loved Aunt Ira, but she was always a bit scared of Uncle Yuri. His short temper and love of alcohol brought conflict to the family.

One day Aunt Ira bustled into the house, smiling from ear to ear. "I found a job for you, Tanya," she cheered. "It's only a few blocks away, and it's a warm place to work. You won't get sick there! And you'll earn almost as much as you did at the sewing factory."

"Seriously?" Tanya sat up on the couch where she had been resting. "Do you think I can do it? Will I be smart enough? What kind of work is it?"

Life in Kyiv

"I'm sure you're smart enough for this job, Tanya! It's actually quite easy. You'll be a dishwasher at the Smakota restaurant just down the road!" Aunt Ira burst into laughter at Tanya's surprised expression. "And don't you dare complain about washing dishes! I think this will be a perfect job for you."

A few days later Tanya began her job as the official dishwasher at Smakota. As a child, she had despised washing dishes, but now when her paycheck depended on it, she found it wasn't such a terrible job. Her managers were impressed with her efficiency, and she soon became one of their favorite employees.

The best part of her new position was clearing the tables. She was allowed to claim any of the leftover food after the customers were finished. Sometimes by the end of the day she had collected enough leftovers to feed the whole family. The food she brought home was enough to pay for her room and board. Everyone was satisfied with this arrangement, even Uncle Yuri, who was usually hard to please.

Because Smakota was known for its kosher foods, Jews frequented this restaurant. Tanya knew very little about Jews, but she found their dress and manners intriguing. Their prayers before they ate seemed endless, but maybe that was because she couldn't understand a word they said. One day as she watched them pray, she remembered what Svetta had told her before she died. She had talked about going to church and praying. *Perhaps Zhenia could tell me more.* She pushed aside the thoughts of prayer and hurried outside for a smoke.

That night Tanya tossed and turned in bed. Memories of the last evening with Svetta flooded her mind. Svetta had said going to church with Zhenia was the highlight of her stay in Kyiv.

"Zhenia," Tanya whispered, nudging her cousin. "Are you sleeping?"

"Not anymore," Zhenia huffed. "I was nearly asleep. What do you want?"

"Oh, I've been wanting to ask you something, but I never think of it at the right time." Tanya rolled over and faced her cousin. "Do you ever go to church?"

"Are you silly, or what?" Zhenia half chuckled. "You woke me up just to ask that? No, I never go to church anymore. Whatever made you ask?"

"Svetta told me how she went to church with you. She said that was the best part of her time here."

"Oh, I remember. Your mom and Svetta did go to church with me one time. I used to go regularly. It was fun to see the rich Germans and Americans that came to church. Sometimes they gave us stuff. You know that warm jacket I wear all the time? It was a gift from them."

"Why did you stop going?"

"Well, the services were so long and boring, and I really didn't need more gifts. I decided there are other ways to spend my Sundays. Probably the biggest reason is because we party so late on Saturdays that I'd rather sleep all day on Sunday." She yawned. "I'd rather be sleeping now than talking. Will you quit your questions and let me sleep?"

"I guess. But, Zhenia, listen. If you ever decide to go to church again, let me know. I want to go with you."

The only answer was a soft snore.

chapter 10

Uncle Yuri

2000

Tanya's long days of work at Smakota sometimes stretched late into the night. Customers who had entered the bar as decent businessmen left as slobbering, staggering drunkards. Sometimes the faint light of morning tinted the sky as she trudged home from a long night at the restaurant.

Tanya dreaded being on duty over the weekends, but spending the weekend at Aunt Ira's apartment was not much better. Uncle Yuri's insatiable thirst for alcohol attracted his cronies. Arguing, drinking, swearing, and blaring radio music were often her lullabies when she finally dropped into bed.

Will I never be able to get away from this awful stuff? Tanya wondered as she came back to the apartment late one night. In the dim light, she could see empty bottles littering the table. Uncle Yuri was lying on the floor snoring, a half-empty bottle of vodka beside him. Tanya tiptoed past him. The worst thing about Uncle Yuri's drinking was his temper. She shuddered as she remembered the fights she had witnessed. He always seemed to have it in for his seventeen-year-old son Bogdon.

More often than not, a bruise or a black eye adorned Bogdon's face. Tanya knew that not all the bruises came from Uncle Yuri, but too many of them did. Somehow the two of them clashed. Bogdon shared his father's appetite for drink and a distaste for work. It was a bad combination.

Worry gnawed at Tanya's heart. She liked Bogdon. He was the cousin closest to her age, and they had grown up together. But something was wrong. He hadn't been himself recently. He had a glazed look in his eyes, and Tanya was concerned. Was he on drugs? She shuddered. Bogdon was too young for that kind of garbage.

Tanya's troubled thoughts drifted from Bogdon to Pavlo, and she smiled. Pavlo was a different sort of fellow. Tanya couldn't help but admire him the first time he had shown up at Smakota. His jolly smile had attracted her like a magnet.

It wasn't long before Pavlo became a regular customer at Smakota. At first he came with his friends, but one day he came alone. Tanya delighted in the chance to serve him. "What can I get for you?" she asked with a shy smile.

"I'll take two coffees with sugar, please." His broad smile sent tingles of delight up her back. "And perhaps you could find someone I can share it with." He gave her a knowing nod. "Coffee doesn't taste half as good when you're drinking it alone."

Tanya felt her face grow warm. "I can bring you the coffee, but I don't think there's anyone available to keep you company. All the girls in the kitchen are busy filling orders."

"I don't need any of the kitchen girls," Pavlo answered with a mischievous grin. "There's only one girl I'd like to drink coffee with—the one right here!"

"Thanks, but—" Tanya paused as she tried to find the right words. "It would never do for the manager to catch me drinking coffee with a customer when I should be working."

"Aw, come on. Are you sure?" Pavlo asked, his voice edged in disappointment. "Well, just bring me one coffee then, and maybe some other time I can share one with you."

To hide her pleasure, Tanya turned toward the kitchen. "I'll be right back," she called over her shoulder. She soon returned with a steaming cup of coffee.

"Thank you, kindly," he said, looking her in the eyes. "Do you work late tonight?"

"Yes. Till midnight." Tanya suppressed a sigh. "And there won't be time for coffee with anyone till my shift is over for the day."

"I understand, but I was wondering…" He looked questioningly at her. "Isn't it scary to walk home alone that late at night?"

She shrugged her shoulders. "I can't say that I like it, but I have no choice. I can't stay here all night."

"True." He smiled at her candidness. "Suppose I walk you home tonight? Would you be opposed?"

Tanya tried to look indifferent. "It couldn't be worse than walking alone," she laughed. "But it'll be late. Don't bother."

But at midnight, Pavlo was waiting for her. They chatted easily as they walked along.

———

As the weeks passed, Pavlo and Tanya's friendship grew. Instead of Tanya dreading the walk home from work, it soon became a daily highlight.

"Tanya," Pavlo said one night as he walked her home from work, "I have really enjoyed getting to know you. But I'd like to learn to know your parents too. I'd like to see where you grew up."

The darkness hid the blush that crept across Tanya's face.

"Let's go to Kryvoshyintsi this weekend." Pavlo slowed his pace and looked questioningly into her eyes. "Would you like that?"

Tanya shrugged. "I don't know." She paused, wondering how she could explain how embarrassed she felt about her parents. "Village life is—well—just different from city life. The people are different. The houses are different. I don't think you would like it."

Pavlo threw back his head in a hearty laugh. "Don't you worry. If it has anything to do with you, I'm going to love it."

Despite Tanya's apprehension, she found herself boarding the bus with Pavlo. She had called Galya and asked her to pass the message to her parents that she was coming home with a friend. She dreaded their reaction.

Just as Tanya feared, the weekend was a nightmare. Her parents were in a drunken stupor and an ill mood. They treated Pavlo indifferently but bossed Tanya around as if she were their servant. It felt as though her two worlds had collided. The stylish, city-girl facade was stripped away, and Pavlo could see who she really was—a poor village girl. A daughter of drunks.

The village looked different when she tried to picture it through his eyes—muddy streets, whitewashed houses with no indoor plumbing, and chickens and ducks roaming the courtyards. A heavy odor of cigarettes and alcohol filled the house. Tanya shuddered.

"I'm sorry, Pavlo," she whispered during the bus ride back to the city. "Sorry for what?"

She dropped her head. "For everything. I'm not a nice city girl like you thought I was. You saw my parents. You saw the house where I grew up. I can't hide it from you. I'm not worth anything."

"It's all right," he said. His sympathetic gaze embraced her. "I like you more than ever. I admire your courage. I'm glad you're my girl."

Aunt Ira's family had been saving every extra hryvnia to prepare for Zhenia's long-awaited sixteenth birthday. When the evening of her birthday arrived, so did the guests. School friends, neighbors, and relatives crowded into the apartment.

The tables were loaded with the choicest foods. The red caviar on the sandwiches shimmered like little jewels. *Olivye*[1] salad, *holodets*,[2] and other delicacies tempted the taste buds. Honey cake and a variety of candies attracted the sweet tooth. Bottles of mineral water and juices stood on the table—along with an abundance of alcohol.

Dread crept into Tanya's heart when Uncle Yuri poured yet another large glass of vodka. His glazed eyes burned with thirst. *I hope he can keep his temper under control*, she worried.

As usual, Bogdon was the life of the party. His quick wit and humor had everyone roaring with laughter. Pushing aside the tables and stools, they made enough room to dance with the music. The singing of throaty chants sprinkled with slurs shook the apartment walls. The party stretched into the wee hours of the morning. Eventually Uncle Yuri's snores replaced his raucous laughter, and one by one the guests slipped from the apartment and headed to their own homes to sleep away the effects of the party.

Candy wrappers, mandarin peels, and bread crumbs littered the couch

---

[1] Ukrainian potato salad.

[2] A traditional jellied meat dish.

that doubled as Tanya and Zhenia's bed. Tanya pushed the trash to the floor before collapsing on the bed. As she drifted off to sleep, the words of an old folk song still danced through her brain.

Tanya awoke with a start. It was still dark. Her head pounded, begging for more sleep. She tried to shake the fog away from her brain. What was happening? A chill crept over her as she heard Uncle Yuri's voice bellow from the kitchen. "Where's my vodka? Give me a drink!"

Uncle Yuri's unsteady footsteps neared the room where the girls lay under the covers. Tanya pinched her eyes shut, willing herself to relax and fake sleep.

The form of Uncle Yuri darkened the doorway. "Get up and give me a drink!"

Tanya trembled under the roar of his voice and reached under the blanket for Zhenia's hand.

"I said give me a drink!" Uncle Yuri leaned closer, losing his balance and nearly toppling on the bed. "Stop hiding it from me. I need a drink—now!"

Aunt Ira hurried in. "Come, Yuri." She grabbed his arm and led him away. "That's no way to act. Leave the girls alone. They are tired." She drew him into the kitchen and pulled out a stool. "Sit down. I'll get you something to drink."

Through the open bedroom door, Tanya could see into the kitchen. She watched as Aunt Ira placed the teakettle on the stove and rummaged in the cupboard. "What kind of tea would you like, black or green?"

"Tea?" His bellow echoed through the apartment. "Not tea! Vodka! Give me a drink!" He struggled to his feet and reached for a bottle on the table. Finding it empty, he threw it on the floor in disgust. It shattered into smithereens. He grabbed another bottle and chucked it on the floor.

Tanya shivered as she saw Uncle Yuri reach for the third bottle.

"How dare you finish all these drinks and leave nothing for me?" He hurled the bottle at Aunt Ira.

Her scream rent the air.

In an instant, Bogdon came running into the kitchen. "Papa, what's going on?" he demanded. "That's no way to treat Mama!" He knocked a bottle from his father's hands.

Uncle Yuri's face purpled with rage. "Don't you dare talk to me like that!" He clenched his fist and glared menacingly at Bogdon. "So you're the one who hid the drink from me. Give it to me now!" He lunged toward Bogdon.

Bogdon stepped aside, and Uncle Yuri nearly toppled against the wall.

"Papa, sit down and be quiet." Bogdon spoke with an air of authority. "Remember, we had company last night. You drank vodka and so did they. Now the bottles are empty, but in the morning we can go to the store and buy more."

Bogdon's logical reasoning only infuriated his father. Uncle Yuri grabbed the butcher knife from the knife rack and lunged at Bogdon.

Tanya stifled a scream. She wanted to hide her face in her blanket, but she couldn't tear her eyes away from the horror before her. She clung to Zhenia in terror.

Bogdon stepped aside just in time. He wrenched the knife from his father's hand and tossed it behind the stove. "Papa, stop this. Go back to bed." His deep voice held a tremor. "We'll buy drinks for you in the morning." His efforts to calm Uncle Yuri fell on deaf ears.

Uncle Yuri's eyes skimmed the room like a crazed animal looking for prey. He stumbled to the closet and rummaged around. Seconds later Tanya saw the glint of steel. She cringed as Yuri brandished the axe and swung at Bogdon.

"Stop! You'll kill him!" Aunt Ira's scream sliced the air. "Stop!"

For a second, Uncle Yuri's fury toward Bogdon paused as he turned toward Aunt Ira. "Who do you think you are, meddling like this?"

In that split second, Bogdon lunged at his father and grabbed the axe. Before Yuri realized what was happening, Bogdon flung the axe out the balcony door. It landed with a faint thud on the ground five floors below.

A furious fistfight followed.

Tanya buried her face in her blanket, willing the blows to stop. Eventually she became aware of an uncanny quiet. Gathering up her courage, she peeked out from her refuge under the covers. Bogdon was slumped against the wall, blood dripping from his nose. His eye was swelling shut and turning an ugly blue. Uncle Yuri lay on the floor where he had fallen.

Aunt Ira returned to the room with a wet washcloth. Her hands shook as she gently wiped Bogdon's face. "Are you all right, son?" Her voice trembled. "I thought he was going to kill you!"

Bogdon groaned and opened one eye. "He almost did! I think I'll be okay, but I don't know what will happen when he wakes up." He nodded toward Uncle Yuri, who still lay motionless on the floor. "I think that last blow knocked him out." He groaned again as he tried to sit up.

Their eyes all turned toward Uncle Yuri. He lay there quietly. *Too quiet,* Tanya thought. "Is he okay?" she asked. "Something seems wrong."

Aunt Ira knelt by Yuri's side and gingerly took his hand, feeling for a pulse. "Call the ambulance," she urged. Her voice dropped to a whisper. "I can't feel anything." She got to her feet. "Even if there is a pulse, we need the ambulance. We have to give him a tranquilizer. I don't want to be around when he wakes up."

The ambulance soon arrived, and so did the police. When the paramedics pronounced Uncle Yuri dead, Zhenia, who had been watching everything in stunned silence, broke into hysterical sobs. The paramedics gave Bogdon an injection of pain reliever, then they lifted Yuri's body onto a stretcher and carried him away.

Then the interrogations began. The next hours passed in a blur. *Surely this is just a nightmare, and I'll soon wake up,* Tanya told herself over and over. While one police officer grilled everyone, another jotted down the information on his clipboard.

Tanya struggled to stay focused and answer accurately. "Bogdon didn't want to kill his father! Uncle Yuri was trying to kill him and Aunt Ira. He might have murdered us all if it hadn't been for Bogdon!"

After hours of interrogation, the police handcuffed Bogdon and led him away. "We know he didn't intend to kill his father," one policeman explained. "But murder, even in self-protection, is breaking the law. Although Bogdon is under eighteen and they can't give him a jail sentence, that is the safest place for him for the next few weeks."

Aunt Ira nodded slowly, trying to understand what the police were explaining. "But the funeral. He needs to be at the funeral!"

"I think not," the policeman answered. "Yuri may have cronies who will want revenge. Like I said, jail is the safest place for Bogdon right now."

The police were right. Tanya shuddered at the malicious comments she heard during the next few days. Uncle Yuri's brother was especially angry. He demanded that Aunt Ira move out of the apartment, which was registered in Yuri's name. Aunt Ira was too worn out to put up a fight. Besides, the apartment held too many memories of Yuri.

She found a small, two-room apartment to rent on the other side of the city. It would be a tight fit with just Aunt Ira and her two children, so Tanya knew she would have to find another place to live.

Pavlo came to her rescue. "Close to my mother's house is an elderly couple looking for someone to live with them. They will give you a room for free if you help take care of them."

Several days later Tanya packed her bags and bid Aunt Ira farewell. "Thank you for everything you have done for me," she murmured. "You gave me a home when I so desperately needed one. I'll always be grateful to you."

chapter 11

More Changes

2000

It didn't take long for Tanya to fall in love with the old couple who gave her a home. *Baba*[1] Marusia was so kind and motherly, and *Dyed*[2] Petya was a grizzled grandpa with a heart and humor that Tanya loved. However, they lived quite far from her job, and it took nearly an hour of travel on public transportation to reach the restaurant where she worked. With the expensive bus fare, she determined that something had to change.

On her next day off work, Tanya decided to search for a new job. Her first stop was at the local market to pick up groceries for Baba

---

[1] An elderly woman or grandmother.

[2] An elderly man or grandfather.

Marusia. As she chatted with a vendor, she mentioned her search for another job.

"Would you like to work here at the market?" the vendor asked. "I saw a notice on one of the clothing stands saying they need a worker."

Tanya wove her way through the market toward the clothing section. Her sharp eyes skimmed the stands, looking for the notice. There it was. Boots, belts, backpacks, and other leather products filled the tables and hung haphazardly around the kiosk.

"How may I help you?" the vendor asked. "Would you like to try on some boots?"

Tanya willed her voice to sound confident. "Actually, I came to see if you still want to hire a saleswoman? I'm looking for a job and saw your notice."

Tanya cringed as the lady scrutinized her from head to toe. "Have you done this type of work before?"

"No." Tanya shook her head. "But I'm willing to learn."

Before the day was over, Tanya was hired at the market. She quit her job at Smakota and learned market lingo. Because she received a percent of her sales, Tanya soon realized it was in her favor to be a good saleswoman. Within a few weeks, she was an expert at extolling the virtues of her products. Much to her delight, her sales began to increase. The pay still wasn't as much as Smakota offered, but Tanya didn't regret her decision. The hours at her new job were nicer, and she didn't miss the drinking at the café.

The market opened early in the morning and closed in the afternoon, giving Tanya a few hours to help Dyed Petya and Baba Marusia. She enjoyed buying their groceries, helping in the little garden, and running errands for them.

Pavlo paid regular visits to Tanya. Often he brought a small gift, some flowers, or other tokens of his friendship. One evening when he brought an expensive bracelet, Tanya protested. "Pavlo, you must quit spoiling me like this. You are wasting your money! Where do you find all these charming things?"

Pavlo laughed and wiped the perspiration from his forehead. "I'm not wasting my money if I'm spending it on you! And don't worry about where I find them. I get them especially for you!" Abruptly he changed the subject. "What would you like to do this evening? Theater or park?"

Sometimes they would go to the theater, but more often they would stroll the city parks. Tanya loved nature; it gave her a connection to her childhood in the village.

Tanya enjoyed the evenings with Baba Marusia and Dyed Petya. Time had a way of slipping by while they sat in the kitchen to drink tea and eat sunflower seeds. Life slipped into a smooth rhythm, and Tanya was happy. She had a comfortable place to live, a good job, and a kind boyfriend. What more could she want?

Early one morning as Tanya was preparing for work, she was startled by a knock at the door. *Who could be coming so early?* Quickly she stepped to the door. To her surprise, it was Katerina, Pavlo's mother. Her face was lined with worry.

"Good morning, Katerina. What brings you here so early? Is everything all right?" Tanya motioned her in.

Katerina shook her head. "They took Pavlo!" she choked.

"Who took Pavlo? What are you talking about?" Tanya demanded.

"The police!"

"What do you mean?" Tanya's voice trembled. "What happened?"

Katerina shook her head. "I don't know. Pavlo has been staying out late some nights. Sometimes it's almost morning till he comes home. He was out again last night. Then early this morning, about an hour after he came home, the police were at our door. They arrested him for stealing." Katerina's voice broke.

Tanya's mind was reeling. It seemed like only yesterday that the police had marched cousin Bogdon away in handcuffs. Now it was Pavlo. Her beloved Pavlo!

Katerina sniffed and continued, "I was worried those nights when he didn't come home. I didn't like the crowd of friends he was in, but I never dreamed they were stealing. My son, a thief!" She buried her head in her hands and sobbed.

Tanya clawed for hope. "Maybe they'll find out he's innocent and let him out. My cousin was in jail for three weeks for murdering his dad, then they let him go free. Even if Pavlo did steal, surely they won't keep him in prison for long."

Katerina wiped her eyes. "I don't know. Oh, Pavlo, my precious son! How could you do this to me?"

Time seemed to crawl after Pavlo's arrest. There were no fun evenings to look forward to. Even the jewelry she used to delight in now just mocked her by bringing back memories. She was surprised at how much she missed him.

When the day of his court appearance arrived, Tanya hurried to Katerina's house after work. She was eager, yet dreading, to hear the verdict. When she stepped inside the house, she could tell the news wasn't good. "What did the judge decide?" she asked, taking a seat across from Katerina.

"He found him guilty and sentenced him to three years in prison." Defeat was written across Katerina's face.

"Three years? For stealing?" Tanya's troubled eyes searched Katerina's face. "Usually they aren't that hard on a first-time thief."

"That's the problem." Katerina's shoulders slumped even further. "It appears this wasn't his first theft. He was found guilty of robbing a jewelry store and a clothing store earlier. He was also accused of robbing a currency exchange service at the market."

Tanya raised her eyebrows. She had heard about the currency exchange robbery, but she hadn't dreamed that Pavlo had been the culprit!

"Somehow Pavlo's friends all escaped, and he refuses to tell the police who they are. That's another reason he was sentenced to three years."

"The poor boy..." Tanya shook her head. The lump in her throat kept her from saying more. Her boyfriend in prison for three years? Could she wait that long for him?

The stigma of having a boyfriend in prison was almost more than Tanya could bear. After the court case, the whole market seemed abuzz with the gossip. People whom Tanya had considered friends now snubbed her, making snide remarks about the awfulness of robbery. Tanya quietly put away all the gifts Pavlo had given her. Even so, people often commented that something she was wearing had probably been stolen.

Tanya was surprised at the conflicting emotions swirling within her. Sometimes she found herself defending Pavlo and persuading herself that he really had a good heart. If his friends hadn't been such a bad influence, he would still be free.

But at other times, cold fingers of fear and resentment gripped her heart. *Do I really want to be in a relationship with a thief? If he wasn't strong enough to stand up for what's right, what kind of man is he? Can I wait on him for three years?* She longed to be loyal to Pavlo, but as the weeks slipped by, she found herself more confused than ever.

One evening Katerina stopped by. "I just came from visiting Pavlo in prison. He sent this to you." She held out a thin envelope and left before Tanya had a chance to open it.

After retreating to her bedroom, Tanya's hands trembled as she slit open the envelope. It had been nearly two months since Pavlo's arrest. Two long months. Now she finally had a letter from him!

> My dearest Tanya,
>
> How sad I am that I can no longer be the friend you deserve. You have given me joy, life, and love like no one else. But now I am stuck behind these bars. You don't want to belong to a jailbird. You don't deserve to be bound to someone who can't give you happiness and life. Although it pains my heart terribly to lose you, I can't ask you to wait for me. Three years is too long. I release you from our friendship. I will miss you, but I know it's best this way. You needn't wait for me. You are free to move on with life. Live it to the fullest.
>
> Goodbye. I wish you the best.
>
> Sincerely,
>
> Your Pavlo

Tanya buried her head in her pillow and allowed the tears to come—tears of both relief and disappointment. It was a relief to know that Pavlo wasn't expecting her to wait for him, but the finality of the goodbye hurt. How she would miss him! Could she ever love another man like she had loved him?

Tanya was grateful for Baba Marusia and Dyed Petya. Now that Pavlo was gone, she spent many evenings at home with them. Dyed Petya loved to talk and had a wealth of stories. Often he would reminisce about his childhood.

One afternoon as Tanya walked home from work, she was startled to see several vehicles parked outside Petya and Marusia's place. *What brings visitors at this time of day?* She quickened her steps, but then stopped short in dismay. A casket lid was propped against the porch, and a hushed group of people stood outside.

Dread gripped Tanya's heart. Had someone died? Her heart pounded as she eased the gate open. One of the neighbors looked up as she approached. "What happened?" she asked in a hushed voice.

"Baba Marusia died."

The color drained from Tanya's cheeks. "What happened? Where's Dyed Petya?"

The neighbor nodded toward the door. "He's in the house. Go on in. He'll be glad to see you."

Tanya stepped inside the house, hesitating a moment before tiptoeing into the living room, which served as the old couple's bedroom. She could see the casket placed on several stools, with Dyed Petya sitting beside it.

"Oh, Dyed Petya!" Tanya whispered, stepping to the old man's side. He clasped her hand in his, and for a moment neither said a word.

"What happened?" Tanya finally managed to ask.

In broken words, Dyed Petya told how he had awakened that morning and found Marusia still asleep. When she wasn't up an hour later, he had tried waking her. "She was already cold," he said. "She died in her sleep."

The following days passed in a blur. Tanya didn't know where she belonged. Petya and Marusia had seemed almost like her own grandparents, and she had felt at home in their house. But now, with their children and grandchildren around, she felt like an intruder. To make matters worse, they seemed to resent Tanya's affection for the old couple.

As Tanya stood by the casket and gazed for the last time at the face of Baba Marusia, her tears flowed freely. There were tears of grief and pain at losing yet another loved one and tears of fear for the future. There were also tears of discouragement. She wondered how many more times her heart could break.

That evening, after everyone except Dyed Petya and his two children and their families had left, Petya's daughter called Tanya aside. "I guess I should tell you what our plans are," she said. Her tired eyes looked straight at Tanya. "We plan to stay here with Papa the rest of the week. But then we'll take him to live with us. You have to find another place to live."

Tanya nodded mutely. *Where can I go? How can I find another place so quickly?* She struggled to maintain her composure. "I understand."

Loneliness gripped Tanya's heart. Returning to the village was not an option. Nor was moving in with Aunt Ira. Tanya found herself alone in a cold, hard world, with seemingly no one who cared about her.

That night she cried herself to sleep.

chapter 12

Adjustments

2000

The next morning Tanya explained her predicament to Lida, her boss. "Do you know of any rooms to rent? I like my job and would be happy to continue working here."

Lida smiled. "Well, I'm opening a store in the Chippievka district. Would you consider working for me there? Why don't you take today off and go see if you can find living quarters in that part of the city?"

Tanya didn't like the idea of moving to another part of the city, but she counted it an honor that her boss wanted to give her a better job at her new store. Although she had often traveled through the Chippievka district, she didn't know anyone who lived there. She decided to begin her search for lodging by asking around at the Chippievka market.

By noon the market was closing for the day and Tanya was exhausted.

She was ready to give up when she saw a young woman selling produce. Her friendly smile gave Tanya courage to ask one more time.

The young woman's smile soon turned into a pleasant chuckle. "Tanya, is it you? Don't you remember me? I'm Katya. We went to boarding school together!"

Tanya's surprise changed to delight. "Of course I remember you! Why didn't I recognize you? But I thought you studied to be a seamstress. Why are you selling produce at the market?"

Katya laughed and threw the question back at her. "What about you? Are you working as a seamstress?"

When Tanya shook her head, Katya continued, "That's how it is. We study one thing and then work at another. But tell me about yourself. You say you will be working here in Chippievka?"

After Tanya briefly explained her situation, Katya chuckled. "I guess we're in the same boat! I'm looking for a place too, and I'm planning to meet someone this afternoon to check out a possibility. Why don't you come along? Maybe she'll have room for both of us."

A few hours later, Tanya fell into step beside Katya as they turned into a side street close to the bus stop. "I believe this is the street," Katya said, looking at a scrap of paper with the address. "Now we need to figure out which is Valya's house."

Right from the start, Tanya liked the location. Although it was near the market and in the city, it had a village-like feel that Tanya craved. The houses sat back-to-back, with small garden plots and fruit trees filling any empty spaces between them.

"I think this is the place," Katya said, comparing the number on the rusty iron gate to her scrap of paper. She rapped on the gate and called out, "Anybody home?"

A chorus of angry barks answered her. Tanya took a quick step back as two snarling dogs lunged at them from the other side of the gate.

Tanya's confidence faded further when the gate suddenly cracked open and a bulky woman peered out. "What do you want?" she asked, her voice cold and coarse.

"My name is Katya, and I'm looking for a room to rent," Katya said timidly. "I made arrangements to meet with Valya Kosenko concerning—"

"That's me!" exclaimed the woman, opening the gate. "Come in. Come in." She stepped aside so the girls could enter. "You needn't be afraid of the dogs. They won't bite unless it's someone I don't like." Valya led the way to the house. The girls followed with a cautious glance at the dogs.

The dogs returned their gaze, looking warily from one girl to the other and sniffing their shoes. "Good doggie," Tanya crooned, reaching out a slow hand toward one of the dogs. "Good dog." Her soft voice put the dog at ease, and soon he was wagging his tail as Tanya scratched his head.

Air thick with cigarette smoke washed over Tanya as she followed the others into the veranda. Sacks of bottles and all kinds of other junk littered the floor. A table pushed against the wall was cluttered with sunflower seed shells and part of a loaf of moldy bread.

The landlady ushered the girls on into the house and opened another door. "This is the room that is for rent," she said. "Come in and sit down." She motioned toward a nearby couch.

Tanya sat down and surveyed the room. Sunshine filtered through the lace curtains, creating a speckled pattern on the floor. Rugs hung on the whitewashed walls, and another rug stretched across the wooden floor. The room exceeded Tanya's expectations after the cluttered veranda. A feeling of nostalgia filled her. The simple house reminded her of home.

Moving was easy. It didn't take Tanya long to pack her meager belongings and move them into the room she shared with Katya. But adjusting to new people and a new place proved challenging. Valya, the landlady, intimidated Tanya. She was clearly the lady of the house. It seemed she was always chiding, scolding, and bossing her tenants. Tanya resented being treated like a child.

And then there was Katya. Although Tanya was grateful for her help in finding a place to rent, she found sharing a room with her more difficult than she had expected. For one, their personalities clashed. Katya was a party girl, always running from one activity to the next. Only rarely did she have a serious thought, and her lack of responsibility grated on Tanya's nerves. Wherever Katya went, she left a trail: clothing on the floor, dirty mugs on the table, and rumpled blankets in her bed. But it wasn't only that. With her sunny disposition and ready smile, Katya had an abundance of friends and was always throwing parties.

Tanya hated these parties. The noise, the laughter, and the hilarity annoyed her. She quickly learned that it worked best if she quietly disappeared when Katya's friends came over.

Often Tanya found refuge in the garden. There she would close her ears to the raucous laughter that pulsed from the open windows. She pretended she was still a little girl at home in Mama's garden. She found joy in pulling weeds, hoeing the long rows of potatoes, and seeing the green plants grow and flourish.

Life soon settled into a routine. Tanya enjoyed her position selling men's clothes at the store. Her hours were longer than what she was used to at the market, but she didn't mind. It meant an increase in pay—and less time to miss Pavlo.

Tanya had hoped to move on with life and forget about him. But she struggled more than she had thought she would. Valya often talked about her son Valentine, who was also in prison. This made Tanya wonder how Pavlo was faring.

Another issue was Roma, Katya's boyfriend, who often came around to see her. Whenever he was off work, he would come and stay with Katya. Seeing them together was hard for Tanya. It brought back memories of when Pavlo was still a part of her life. She couldn't help but miss him.

chapter 13

The Landlady's Son

2001

"Girls, you have to move out."

Tanya stared in surprise at Valya. Why would they have to move? Where would she go?

"Valentine will soon be released from prison. This is his room, and you need to move out so he can have his room back."

Tanya involuntarily looked at the picture on the wall. The handsome young man stared back at her, just as he had ever since they had moved in. His face had become quite familiar. Tanya often wondered what he was like in real life. Was he as hard to live with as his mother?

She dreaded finding another place to live, but it couldn't be much worse than where she was now.

Over a year had passed since the girls had moved in with Valya.

Things had improved slightly after Valya kicked Roma out of the house. Tanya shuddered as she remembered the terrible nights when he came home drunk. Many a night, Tanya and Valya had risked their own safety while trying to protect Katya and her tiny son. Katya had not been the only one with bruises.

With Roma gone now, things had settled down a bit. But there were still arguments, and it seemed hardly a day went by without a disagreement. Sometimes it was the two girls against Valya. And other times, Valya and Katya were against Tanya. *It's a wonder Valya puts up with us,* Tanya thought. *If it weren't for the rent money she needs for drink and cigarettes, she would have kicked us out long ago.*

But now, with Valentine coming home, the time had come to move.

"How soon do we need to be out?" Katya's voice was laced with weariness. She bounced her little boy up and down to quiet his complaining cry.

Little Anton was now almost six months old, and Tanya had never seen such a clingy, fussy child. But then, what did she know about babies? She had been only five years old when Svetta was born, and that was a long time ago. But one thing she did know—she never wanted to be a mother if she had to do it like Katya.

It didn't seem to bother Katya that her baby spent his days at the daycare while she worked at the market. And it didn't seem to faze her that her son was facing life without a father. There was no doubt that Katya loved her son, but her love was tinged with resentment. The child had stolen her freedom. No longer could Katya enjoy her party life without feeling guilty. But she still did her share of partying, usually leaving Anton under Valya's care.

"You don't need to leave right away." Valya's brisk voice interrupted Tanya's reverie. "I'm not exactly sure when Valentine is coming home, so stay till he comes. He can spend the first few nights in the dining room."

The dining room was more like a hall than a room. Tanya didn't relish the idea of having a jailbird sleeping in the room next to hers. She shivered at the thought and determined to be gone before Valentine came home.

Gradually the warm days of summer gave way to the brisk chill of fall. One evening as Tanya stepped inside the house after a day at work, she noticed an unfamiliar pair of well-worn men's shoes inside the door. She wondered who could be visiting, when suddenly it dawned on her. *Has Valentine come home?*

She dreaded meeting this stranger whom she had heard so much about. Was he really the man his mom had described? She shook her head. *The sooner I move out, the better. If only I could have found a place to stay!* Evening after evening, she had scoured the area looking for a room. Most of the apartments were far more than her budget could afford. And now Valya's son had come home.

Tanya slipped through the dining room to her bedroom, hoping to remain unnoticed. The aromas that floated from the kitchen told her a feast was in the making. Normally she would have gone to the kitchen and offered to help, but not tonight. Not if Valentine was in there.

"Supper's ready!" Valya called, sticking her head into the girls' room. "And guess who's here! Valentine has come home!"

"Congratulations!" Katya chirped. "How exciting! By the smell of things, you are making a real feast!"

"Of course!" Valya chuckled. "It's time to celebrate!"

The girls followed Valya to the kitchen. Tanya gulped when she saw the man sitting at the table. So this was Valentine. He was not the handsome young man in the portrait. There was a resemblance, to be sure, but this man looked older than she had expected.

Despite the tasty food, supper was an awkward affair. Valentine picked at his food and seemed aloof. Tanya couldn't help but wonder if he was always this way, or if it was just the newness of freedom that left him so withdrawn. In times of stress, Tanya's tongue always felt clumsy, and tonight was no exception. Feeling uncomfortable, she rose to leave before the others were finished eating. "Shall I milk the goats tonight?" she asked Valya, who was pouring herself another drink.

Valya nodded. "Yes, please."

As Tanya stepped out the door, she heard Valentine ask, "Does she often do that for you?"

She paused and listened for the answer. "Yes, she's a great helper. She grew up in the village and is used to hard work."

"A simple village girl! That's what she is!" Katya's titter rose above Valentine's chuckle.

Tanya bit her lip, her cheeks burning. She didn't wait to listen for more but hurried to the barn where she could be alone with her thoughts. *Yes, that's who I am*, she thought bitterly. *Just a simple village girl. I don't belong here, but I can't find anywhere else to stay. Maybe I should just move to the village.* She set her stool next to the goat and began stripping the milk from its swollen teats. She wished her troubles could be stripped away as easily.

Tanya knew moving back to her childhood home was not an option. She still visited her parents occasionally, but each time the house was more rundown and her parents more irritable than before. She couldn't remember a visit when they hadn't had a disagreement about something. Finding a job would also be almost impossible. No, she could not go back to Kryvoshyintsi. She would have to stay in Kyiv. Tomorrow she would continue her search.

Valentine and his mother were in no hurry to go to bed. They sat up late into the night visiting and catching up on the last two years. Finally their voices quieted and gave way to muffled snoring. Tanya lay on her bed and shivered. A feeling of claustrophobia overwhelmed her. She felt trapped in her room. If she wanted to go anywhere, she would have to walk through the dining room where Valentine lay. The past years had taught her to trust no one, especially not a man. She struggled to push away her fears and go to sleep.

Days passed, and still Tanya couldn't find a place to stay. Katya was also looking for a new place. At one time Tanya had been open to the idea of sharing a room with Katya at another location, but since Valentine's arrival, their relationship had become more strained.

She wasn't sure what to think about this man. But as they learned to know each other better, she lost her paralyzing fear. She tried to keep a healthy distance, but that was hard to do while living in such tight quarters.

Katya seemed to enjoy Valentine's presence. She was always telling jokes and bantering with him. Her lack of reserve nauseated Tanya. She felt herself overreacting, causing her to become more tightlipped and reserved than ever.

Valentine was usually still sleeping when Tanya slipped out of the house to go to work. But one morning he was sitting at the table drinking coffee when Tanya walked past. "Good morning, Tanya," he said. "Ready for work?" He smiled and motioned to the chair next to him. "Do you have time to sit and drink coffee with me?"

Tanya glanced at the clock and hesitated. "Hardly. I don't want to be late for work. Thanks, though."

"I understand. Tell you what, Tanya, I'd really like to get to know you better. But with Katya around all the time, I can hardly get a word out of you." He gave her a teasing smile. "How about spending the evening with me? We could go to the theater and get some ice cream afterward. What do you say?"

"I was going to continue looking for an apartment this evening," she said, trying to process what he was saying. "I can't find anything."

"Oh, just skip that tonight. There's no rush. No one is pushing you out. You haven't heard me complaining about sleeping in the dining room, have you? Katya doesn't seem to be in a hurry to move, so why should you?"

Tanya struggled to concentrate on her work that day. She thought of Pavlo and remembered the fun they had together. Was she betraying him if she spent the evening with Valentine? He had told her to move on. But did she even like Valentine? *I guess one evening can't hurt,* she finally decided. *I'll see what he's like.*

Tanya surprised herself by enjoying the evening more than she had thought possible. Valentine wasn't so bad after all. She had forgotten how good it felt to walk down the street with someone at her side. Valentine wasn't young or overly handsome, but that didn't bother Tanya. He was a natural conversationalist, and she enjoyed his sense of humor.

Katya was still awake when Tanya got back home. The sneer on her face sent daggers into Tanya's heart. "So you found a new boyfriend?" Katya's voice was hushed. Tanya wasn't sure if it was because little Anton was sleeping, or because she didn't want anyone on the other side of the wall to overhear.

Tanya shrugged and gave a little laugh. "Was I supposed to ask you before I let him take me out? Since when are you my boss?"

"I'm not your boss, but I know your motives. You just don't want to move out. You think if you get on the good side of Valentine, you can stay here. Sly girl you are!"

Angry words threatened to spew out of Tanya's mouth, but she choked them back. They would do more harm than good. Silently she prepared for bed.

Sleep was slow in coming.

chapter 14

Is This Love?

2001

Tanya had enjoyed the evening with Valentine, but she hardly dared admit it, even to herself. As the days passed, she was a little disappointed when Valentine made no effort to spend more time with her. She resented the way he spent evenings with his old friends, cronies he had run around with before his time in jail. But it was Katya's attitude that frustrated her the most. Katya knew how to make Valentine laugh, and her joking and teasing grated on Tanya's nerves. The degrading way she treated Tanya hurt most of all.

After the arrival of little Anton, Katya had quit bringing friends home to party. But now, with Valentine at home, things changed. Once again late-night parties were held in their room. Valentine brought his friends and Katya hers, and they often partied late into the night.

Tanya dreaded those evenings, but she didn't want to give Valentine the impression that she was unsociable. Sometimes she would look for an excuse to stay away, but other times she would join the party, trying to act happy and carefree. The smoke from the cigarettes and the pounding of the music often gave her a throbbing headache. She knew the effects of too much drink, so she tried not to drink more than a shot glass or two. She couldn't risk losing her job.

Tanya regularly did the evening chores, and the barn became her place of refuge. There she could be herself without worrying about making an impression. The animals never gave her sneering glances like Katya did.

One evening as Tanya carried the bucket of milk to the house, she stopped short. Loud voices floated through the window. Arguments were not unusual, but she didn't want to walk in on one.

"Why do you keep hanging out with city girls?" Valya's voice was sharp and critical, as usual. "Don't you know they are lazy and good for nothing? How many times do I have to tell you that the girl you need is Tanya?"

Tanya cringed, but she didn't move from where she was standing in the shadows near the window. She felt rooted to the spot.

"You will never get far in life with a city girl. What you need is a good, hardworking village girl like Tanya."

"I will choose my own girl! I don't need you telling me what to do," Valentine said with disgust. "Who said I even want to get married? The last thing I need is to be tied to some woman for the rest of my life. Let me have fun with the ones I want. You mind your own business, and I'll mind mine." A door slammed, and Tanya heard Valentine's heavy footsteps receding.

She turned and went back to the barn. She wasn't ready to go in and face them. Tears stung her eyes, but she wasn't sure why. In a way, it was a relief to know that Valentine wasn't interested in her. As much as she had enjoyed their evening at the theater, Tanya wasn't sure she wanted to be married to someone like Valentine for the rest of her life.

He could be so nice—so gentlemanly and polite. But after weeks of living under the same roof, Tanya knew the other side of him as well. There were days when everything displeased him, and everyone knew to stay out of his way. As for his other habits, he drank, but not a lot. He smoked too, but Tanya couldn't fault him for that. She was also addicted to cigarettes. But at least she knew how to limit them to one or two a day. Valentine went through a whole pack each day.

Hardworking. Is that the only good thing about me? Tanya's thoughts rambled on. *I never want someone to marry me just because they think I'm a hard worker. I want to be loved and appreciated for who I am, not just for what I do.*

Tanya glanced down at the milk in the pail. She must strain it and put it into the fridge before it soured. She wiped her eyes and pasted on a smile, determined to keep the feelings of her heart hidden.

It happened slowly. So slowly that Tanya hardly noticed. Although she still hated when Valentine drank, she found herself enjoying him more and more. And he seemed to feel the same way, finding more and more excuses to spend time with her. Sometimes he would stop by at closing time and walk home with her from work. Other times they would go out for coffee or attend a movie.

But when she was alone, it was different. At those times she found herself doubting. She wondered why she ever gave in to his attention. But try as she might, she always forgot herself in his presence. She felt helpless to keep her distance and reserve. He had a way of pulling her right into the fun. She began to enjoy the parties and the dancing.

One evening they partied late, as usual. One by one the guests left until only Valentine remained in the room with Katya, Tanya, and little Anton. Valentine settled back on the couch and yawned loudly. "I'm so tired I think I could sleep right here. This used to be my bed, you know."

By the time the girls had finished clearing the bottles away from the table, he was snoring, stretched across the couch—Tanya's bed.

"Shall I wake him?" Tanya asked uncertainly.

"Don't you dare!" Katya whispered back. "You saw how much he drank this evening. And you know how easily he gets upset. I'm guessing if we don't disturb him, he'll sleep till morning."

"But where should I sleep?" Tanya asked, feeling like a needy little girl. "May I join you on your couch?"

Katya shrugged her shoulders. "I guess." She reached out to unfold the bed. "But this *is* Valentine's room, you know. It's high time you move out."

"What about you?" Tanya hissed. Her eyes burned with anger. "You need to move out as much as I do!"

Tanya lay awake long into the night. When she finally dozed off to sleep, nightmares chased her. She awoke in terror. She could not go on like this. *I have to move out as soon as possible.*

The next morning Tanya talked with Valya while they were doing the chores. She explained what had happened the evening before. "This has become too awkward. I must move out."

Valya laughed. "Don't worry, Tanya dear. There's no hurry for you to move. Haven't you noticed that Valentine likes you? You would make the perfect wife for him. Give him some time, and everything will work out."

Tanya shook her head. "No, I must move out." She glanced at her watch and realized she had to hurry or she would be late for work.

She struggled to keep her mind on her work. By noon, Tanya knew what she would do. She closed the store early and caught a bus to the metro station. She would go see if Aunt Ira had some advice.

Aunt Ira welcomed her with open arms. Time passed quickly as Tanya shared the struggles she was facing. For so long she had kept everything inside, telling no one. Now, putting her fears and feelings into words was harder than she had imagined.

Aunt Ira listened patiently, interrupting now and then to ask a question. "I think it comes down to one question," she said. "Do you think he really loves you?"

Tanya sat deep in thought. Finally she answered, "I don't know. I think he does, but I don't know how much. I'm afraid he loves his drink more than me."

"Hmm. That's a problem. Drinking men are not fun to live with." Tanya knew from the pained look in her eyes that she was remembering Uncle Yuri.

"I know that!" Tanya answered. "It was terrible to be around Papa when he was drunk—and Valentine is not much better!"

"You said he was in jail. What was he arrested for?"

"I'm not sure." Tanya felt her cheeks get warm. "I never asked him about it. But I think it was for stealing."

"That's something you should look into," Aunt Ira said with finality. "Give him some time. If he truly loves you, he might change. Maybe with a wife like you, he'd become a real man."

"Is that the way it works?" Tanya knew she was treading on dangerous ground, but she had to know how Aunt Ira felt.

Aunt Ira's face tightened. "Sometimes, but not always. For Yuri it didn't."

Is This Love?

Reluctantly Tanya stood to leave. She looked around the apartment one last time. "Are you sure there's no room here?"

"No, you can see that for yourself. This apartment isn't much more than a closet. Everything is piled on top of everything else. I'm sorry, dear, but you must go."

Tanya gave her aunt a hug and stepped outside. If she hurried, she could catch the last bus. She made it in time for the metro, but by the time she arrived at the bus station, no buses were left. She would have to walk the last stretch. She quickened her steps. It was an hour's hike from the metro to the house. Thick clouds covered the sky, hiding the stars.

The occasional streetlights cast an eerie glow over the street. Tanya shivered as she passed a homeless man lying on a park bench. Up ahead she noticed some teenagers partying on the street. "Lord, have mercy!" she prayed. "Help me get home safely!" She skirted the crowd, resisting the urge to run. Her heart pounded when she noticed a lone man walking in her direction. He stopped under a streetlight, but she didn't dare look at him. She kept her eyes on the sidewalk and continued her brisk pace.

"Tanya, is it you?"

The voice calling from under the streetlight startled her, but the cold fingers of fear melted away when Tanya looked up and realized it was Valentine.

"Valentine! You scared me! What are you doing out here?" Tanya's breath came in short gasps. She couldn't hide her relief.

"I have the same question for you!" Valentine said, holding Tanya close. "We were worried about you! I've been out here looking for you for the last hour. Where have you been?"

As Tanya laid her head on his shoulder, she couldn't help but feel safe and secure and a little foolish. *How could I have doubted his love? Why didn't I trust him?*

As they walked the last kilometers toward home, she explained to Valentine where she had gone. She didn't tell him why she had needed to talk with Aunt Ira, and to her relief, he didn't press for an explanation.

"Please don't do that again," he said. "I was so worried about you. It's not safe to be out alone in the dark. Next time let me go with you."

"All right," Tanya said, trying to keep the tremble out of her voice. She realized with a start that her freedom was being taken from her. But to her surprise, it felt good. She felt more loved and secure than she had for a long time.

"What's going on?" Tanya asked as she stared at the bedroom. Something was amiss. The cupboard door was hanging open, and half of the shelves were empty. A few pieces of trash littered the floor, along with one of Katya's old housecoats. The blankets and pillows that were usually on Katya's bed lay in a heap on the floor, and the bedsheet was missing.

Tanya hurried to the kitchen to find Valya. "What's with Katya?" she asked.

"What do you mean?" Valya asked, perplexed.

"Come and see." Tanya led the way to her room. "Look at this!"

Valya took in the scene. "Hmm, it looks like most of her clothes are gone. Even Anton's toys are missing. I wonder if she left for good."

Tanya disappeared into the veranda for a moment. "Her shoes and boots are gone too," she announced when she returned. "Did she tell you she was leaving?"

"No. You didn't know anything either?"

Tanya shook her head. "A week or so ago, she told me I'd better move out soon. But I didn't know *she* was planning to leave. Why wouldn't she have told us?"

"She had a good reason not to tell," Valya snorted. "She was several months behind in paying her rent. I guess she thought if she leaves this way, she'll get out of paying it."

"But now what?" Tanya's voice trembled a bit. "I don't want to stay here alone."

As much as Katya had grated on Tanya's nerves, having her nearby had given a measure of security. True, they argued and were constantly in each other's hair, but the thought of staying alone made Tanya feel vulnerable.

"Tanya dear, don't look so worried! I think this is just the way it's supposed to be. You'll soon feel like part of the family. It's just as good that Katya got out of the way."

Valentine's reaction confirmed Tanya's fears. "It was high time that girl and her baby got out of here! Now I can have my own bed back without crowding anybody."

That night Valentine moved his things into the space vacated by Katya.

Tanya lay awake late into the night, plagued by doubts and guilt. *What kind of mess have I gotten myself into?*

chapter 15

A Renter No Longer

2001-2002

*L*ife settled into a new routine, and Tanya found it a relief to have Katya gone. Now she could be herself without worrying about snide remarks or accusations. Even Valentine and his mom seemed more relaxed and amiable.

Without Katya to plan the parties, Valentine drank less and was more congenial. He found a job fueling cars at a local gas station, but Tanya wasn't sure how much of his paycheck ever came home. She suspected that the larger portion went toward his cigarettes and alcohol, but at least he wasn't sponging off his mother.

As usual, at the end of the month, Tanya gave part of her paycheck to Valya for rent.

"Listen, daughter, your days of paying rent are over," Valya said, handing back the money. "You are part of the family now. I can't take rent from you."

Tanya didn't know whether to laugh or cry. It felt good to be loved and accepted, but was this where she wanted to spend the rest of her life? She forced a laugh. "Thank you!" she said as she pocketed the money. She determined to save the money. That way, if things got too bad, she could always leave. But until then, she would enjoy being Valentine's girl.

One morning Tanya dragged herself out of bed, dreading another day. A wave of nausea washed over her. *How long will this flu last?* She forced herself to eat a bite of breakfast and drink a little tea. She left for work early so she could stop at the pharmacy. *Maybe they will have something to help me.*

The pharmacist listened with professional sympathy as Tanya explained how she was feeling and then asked for something to help with her nausea.

"Are you sure it's the flu?" the pharmacist asked. "Your symptoms sound suspiciously like morning sickness."

Tanya's face paled, and she struggled to keep her breakfast down. "I'm not sure what it is," she admitted.

She left the pharmacy with some pills for nausea and a pregnancy test.

Somehow she made it through the day. Twice she gave a customer the wrong change, and another time she quoted the wrong price for a leather belt. Her stomach churned and her mind raced. *What if it isn't just the flu?*

Tanya's hands trembled the next morning as she held the test toward the faint light coming from the eastern sky. Her heart sank as she saw the result. *Positive.*

Now what? A myriad of emotions flooded her heart. She needed time alone to think. She called Lida, her boss, and asked for the day off. Lida agreed reluctantly but said it would come off her paycheck at the end of the month.

Tanya left the house at her usual time, not wanting to raise questions. She was not ready to talk about this to anyone yet. But instead of heading into the city, she took the path that led toward the river. The river was hardly big enough to be called a river. It was just a narrow stream that eventually flowed into the much larger Dnieper River. She had often come here when she needed time alone.

It was cold, and the February winds beat across her slender shoulders, threatening to blow her into the river. The gray sky hung like a heavy blanket over the city. As the cold crept through the layers of clothing, numbness gripped her heart, and she realized it was too cold to be outside for long. She was foolish to even think about spending the day at the river in this kind of weather.

Wearily she turned her footsteps back the way she had come. She was still not ready to talk with anyone, but she felt too sick and chilled to stay outside.

Valya looked up in surprise when Tanya entered the house a little later. "I thought you went to work," she said. "What's the deal?"

"I'm sick, so I came home," Tanya said as she slid off her boots. She leaned wearily against the doorframe. "Could you bring me a bucket? I think I'm going to throw up."

Valya looked alarmed. She quickly fetched a bucket—just in time to catch the contents of Tanya's meager breakfast.

"I'll be all right," Tanya said, giving her a weak smile. "I just need to rest."

Valya followed her into the bedroom. "Lie down, dear, and let me feel your forehead. Maybe you have a temperature."

A Renter No Longer

Tanya's cheeks were flushed from the cold wind, but her forehead was cool.

"I don't believe you have a fever. I'll bring you a cup of tea."

Tanya nodded. There was no use protesting. And she didn't feel up to talking right now anyway. She closed her eyes and tried to sleep.

Instead of sleep came tears—bitter, salty tears that coursed down her cheeks. *What have I gotten myself into? Now I'm trapped! Is there any way out?* Her mind traveled back over the past few months. She could still hear Valentine's voice coming through the window that night as he argued with his mother. *"Who said I even want to get married? The last thing I need is to be tied to some woman for the rest of my life. Let me have fun with the ones I want."*

She shuddered at the memory. Had Valentine grown up since then? Would he accept responsibility, or would he get angry and kick her out? Or worse yet, would he insist on an abortion? She trembled at the thought.

Whatever the case, she had to tell him, and the sooner the better. His response couldn't be worse than the dread she felt. Her decision made, she fell into a fitful sleep.

She awoke hours later, feeling refreshed. The intense nausea had lessened, but her body ached as though she had chopped wood all day.

As Tanya pulled the comb through her brown hair, she studied the face of the girl staring back. The face looked old and burdened for being only twenty years old. "You're no longer a young girl," she whispered ruefully to the face. "You are becoming a mother." For a moment she felt a thrill of excitement. *How exciting to have a child of my own!* But fear quickly squelched her excitement. *How will Valentine respond?*

Resolutely she set down her comb and reached for her makeup. She would do her part to make Valentine pleased with her.

"Good evening, Tanya. How's my pretty girl?" Valentine settled on the couch beside her. "Mama told me you weren't feeling well this morning. Are you feeling better now?"

Tanya blushed, more from the secret she was hiding than from the compliment. "Yes, I feel better than I did this morning. Shall we check if supper is ready?"

The aroma of *rassolnik*[1] soup filled the air, tantalizing their taste buds. The flavors of rice, chicken, and sour pickles melded together into a flavorful broth. To Tanya's surprise, she actually felt hungry.

"Ah, what tastes better than a bowl of rassolnik on a cold winter night?" Valentine said, slurping the hot broth from his large spoon. "I got so cold fueling cars today! At least I can buy coffee. I don't know how many cups I drank today."

"Doesn't that get expensive?" Tanya wondered.

Valentine laughed. "Not the way I do it! You see, for every two hundred hryvnia's worth of fuel someone buys, they get a free coffee. Some people don't know about that offer or don't want to bother with it. So if they leave their receipts behind, I can use them to get my coffee for free."

Tanya wrinkled her brow. "What if you get caught?"

"You silly goose! It's not stealing. It's only drinking free coffee that someone else didn't get."

Tanya shrugged. "I just don't want you to be put in prison again!"

"You need to do worse things than that to land in prison," Valentine said. "I have no intention of ever landing there again!" He grimaced and shook his head.

After supper, Tanya sat beside Valentine as usual to watch his favorite TV show. Her thoughts were far away, however, and fear clawed at

---

[1] A traditional soup famous for its sour pickles.

A Renter No Longer

her heart. How would Valentine react when he found out?

"That was a good show!" Valentine said with pleasure at the end of the show.

"I actually didn't notice," Tanya said, dropping her eyes. "I guess I have other things on my mind."

"What do you mean?" Valentine asked. "Are you still not feeling well from the flu?" This wasn't like Tanya to act so subdued.

The lump in Tanya's throat grew until she wondered how she could say what she knew she needed to say. Tears glazed her eyes. "I really don't have the flu," she said. She bit her lip to try to keep back the tears. "I'm pregnant."

The silence was thick as the reality hit.

"So I'm going to be a papa?"

Tanya nodded. "Yes."

A smile slowly spread across Valentine's face. "Exciting! You'll make a wonderful mother! When shall we get married?"

Tanya sighed with relief. This was better than she had dared to hope. Life would be good after they got married.

chapter 16

Mama's Story

2002

Tanya's thoughts whirled as she went to work the next morning. She felt giddy with excitement. Soon she would be more than just Valentine's girl, she would be his wife—and the mother of his baby! Her heart fluttered as she remembered how excited Valya had been when they told her of their plans. To think that her landlady would actually become her mother-in-law! Tanya smiled, and for a moment all her earlier conflicts with Valya faded.

She couldn't help but wonder how her parents would respond. *Most likely they won't even care. But I hope they at least come to the wedding.*

The next Saturday, Valentine and Tanya boarded the bus for Kryvoshyintsi. She had asked Galya to let Mama and Papa know she was coming home and bringing her boyfriend. Apprehension and excitement twisted Tanya's stomach as the bus neared the village. The familiar buildings, the empty stork nests, and the bustling village store brought back a flood of nostalgia. This was where her roots were. This was where she belonged.

"Shall we stop at the store and buy some food to take to your parents?" Valentine asked.

"Good idea!" Tanya grabbed his hand and led the way to the store.

Masha Klimenko, the store owner, looked up in surprise as Tanya entered. "Why, Tanya!" she said. "I didn't know you were around! It's been a long time since I saw you. Who do you have with you?" She gave Valentine a friendly smile.

"This is Valentine, my fiancé," Tanya replied, giving him a pleased smile. It was fun to introduce him to her old village friends.

"And when is the wedding?" Masha wondered. "Will it be here in the village?"

Tanya laughed. "No, not here. We're getting married in Kyiv a month from today."

"Congratulations!"

Valentine helped Tanya pick out some lunch meat and cheese. They also bought several poppy seed rolls, Papa's favorite.

The weekend went better than Tanya had dared hope. Mikoli liked Valentine from the start. The first evening they sat up late, drinking, joking, and laughing. Tanya shook her head. Why was it that sometimes alcohol only led to hilarity, but other times it turned people into vicious beasts? She couldn't understand.

Mikoli took Valentine to the collective farm where he worked to show him around. This was Tanya's chance to talk with her mother. She took a deep breath and gathered up her courage. "Mama, what do you think about Valentine? Should I marry him?"

Natasha looked up from where she was picking walnuts out of the shells. "I don't know, daughter. Do you love him?"

Tanya studied the walnut in her hand before answering. "I don't know. Some days I think I do. Other times I'm not sure." With a hammer she tapped the nut gently, and it cracked open. She shoved it onto the pile of cracked nuts on the table.

"Maybe there's a more important question. Does he love you?" Natasha blinked as an unbidden tear sprang into her eye. She wiped it away, hoping Tanya had not noticed. "You don't want to be married to a man who does not love you."

Tanya nodded. "You're right. And I do think he loves me. He's so kind and considerate. He acts like he loves me. But how can I know for sure?"

"I don't know." Natasha's shoulders slumped further. "All I can tell you is to please be careful. Don't repeat my mistakes!"

Tanya was startled by the pain in her mother's eyes. "Tell me, Mama, how was it for you? I don't think you ever told me the whole story."

Natasha shelled several more walnuts before beginning her story. "I never told you this story before because it's too painful. I don't like to remember it. But today I feel I must tell you. Maybe it can help spare you a miserable marriage." She looked out the window, a faraway look in her eyes. "You know I'm not from this village. I grew up in Tsapiivka."

Tanya nodded. As a child she had often gone with her mother to Tsapiivka, a neighboring village, to visit relatives.

"My babushka lived here in Kryvoshyintsi. She was getting older and needed someone to look after her, and I needed a job. I had a better chance of finding a job here since Kryvoshyintsi is a larger village. So when I was twenty, I moved here and got a job at the collective farm. It was hard work, but I was young and strong.

"I was a quiet girl and didn't have many friends. I preferred spending the evenings at home with Babushka instead of partying with the other young people."

Mama's Story

Tanya tried to keep back a smile. She had not realized how much she and her mother were alike.

"When I was twenty-two, a young man named Mikoli returned from serving in the army."

Tanya nodded. She remembered the picture of Papa in his uniform. He had looked so young and handsome back then.

"Everyone spoke highly of him, but I paid no attention to him. I was absorbed in my work and had no interest in pursuing boys. In fact, sometimes Babushka would chide me. She told me I should find myself a boyfriend or I'd be an old maid.

"One evening Babushka and I were sitting out in the veranda shelling the beans we had harvested from the garden. Suddenly the gate opened, and I was startled to see Mikoli come striding up the walk. Behind him came his mother, his sister, and his elderly grandfather, Prokip.

"Babushka and I looked at each other in surprise. What could these people want? When Mikoli knocked sharply, Babushka hurried to open the door and welcome them in. I stayed where I was sitting.

"Mikoli bowed politely and said, 'I came to talk to Natasha Victorivna.' He looked at me, and my mind started racing in all directions. I wondered what he could want.

"'That's me,' I said. 'What can I do for you?' I was so scared I could hardly speak."

By now Tanya was sitting on the edge of her chair, wide-eyed. She had never heard this story before. The walnuts lay untouched on the table as she listened, spellbound.

"Mikoli bowed again and asked, 'Natasha Victorivna, will you please marry me?' His question shocked me. It was as if lightning had struck our house. I couldn't believe my ears. Why would this 27-year-old want to marry me? Quiet, shy me? I had never even talked to him, and now he was asking me to marry him. A thousand thoughts surged through my mind. *What should I do? Should I marry him?* I remembered all the smart remarks the other girls had made about him. I knew he was well liked throughout the village.

"Babushka then urged me. 'Well, Natasha, will you or won't you?' I looked around at the eager faces, and their excitement had a way of pulling me in. I could hardly believe my ears when I heard myself saying, 'Yes, Mikoli, I will be happy to marry you.'

"My life was never the same after that." Natasha gazed out the window, into the distance, as if she had forgotten Tanya's presence.

Finally Tanya spoke. "But, Mama! How could you? Did you even love him?"

Natasha shrugged. "I don't know why I did it; I guess I was young and naive. I wanted to get married, and I knew Mikoli was popular. I couldn't think of any reason to say no. But I was scared. Terribly scared.

"After he had proposed, we spent some time together. He took me to Tsapiivka so I could introduce him to my family. Everyone was excited for us, and I became excited too. A few months later we were married. He was still nearly a stranger, but I was happy. I resolved to do all I could to be a good wife.

"I moved into his house. This house." Natasha studied the whitewashed beams on the ceiling, remembering those days of long ago. "It was his grandpa's house. Prokip was a good man." A look of tenderness filled her eyes. "You don't remember him, Tanya, do you?"

Tanya shook her head.

"He loved you. He couldn't have loved his own daughter more. When you were only three weeks old, I had to return to work. You stayed with Prokip, and he took good care of you." Her mother smiled.

"How old was I when he died?" Tanya wondered. "I don't remember him at all except from the photo where he is holding me."

"You were only two years old when he died. Our marriage was strained right from the start, but the tension increased after Prokip was gone. Mikoli had great respect for him and tried to please him. But after he was gone, Mikoli began to do as he pleased.

"Since he worked as a truck driver, he sometimes had to work the night shift. I trusted him and was faithful to him. But soon rumors reached me that he was using the night shift to hang out with other girls."

The bitterness in her mother's voice startled Tanya. Sympathy welled in her heart for her dear mother. As a child, she had been blissfully unaware of all the grief her mother bore. She knew Papa and Mama didn't always get along, but she hadn't realized it was this bad.

"The hardest part for me…" Natasha swallowed the lump in her throat, "was when I found out that he had never even loved me. He married me out of spite."

"Out of spite? What do you mean?"

"After we were married, I found out that he had been engaged to marry another girl. He loved this girl, but Prokip didn't like her. He said her hands were too tender to ever be of any good use. 'You need someone who can work hard, bear you children, and be a good housekeeper.'

"Surprisingly, Mikoli took his advice and called off the engagement. One day his mother and sister were visiting and began to pressure Mikoli to get married. They were giving him a hard time when I happened to walk by. I was clueless, of course, but they saw me through the window. 'Look at that girl,' Prokip said. 'She's young and pretty, and it's easy to see that she's hardworking. That's the kind of girl you should marry.'

"Mikoli was tired of their pressure, so he replied, 'All right. We'll get engaged today.' And that's what happened."

Tanya looked away. The story sounded strangely familiar. *Does Valentine want to marry me just because his mother pressured him to? Just because I'm hardworking?*

"Mama, did you ever think about leaving Papa and moving back to Tsapiivka?"

The sadness on Natasha's face deepened. "Yes, I did. There were many times I wanted to run away. In fact, one time I did leave him. I took you to my parents in Tsapiivka. I told them I was ready to divorce Mikoli and start a new life. But they said it had been my choice to marry him and that I dare not disgrace them by coming home as a single mother. They told me divorce was not an option."

Silence hung between them as Tanya picked up the hammer and began gently tapping the walnuts again. Her thoughts swirled. Would she end up trapped in a marriage like Mama's? She shook her head. Surely Valentine would never be as cruel as Papa.

A single mother. Disgrace. A single mother. Disgrace. A single mother… The tap-tap of the hammer on the nuts seemed to chant the words. *Disgrace. A single mother. Disgrace…* Tears welled in her eyes. She did not want to be a disgrace to her family. She wanted to prove that something good could come out of her family.

Natasha broke the silence. "That's my story, Tanya. I hope yours will be different. I hope you never have to live through pain like that."

For a moment, Tanya and her mother looked deeply into each other's eyes. "I never dreamed it was like this," Tanya said. "Thank you, Mama, for all you did to try to give me a happy childhood." Her voice broke and dropped to a whisper. "I want to do the same for my baby."

Natasha looked up sharply. "Your baby?"

"Yes, my baby and Valentine's baby." Tanya looked away. Unfamiliar emotions surged through her heart. She felt an overwhelming love for her baby, a fierce desire to give this unborn child the best future she could.

"Then it is decided, Tanya," her mother said resolutely. "You have no choice but to get married. You don't want to be a single mother."

Tanya nodded. "I know."

chapter 17

The Wedding

2002

The wedding day arrived—March 30, 2002. This was the day Tanya's life would change forever. She smiled as she looked into the mirror, past the layers of makeup, and into the brown eyes sparkling back at her. This was her special day.

The morning passed in a flurry of activity as Tanya helped Valya in the kitchen. Their wedding would not be a royal event. There wouldn't be a large crowd, dinner at a banquet hall, or a luscious cake. There wouldn't be wedding gowns and flower girls. Tanya told herself that only in fairy tales was life that wonderful.

They had invited her parents and a few friends. Valya had borrowed money to make a feast. It would be simple but special.

Valentine rearranged the furniture in their bedroom to make room for the tables. By laying a plank of wood across two chairs, they were able to make a long bench.

Tanya deftly lifted another blanched cabbage leaf from the kettle. She spooned some of the rice and hamburger mixture onto it and folded the ends over and rolled it tightly. She added it to the pot and reached for another leaf.

Valya added mayonnaise to the vegetables she had cooked and chopped earlier. She opened a can of peas, quickly adding them and some chopped pickles to the bowl. With a large spoon, she gently mixed the Olivye salad, being careful not to mash the cubed potatoes and carrots.

The savory aroma of meat cooking and fish frying filled the air. Tanya wiped a strand of sticky hair from her forehead. "May I go when I'm finished with these cabbage rolls?" she asked.

Valya nodded. "Yes, and thanks for your help." She glanced at the clock. "You'd better hurry, girl. You don't want to be late!"

Tanya's hands tingled with excitement as she buttoned the pearl buttons on her suit. It was not the wedding dress she had dreamed of; those dreams had faded when she saw the price tag. She had finally settled on a beautiful pink suit. It was more expensive and more beautiful than any piece of clothing she had ever owned, but she could also wear it for special occasions in the future. It made her look like a woman in style. Tanya smiled at the girl in the mirror. The face that looked back at her shone brightly with anticipation.

Valentine entered the room carrying a bouquet. "Here are the flowers for my beautiful bride!"

Tanya's heart skipped a beat as she took the bouquet he extended to her. She buried her face in the silky petals of the roses and inhaled deeply. "Thank you, my love. They're beautiful."

For a moment she gazed deeply into his eyes. Her heart melted as she saw the love and admiration they held. Why had she ever doubted him? He was a real man.

A car horn honked, and Valentine grinned. "Vladic must be here to pick us up! Are you ready to go?"

"Almost." Tanya smiled as she slipped her feet into her new white heels. They were hardly practical, but right now she didn't care.

"Are you excited?" Vladic asked as they entered the car. "I feel pretty privileged to be taking such a charming couple to get their marriage license."

Valentine chuckled. "Let's be on our way. We don't want to be late."

The young couple was grateful that Vladic and his girlfriend Rina had agreed to be witnesses at their wedding. Vladic was a good friend of Valentine's and often brought Rina along to the parties they held at the Kosenko home. Tanya hadn't known who to ask to be her bridesmaid, so when Valentine suggested asking Rina and Vladic, she agreed.

The biggest plus about asking them was that Vladic had a car. Tanya was relieved that they did not have to travel to the notary on the bus. This was the normal way of life for her, but today on her wedding day, she felt like a queen riding in a chariot.

Tanya's stomach churned as the vehicle sped along the crowded city roads, dodging potholes, pedestrians, and vehicles. She couldn't decide if it was carsickness, morning sickness, or just the excitement of the day. She buried her face in her bouquet, breathing deeply the sweetness of the flowers.

The notary was a majestic building near the center of the city. Tanya shivered as she walked inside the large doors. The concrete walls had soaked up the winter's cold, and even though the sun shone warm outside, the building was an icebox.

The minutes ticked by slowly as they waited to be admitted. Tanya felt giddy from the excitement and the cold. Valentine reached for her hand and pulled her close. "My dear Tanyechka, today you will become mine."

"Next," the judge called.

Valentine and Tanya entered the large room. Vladic and Rina followed close behind. Valentine laid the documents on the desk in front of the judge. "We are here to receive our marriage certificate," he said.

The judge paged through the papers, then looked up. "Valentine Kosenko and Tatianna Dmitruk, a month ago you stated your desire to get married. Is that still your desire?"

"Yes, it is." Valentine's voice echoed in the large building.

The judge looked at Tanya.

"Yes, I do desire to get married." Her voice was barely above a whisper.

"Please sign these declarations." He handed each of them a sheet of paper. Tanya glanced over it. *Over eighteen years of age. Not legally married to someone else. Not directly related to each other.* She smiled and quickly signed her name.

The judge entered their information into the computer. "Will either of you be changing your last name?" he asked.

Tanya looked in surprise at Valentine. They had not discussed this.

Valentine smiled and whispered, "Take my last name."

Tanya's voice trembled, but she spoke clearly, "I would like to become a Kosenko."

The judge nodded and finished filling out the certificate. He printed the document and handed it to the couple. "Please look over it carefully and make sure all the information is correct."

Tanya's heart beat faster as she saw the official-looking document with their names on it. This was for real!

She nodded slightly. "Looks good."

Valentine handed the paper back to the judge. "Everything looks correct."

The judge scribbled his signature and inked the stamp, then pressed it on the bottom left corner. The blue ink contrasted with the red certificate. "I pronounce you husband and wife," he said. "Go in peace."

Valentine took the proffered certificate and the folder with the documents. He looked at Tanya with a triumphant smile. "We're married!" He held her close.

Tanya relaxed in his embrace, happiness bubbling within. "I feel like I could fly!" she whispered as they stepped out into the sunshine.

The whole world shone. Though the stark trees and melting snow still spoke of winter, summer was in the air. The clear blue of the sky and the warmth of the sun seemed to reflect the joy of the young couple. "I'm so happy!" Tanya murmured. She leaned her head on Valentine's shoulder.

The young couple was met with cheers and congratulations when they arrived home. Most of the guests were already there. Papa and Mama had come all the way from Kryvoshyintsi to share in this special day.

There was a tremor in Natasha's voice as she wrapped her arms around Tanya. "My dear daughter, may you always be happy," she said, holding her close.

Tanya's heart suddenly swelled with an intense longing for her sister Svetta. She remembered Svetta's dream and her own reply, *"You'll probably get married before I do."* Now it was her wedding day, and Svetta was gone. *But in a way I was right,* Tanya thought. She remembered her sister lying in the coffin dressed in a wedding dress. *You did get married first! Oh, Svetta, I miss you!*

"What's wrong, Tanya?" Valentine asked, concerned about the teary eyes of his bride. "Are you all right?"

Tanya nodded. "I just miss Svetta, my little sister. She would have loved being here."

Valentine nodded and squeezed her hand. "I can understand why you think about her at a time like this. I wish I could have met her."

The Wedding

Tanya pushed aside her grief and tried to put her heart into the celebration. But even in the midst of her happiness, her heart ached.

After eating all they could hold, they cleared away the tables so they could dance. Alcohol flowed freely, and emotions soared with the blaring music. The party lasted until the early morning hours. Tanya fell into bed utterly exhausted. She was glad the next day was Sunday, and she wouldn't need to work.

The celebration continued on Sunday. Although most of the guests had gone home, Papa and Mama had stayed overnight. Valentine had planned an afternoon *shashlik*[1] party by the river. The chunks of pork had been marinating for several days in mayonnaise and onions. Tanya planned to take along some leftover food from the evening before.

It was a good-natured group that gathered by the river that afternoon. The aroma of grilled shashlik tantalized the taste buds. Some of the men had brought their fishing gear and were soon trying their luck in catching fish. Tanya's heart filled with gratitude as she looked around at the small group of people.

She could not help but remember the last time she had come to the river. That time she had come alone—overwhelmed at the thought of motherhood. How quickly that had changed. Now here she was, married to the man who had promised to love both her and their unborn child. The future looked bright. They would have a happy home. A passionate love for her little one welled in her chest. She would do all she could to give her baby a happy life.

Their honeymoon consisted of only that one special day on the bank of the river. After that, real life resumed. On Monday morning, Tanya

---

[1] A traditional Ukrainian dish of meat grilled on skewers.

went to her job as a store clerk and Valentine to his job at the gas station. In many ways, life felt no different than it had the week before. Tanya glanced at the ring on her finger. That had changed. It was a symbol to everyone that she was married. It gave her a comforting feeling; she belonged to Valentine and he to her. She purposed in her heart to always be true to him.

The honeymoon glow did not last long. As the trees unfolded their green leaves and the daffodils filled the spring air with sunshine and fragrance, Tanya felt the joy of the wedding day waning. Valentine, who had been considerate and loving during their friendship and engagement, now barely acknowledged her existence. When his friends came to party, she felt cheated out of his time and attention. Tanya tried to not let it bother her. She loved her little one more than ever and hoped her baby would fill the aching void in her heart.

She had thought getting married would bring satisfaction, but it had not. Happiness seemed like a fluttering butterfly—so near, yet always out of reach. *Will I ever find happiness anywhere?*

chapter 18

Motherhood

2002

As the summer months sped by, Tanya continued working full time until a month before her due date. She knew they would need the money. As she left her job for the last time, she tried to sort through her feelings. She had learned to enjoy her work as a saleswoman and the interaction it gave her with others. But now she was excited about staying at home. She could hardly wait to meet this child of hers—a girl, the doctors were saying. Would the baby look like her or like Valentine?

Another question worried her. *Will I know how to care for my baby?* She remembered when Svetta was born, but she had been a little girl back then. *Can I be the kind of mother this child deserves?* Her thoughts turned toward her husband. *Will he be a good father to our little girl?*

The thought troubled her. Valentine paid little attention to her pregnancy. He never asked how she was feeling or what the doctor had said. She tried to brush her fears aside. *Surely when the baby arrives, things will be different.*

As her due date drew nearer, Tanya found herself plagued with dread and fear. She tried to drown her morbid thoughts by throwing herself into the fall work of canning and preparing for winter. But it was not easy. Being great with child complicated even simple things like picking up fallen fruit. Never had she felt so clumsy.

There were nuts to gather and fruits to prepare. Valya had an ample supply of empty canning jars, and Tanya found it satisfying to prepare food for the winter. Jars of rich-flavored compote made with a variety of fruit lined the cellar shelves. Spicy tomato sauce and whole pickled tomatoes joined the sour pickles, the zucchini salad, and other jars in the dim cellar.

A soft smile played on Tanya's lips as she held the baby in her arms for the first time. It was September 17, 2002, the birthdate of her little daughter. She gazed at the innocent bundle in her arms. It was her baby, her very own child. As she caressed the baby's soft cheeks, she whispered, "My precious daughter." Emotion kept her from saying more.

Time slipped by rapidly in the hospital as Tanya rested, recuperated, and enjoyed her precious baby. By the third day, she was feeling restless; she could hardly wait for Valentine to meet their little daughter. He had stopped by after work one day, but since visitors were not allowed into the hospital, he had been unable to talk to Tanya or meet their little girl.

He had given the nurses a bag of food for her that Valya had prepared. Tanya was grateful for the home cooking, but the real treasure was the scribbled note she found with the food:

How's my darling Tanya and the little baby? I can hardly wait to meet her. I'll be here to pick you up on Friday after work.
I love you both.
Valentine

Tanya watched the clock eagerly that Friday afternoon. The doctor had signed the papers; now she was free to go home. She packed her bags and bundled up the baby. Even though it was only September, the air had a chill to it and she didn't want to risk her baby getting sick.

It was nearing six o'clock when the nurse tapped on her door. "I think someone is here for you," she said with a smile. "Here, I'll carry your baby so you can take your bags."

Tanya gave the nurse her baby and shouldered her bags. She hurried along the long corridor and down the three flights of stairs. She paused to catch her breath.

The nurse smiled when she caught up to her. "Take it easy, Tanya," she said with a laugh. "There's no rush."

"I can hardly wait to see my husband!" Tanya panted with a sheepish grin. "I guess I'm not as strong as I used to be."

She picked up her bags again and continued the short distance to the waiting room. There stood Valentine. Tanya collapsed into his arms. "My dear Valentine, I missed you!"

He squeezed her tightly. "And I missed you too, my dear. Now where is this daughter of ours?"

Just then the nurse came around the corner. "Congratulations, Papa!" she said. "Here is your daughter!" She held out the baby for Valentine.

He looked questioningly at Tanya. She nodded and whispered, "Yes, it's our baby."

Gingerly he took the little bundle from the nurse. His hands looked clumsy as he tried to situate the baby in his arms. Pride and joy shone on his face. "My little daughter!" He looked at his wife. "Oh, Tanya, can this be true?"

Tears of joy stung her eyes. Maybe he would be a good papa and give their baby a happier childhood than either of them had.

"Come, Tanya. Let's go. Vladic is waiting in the car." Valentine handed the baby to Tanya and picked up her bags.

She followed him down the steps and into the sunshine. She stopped for a moment to catch her breath and to breathe in the beauty that surrounded her. The air was fresh and cool, so different from the musty air of the hospital. The trees were turning color, the rich green fading into yellow and brown. The whine of cars on the road reminded her that she was still in the city, but for the moment, she did not mind. Life was beautiful. Could it ever get any better?

"What are we going to name this baby?" Valentine asked one evening a few days later as he held his little daughter. "I can already tell that she's going to be a smart little girl. She needs a good name!"

"You should call her Elena," suggested Valya, looking up from the magazine she was reading. "That would fit her perfectly."

"I think we should call her Nadia," Valentine said.

For Tanya, there was no doubt what the baby's name should be. "I would like to name our daughter Marina." She spoke with such firmness that both Valentine and his mother looked up in surprise.

Before they could protest, she held up her hand. "Please listen closely, and I will tell you why. Remember my sister Svetta?"

They nodded and looked at her curiously. What did Svetta have to do with naming the baby?

"The summer before she died, she had a dream. In her dream, she saw me, and I was married to a nice man." Tanya flashed Valentine a warm smile. "I was holding the sweetest baby, my own baby, and her name was Marina. That's why I think we must name this baby Marina."

Valentine began to protest, but to Tanya's relief, her mother-in-law stuck up for her. "Tanya is right. If Svetta dreamed that the baby was named Marina, we should listen. We wouldn't want to anger her spirit by not choosing the name that was revealed to her."

On the fortieth day after Marina was born, Valentine and Tanya took her to an Orthodox cathedral. The dim interior and the gold icons exuded a feeling of hushed reverence. Tanya trembled as she handed Marina to her friend Rina, whom they had chosen as the baby's godmother. Tanya had thought she was doing the right thing by having her baby baptized, but now that it was happening, she wasn't sure.

The priest chanted a long prayer in the Old Slavic tongue, and Tanya tried to follow what he was saying. Although she could not understand everything, she knew he was blessing her and her baby and pleading for God's mercy and protection. Rina held the little bundle while the priest christened the baby. He sprinkled holy water on the baby's head, then began another long chant.

Tanya's heart thumped and her head throbbed. Were they doing the right thing by having their baby christened? She hoped so. As a young child in school, she had been taught that there was no God. But with the fall of communism eleven years ago, things had changed.

Tanya didn't know what to believe when it came to God and religion. But one thing she knew: she wanted her baby to grow up loved, happy, and safe. Maybe this baptism would ensure that.

She was relieved when she finally had little Marina back in her arms. Now that her little one was baptized, she would go to heaven no matter what happened to her. But somehow the baptism did not calm Tanya's fears like she had hoped. Peace still eluded her. *Maybe my baby is safe, but what about me? Will God accept me into His kingdom?*

Motherhood

Fall faded into winter, with short, dreary days and cold weather. Marina grew into an alert little miss who loved to be wherever her mama was. A deep satisfaction filled Tanya's heart as she tended to her daughter. It was a beautiful season of her life, unlike the previous years where she always had to hold a job or attend school. Now she was a mother and a homemaker, and she loved it.

She found pleasure in preparing food for the family and keeping the house tidy. She enjoyed keeping the fire in the wood stove burning so the house would stay cozy and warm. But most of all, she loved being with her precious daughter. Never in all her life had she felt so loved and needed as she did now.

There was no need to put on a front—her baby loved and accepted her just as she was.

chapter 19

Answered Through Lilacs

2003

Tanya eagerly welcomed the arrival of spring. She was anxious to get little Marina out into the fresh air. She was worried about her; she seemed pale and listless. Tanya hoped more sunshine would bring the color back to her little girl's cheeks.

As the days lengthened, the cheery daffodils opened their petals, like little pools of sunshine reflecting the golden sun above. Marina lay in her baby carriage, her alert eyes following her mother as Tanya loosened the dark earth and planted rows of vegetables in the garden.

But the spring sunshine did not bring the color back to Marina's cheeks as Tanya so desperately hoped. Instead, she grew weaker and more listless by the day. Tanya's heart twisted with worry as she coaxed her little girl to drink her bottle. But Marina just turned away and cried miserably.

It was a tough time of year, with the canned goods and vegetables in the cellar nearly gone. Valentine's income should have been enough to provide for his little family, but much of it was spent on drink and cigarettes. Valya worked hard and shared what she could with her daughter-in-law, but it upset her when she needed to take care of her able-bodied son's family. Arguments increased.

And now little Marina was sick.

Tanya dreaded asking Valentine for money, but their little girl needed help. She waited until after supper, hoping he would be more congenial after his hunger was satisfied.

"Marina is sick, Valentine."

"I can see that!" he snapped. "She's been crying ever since I came home this evening. Can't you do something to keep her quiet?"

"I've tried everything I know." Tanya blinked back the tears that pooled in her eyes. "I think she needs to go see the doctor."

"Then take her! What are you waiting for?"

"Money. I can't go to the doctor without money." Tanya's nerves were frazzled, and she couldn't keep the anger out of her voice. "I'll take her as soon as you give me the money."

"There is no money," he growled.

"If you wouldn't waste it all on vodka and cigarettes, there would be!"

"Why did I ever get married?" he snarled. "I'm sick of being tied to a needy woman and a fussy baby! I work hard all day, and you just sit around, babying your baby. If Marina's sick, it's up to you to take care of her!"

Tanya bit her lip and walked out of the room, slamming the door behind her. Marina's whimpers followed her, but she tuned out the noise. *It won't hurt Valentine to sit with her for a while,* she fumed. In the shelter of their bedroom, she collapsed on the bed and let the bitter tears flow.

A heavy dread hung over Tanya when she rose from the bed. Through her tears, she caught a glimpse of the icon of Mother Mary holding her holy Son. Valya wasn't a religious woman, but she always kept an icon on the shelf. When faced with a crisis, she turned to it in prayer.

Maybe praying would help, Tanya thought. She stood in front of the icon and crossed herself. Bowing her head, she whispered, "Mary, mother of Jesus, have mercy on me and my baby. Please heal my little daughter." She stood in silence—every heartbeat a silent plea for healing.

As the burden lifted slightly, Tanya left the room with a lighter heart. She hurried outside to do her chores. The cool evening air brushed her face like a gentle feather, and the glow of the sunset filled the sky. Tanya paused on the doorstep to soak in the beauty. As she inhaled deeply, she suddenly became aware of the fragrance of the lilacs. She turned to the lilac bush by the corner of the house. In the stress of the past days, she had not noticed the cloud of purple blossoms. She buried her face in the blossoms and took a deep breath. Perhaps everything would turn out all right.

Lying in bed that night, she mulled over her problems, searching for solutions. Was there any way she could make a little money so she could take Marina to the doctor?

The lilacs! Why didn't I think of that before? I can pick the lilacs and sell the bouquets at the market. Even if it doesn't work, it will be better than sitting at home doing nothing! She fell asleep, her heart lighter than it had been for days.

By nine o'clock the next morning, Tanya had found a place to stand at the market. She was worn out from the long walk. It would have been quicker to take the bus, but she had no money for bus fare. Little Marina had enjoyed the ride in the baby carriage, which Tanya had filled with all the bouquets she could.

After standing for an hour and selling no flowers, Tanya decided it might be better to walk through the market, offering her flowers to the other vendors. She knew many of them, since the store where she had worked for several years was right next to the market. Her face flushed warm at the thought of the vendors seeing how poor she was, but she pasted on a smile. *They don't need to know about our dire situation.* She would carry herself like a confident woman who was satisfied with life. Not like the broken, worried mother she really was.

To her surprise, the flowers sold quickly. Some of the vendors did not recognize Tanya. Others did and were delighted to see her and meet her baby. Tanya suspected that many of them bought flowers out of pity for her and her baby, but she determined to not let it bother her.

As Tanya walked home that afternoon, her heart swelled with relief and thanksgiving. The money from the lilacs had been enough to pay for the medicine the doctor had prescribed. He had assured her that with the medication, Marina would soon perk up and be her happy self.

That night Tanya again crossed herself before the icon. "Thank you, Mother Mary, for having mercy on me and my daughter," she whispered.

Maybe God really does care.

chapter 20

Growing Pains

2004

"I guess we'll have to make room for a few more people in this little house," Valya announced one evening at supper.

"What do you mean?" Valentine demanded, setting down his cup so abruptly that tea splashed over the edge. "Who?"

"Your brother. Vova was kicked out of the house where he was living because he couldn't pay the rent. Tomorrow he and his wife and little child are coming here. Hopefully it won't be for long. But who knows?"

Tanya could hardly keep back a groan of dismay. Vova was Valentine's only brother, and what an uncouth man he was! "Where do you expect them to sleep?" she wondered. "This house is full the way it is!"

"I'm not sure," Valya admitted. "Their baby is still small enough to sleep in his stroller." She stirred another spoonful of sugar into her tea. "I guess Vova and Tetyana could sleep on the other couch in your room. Or we could move that couch out to the dining room and move the table and chairs into your room."

Valentine grimaced and looked at Tanya. "What do you think? I don't want to share our room with them!"

"Same here," Tanya replied. "But it will be inconvenient to always carry the food into our room to eat. And we'll be walking through their room to get to ours."

"I know," Valentine sighed. "But what else can we do?"

It was as bad as they expected. Gone were the quiet mornings Tanya had enjoyed with her little girl while the rest were at work. Now Vova's wife and their little boy were always there. At first Tanya resented their presence and felt intimidated by her sister-in-law. But as time went on, Tanya realized she was a decent woman.

Vova was a bigger adjustment. If one had chanced to meet him on the street, Vova would have appeared quite respectful, looking like a fine gentleman. But his fine features did not add to his character. He was almost always drunk and soon began enticing Valentine to drink as well. His churlish character made Tanya feel edgy when he was in the house.

Tanya and Tetyana soon became friends. Little Marina loved playing with her cousin Rostic, who was a year younger than she was. *There are benefits of having two women in a house,* Tanya decided one day as she bounced little Rostic on her hip while also entertaining Marina. Her sister-in-law had gone to the market to stock up on the week's supply of groceries while Tanya watched the children.

"Shall we go mushroom hunting?" her sister-in-law asked one day. Like Tanya, she was a nature lover, and they shared many of the same interests.

Marina and Rostic sat in the baby carriage while Tanya pushed them.

The children had caught on to the enthusiasm of their mothers and were laughing and chortling, jabbering in a language only they could understand. Tetyana carried a bucket for the mushrooms.

The sun had taken the bite out of the air, and it was a glorious day to be outside. Autumn had garbed the forest in golden hues, and a layer of leaves carpeted the floor, camouflaging the mushrooms. It took a sharp eye to find them, but they were there.

"Mama, look! Mush'oom?" Marina toddled up to her mother carrying a large speckled fungus. Already the two-year-old was repeating words and phrases. She was a bright little girl and took a keen interest in the world around her.

"Yes, that's a mushroom, Marina. But it's a bad mushroom. Phew! Bad mushroom! Mama will help you find a good one."

One could not afford to be careless with mushrooms. One wrong mushroom and the whole family could be poisoned. As Tanya helped her daughter look for mushrooms, her thoughts returned to the problem that had been troubling her for days.

After a child reached his second birthday, he was sent to daycare while his mother returned to work. Ever since Tanya held her baby for the first time, she had been dreading this day. And now Marina had passed her second birthday. After tasting the joys of motherhood and homemaking, Tanya dreaded returning to the life of a career woman. But they needed the money. They could not continue limping along on the meager wages Valentine brought home.

"Tetyana," she called to her sister-in-law, who was scavenging the ground for mushrooms a bit ahead of her, "I suppose it's time for me to get a job. There's no need for both of us to stay at home when we so desperately need money. I dread leaving Marina though."

Her sister-in-law paused, waiting until Tanya caught up to her. "I can watch Marina for you, if that's what you are wondering." She picked another mushroom and added it to the growing pile in her bucket. "Where do you plan to work?"

"I don't know. I'm not a specialist in anything except as a seamstress, and I don't expect to work at a sewing factory!" She kicked the leaves in front of her.

"Do you think you could get a job at the store where you used to work? You have the natural knack of a saleswoman." Tetyana smiled teasingly.

"I suppose, but right now that's the last thing I feel like doing. It's strange the way I've changed. I'd rather just stay at home with my little girl." Tanya squeezed Marina's hand and kissed her upturned forehead. "I wish there would be a job where I could take her with me."

"I doubt if you'll find a job like that!" Tetyana laughed.

The women continued searching for mushrooms in silence, each deep in thought. Suddenly Tetyana said, "I know what! Do you think the daycare would hire you?"

Tanya stopped short. "Now that's an idea! I didn't study to be a teacher or a childcare worker, but maybe they'd hire me anyway." Tanya renewed her search for mushrooms with new vigor. *That would be too good to be true,* she thought. *A job where I can take my daughter with me!*

The slanted rays of sunlight coming through the trees and the chill in the air reminded the women that evening was approaching. Tanya's heart skipped as she walked home with her bucket full of mushrooms. The idea of working with children was new to her, but it sounded appealing.

Tanya's hands trembled as she stepped up to the daycare center. She held her worker's book, the pamphlet that recorded all her former places of employment.

"Hello," a friendly voice greeted her as Tanya stepped into the cheery building. "Are you here to enroll a child?"

"Maybe," Tanya said, taking in her surroundings. The sound of laughter and children at play floated in the air as the woman welcomed her in.

"You may follow me to my office."

Tanya followed the clicking heels down a short hallway. She was impressed with the clean, cheery atmosphere. Seated in the office, she shifted nervously.

"My name is Margarita Gordienko," the woman said. "I am the director. How may I help you?"

"I have a two-year-old daughter that I am considering sending to this daycare. But I am also looking for work, and I was wondering if you have any job openings."

"I'll take your worker's pamphlet, please," the director said. She paged through the booklet, skimming over the information.

Tanya held her breath.

"I see you've worked at a sewing factory, a café, and a store. Do you have any experience working with children?" Margarita's question, while not unkind, was challenging.

Tanya shook her head. "Not except raising my own daughter."

Margarita smiled. "Working with one's own child is totally different from working with other people's children. We get all kinds of children here. It can be rather interesting at times." She studied Tanya. "Right now all our childcare positions are filled. And besides, you would need to have experience working with children—or be a certified teacher."

Tanya's hopes crumbled. She had not realized how badly she had been hoping for a job here. "I understand," she said softly, rising to her feet. "Thank you for your time."

"Just a minute," Margarita interrupted. "I'm not finished. We do have a job opening for a domestic worker. That job will not pay as well, but it might suit you."

Growing Pains

Tanya picked up a shard of hope. "What kind of work does it include?"

"Things like cleaning and washing dishes. You know, the dirty work. Instead of working directly with the children, you would do a lot of behind-the-scenes work."

Tanya nodded. "And what about my little girl?"

"Well, if you work here, she can come to the daycare for free."

By the time the interview was over, Tanya was looking forward to the first day of work. She had agreed to try it for a month before signing a contract.

Valentine did not share her enthusiasm. "That sounds like a lot of work for not much pay," he frowned. "You should get a job at the gas station, like me. You could make double what you will get at the daycare."

Tanya shook her head. "That may be true, but being a gas station attendant is no job for a lady. And it's definitely not a place for a little girl."

Tanya smiled fondly at Marina, who had fallen asleep at the table, her silky brown hair resting on the edge of her soup bowl. "Look at it this way. I will continue to take care of Marina, just as I have for the last two years. But I'll also be helping other children and bringing home a paycheck."

"You and your baby!" Valentine shook his head. "It doesn't make sense to me. But it's up to you. If you don't mind cleaning up other people's dirt and wiping other babies' noses, then go ahead."

chapter 21

Daycare Daze

2004

The job was harder than Tanya had expected. She had always enjoyed quiet, but now at the daycare she was bombarded with nonstop noise. And it seemed she was constantly cleaning up other people's dirt. Toddlers could turn a room upside down in no time. Tanya felt like she was fighting a losing battle at keeping the place clean.

But she loved the children. Marina, of course, was her favorite, but Tanya found a sense of satisfaction in showering her little "sparrows," as she called them, with love. They were always running about, chirping to each other.

Marina adjusted well to the change from being an only child to belonging to a group of children in the daycare. She had always been a social butterfly, and now she flitted from one friend to the next. Her bright smile and quick wit made her a favorite among the workers.

By the end of the month, Tanya had found her niche at the daycare and was ready to sign a contract for a year. As always, the paperwork was a hassle. "I need to take a trip to Kryvoshyintsi," she announced one evening at the supper table.

"Why so?" Valentine wondered, sipping the last of his tea.

"I need to transfer my place of residency from Kryvoshyintsi to Chippievka," Tanya explained. "It shouldn't take long. I'm hoping if I go tomorrow afternoon, I can be home by the next evening."

"Mama, me go too?" Marina looked at her mother in anticipation.

"You want to go with me?" Tanya laughed, squeezing her little girl's shoulder. She looked at Valentine, eyebrows raised in question. "Should I take her with me?"

He shrugged. "You might as well. It won't cost anything to take her along." He leaned forward and said in an undertone, "And it might do your mama good to have a little girl like her around."

Tanya suppressed a sigh. "Perhaps." There was something about Marina that always brought a bit of light to her mother's dim eyes. After all, Marina was her only granddaughter. Maybe it brought memories of her own daughters when they were little. At any rate, it could not hurt to take Marina along.

The next afternoon Tanya and Marina boarded the bus that would take them to Kryvoshyintsi. Tanya had not bothered to call her parents to tell them she was coming. Her heart sank as her childhood home came into view. The raspberry patch in front of the house was hidden by a jungle of weeds. Trash and more weeds littered the courtyard. The gate hung partly open, its hinges creaking in the cold wind.

The place looks deserted, Tanya thought as she made her way up the narrow path toward the door. She rapped at the door, calling, "Anybody home?"

The dog barked furiously, but no answer came from within. Tanya tried the door but then noticed the padlock on the door.

"Babushka!" Marina called, pounding her little fist on the door. "Babushka!"

"I'm sorry, dear. I'm afraid Babushka is not at home," Tanya said, taking her daughter by the hand. "Let's go visit neighbor Galya. Maybe she can tell us where Babushka is."

Galya was just returning from the barn with a bucket of foamy milk when Tanya and Marina entered the gate.

"Well, well, who do I see?" Galya called out in surprise. "Tanya, is it you? What brings you here this evening?" Without waiting for a reply, she hurried on. "Come in, come in! You must sit down and have some tea."

Galya held the door open and motioned them inside. "And this is your little daughter? She is just a copy of how I remember you years ago."

Tanya slipped off her shoes and helped Marina with hers. Soon they were seated at Galya's table—Tanya with a cup of tea and Marina with a glass of fresh, warm milk. A flood of memories surged through Tanya as she remembered the night some years before when she had also come home to an empty house. That time Galya had been able to help her. Memories and emotions of Svetta's sickness came flooding back.

Tanya explained what had brought her. "Maybe I should have called before coming, but I just expected them to be home. Do you have any idea where they could be?"

"I can't tell you for sure, but they are probably at some drinking party." Galya shook her head. "They can't seem to stay away from them."

"It wouldn't have to be like this!" Tanya clenched her teeth and plunked her cup on the table. "It seems like a part of Mama died when Svetta was buried. She doesn't care about anyone or anything these days. If only she would realize that she still has one daughter to live for!" Tears stung her eyes.

Daycare Daze

"But if they are drunk," she continued, "I don't want to see them. I'm ashamed to be the daughter of bums!" Bitterness laced every word. "Could I stay here for the night?" Tanya felt her face burn with shame. She hated asking for help. Or worse yet, pity.

"Of course you may, my dear! You know you are always welcome here." Galya reached over and patted Tanya's shoulder. "I would be honored to have you stay here. In fact," she said with a mischievous spark in her eye, "it might do your parents good to know that you came home to the village but chose not to stay with them. Maybe it will help them come to their senses and realize they should treasure their daughter and granddaughter more."

The next morning Tanya left Marina with Galya while she went to the village head's office to get her document of residency transfer.

"So, Tanya, are you officially moving away from us?" the secretary asked with a teasing smile as she entered Tanya's information and prepared the document.

"I guess so." Tanya shifted her purse from one hand to another. "But Kryvoshyintsi will always have a special spot in my heart. I have so many memories of growing up here."

The secretary chuckled. "But watch out or you'll become too uppity to feel at home here in the village. Once people leave the village for the city, most of them never return." She handed Tanya the document. "Here you go. Sign your name in the corner, and I'll stamp it for you."

With her document in hand, Tanya returned to Galya's house to pick up Marina. Galya insisted that she eat lunch before leaving.

"You're too kind to me," Tanya protested.

"It's my privilege!" Galya reached over and stroked Marina's silky hair. "I had so much fun learning to know this little lady while you were gone. She's quite the talker for one so young!"

After a quick lunch with Galya, Tanya and Marina hurried to the village center to catch the bus. Tanya looked at her watch. *The bus should be here any minute. There it comes!* She was so intent on watching the bus pull in that she did not notice someone approaching.

"Mama, look!" Marina tugged on her coat. "Babushka!"

Startled, Tanya looked to where Marina was pointing. Sure enough, her mother was hurrying across the road in their direction. "Tanya, don't leave yet!" she called. "I want to talk to you!"

By now the bus had screeched to a stop. Tanya's mind whirled. Another bus left in two hours, but that would mean she would get home long after dark. The hurt from the evening before welled into a simmering resentment. She grabbed Marina and started toward the bus.

"Sorry, Mama," she said. "You're too late. If you wanted to talk to me, you should have been at home when I came last night."

Natasha reached for Tanya and grabbed her by the arm. "Please don't hurry off! I want to see Marina! You hardly ever come. Stay longer! Tanya, my dear. Please!"

Tanya jerked away and headed for the bus. "I'm sorry, but you missed your chance." She handed the driver the bus fare and collapsed on the nearest empty seat, her fists clenched in anger and frustration.

Marina wriggled from her mother's grip and slid into the empty seat next to the window. Wide-eyed, she peered out the window. "Mama, look!" Marina tugged Tanya's sleeve. "Babushka is crying!"

Tanya stole a quick look out the window and then looked stoically ahead. Her mother had asked for this. There was no use feeling guilty about it. And yet, try as she might, she could not shake the guilt that niggled at her conscience.

Tanya spent the next day doing the necessary paperwork to become a legal worker at the daycare. Most of the documents were not that hard to get. The medical checkup was the one she dreaded the most. Hospitals and doctors spelled stress to her. Just the smell of Clorox was enough to make her stomach churn.

I should have done this in Skvira before I changed my place of residency, Tanya thought as she looked up and down the hospital hall. *This Kyiv hospital is much bigger than the Skvira hospital. How will I ever find my way around?*

She turned and started down the hall. The first office was the dentist. She waited in line until it was her turn. "I'm here to renew my medical card for work," she explained.

"Do you have any complaints?" the dentist asked.

"No," Tanya fibbed, hoping he would not bother looking into her mouth. She actually had some cavities, but they could not afford dentist bills right now.

"Give me your medical book," the dentist requested.

He scribbled a few notes and signed it. "You're good to go!" he said, handing the book back to her.

With a quick thank-you, Tanya stepped out into the corridor. She eagerly opened the medical book. "Mouth in excellent condition," she read, a smile stretching across her face. *That was easy enough!*

Not all the doctors were quite that easy to convince, but Tanya knew she should not complain. After all, they had to do their job. Tanya sighed with relief when the lung doctor checked her X-ray and said she did not have tuberculosis. That was one of her worst fears. Besides being a painful disease, it was contagious and carried a social stigma.

One by one, Tanya visited the different doctors. The psychologist asked a few questions and pronounced her mentally clear. Tanya couldn't keep back the smile at that one. Now if anyone questioned her sanity, she had a paper to prove it.

By the end of the day, Tanya was more exhausted than if she had spent the day chopping wood. "I hate hospitals!" she declared to Valentine that night.

chapter 22

The Reflection in the Mirror

2004-2007

Signing a contract for a year's work brought a sense of security to Tanya. She was surprised at how good it felt to know that for the next year at least, this was where she belonged.

As the winter weeks slipped by, one cold day after another, Tanya missed the sparkling snow of her childhood. Here the snow quickly dissolved into a dirty slush. Accompanying it was a damp air that seeped through her thick coat. On some of the coldest days, Tanya left Marina at home with Tetyana instead of dragging her through the cold. Other mothers must have had the same idea, because the number of children at the daycare dropped with the temperature.

As Tanya walked home one day, she shivered. The wind hurled biting flakes of snow into her face. On these short winter days, it was dark when she left in the morning and dark again by the time she headed home after cleaning the daycare. As Tanya strode along, she noticed the Christmas lights strung on a store close by. It was that time of year again, but Tanya did not feel the usual anticipation of the holidays. New Year's and Christmas always brought bittersweet memories of her childhood. It made her miss Svetta. And her parents. Or at least the parents she used to have. Tanya shook her head. Was it even worth keeping up her relationship with them?

"Brrr. It's sure cold out there," Tanya said as she slipped off her boots and hurried to stand by the radiator. She curled her numb fingers around the warm pipes that carried water through the house, keeping the house comfortable during the cold winter weather.

Marina came running to meet her. "Mama's home!" she chortled.

Tanya gave her daughter a hug. "Were you a good girl while Mama was gone?" She planted a kiss on her daughter's silky hair.

Marina nodded and scampered away after her cousin Rostic.

"And how was your day?" Tanya wondered, turning to her sister-in-law.

"All right, I guess." Tetyana shrugged her shoulders.

"Something's wrong," Tanya said, looking her in the eye. "You're not yourself. Is everything all right?"

She shook her head. "I'll let Valya tell you."

Tanya hurried to the kitchen where her mother-in-law stood by the stove, stirring a pot of soup. "Valya, what's wrong? I can see that something happened. Please tell me what it is."

Valya reached toward Tanya. "Come, my daughter, I will tell you."

Dread gripped Tanya's heart as she saw the look on Valya's face. "What happened? Tell me quickly! Did something happen to Valentine?"

"No." Valya looked away, as if searching for the right words. "I just got a phone call from Galya in Kryvoshyintsi. Your mama is dead. She died this afternoon."

The shock hit Tanya like a wall of water. She buried her head in her arms and sat in stunned silence. Finally she lifted her head and looked at Valya. "No! Not Mama! It can't be! What happened?"

"I don't know. All I know is that the funeral is tomorrow, and you are supposed to go home as soon as possible."

"This can't be true. I will call Galya. It can't be true." Tanya's fingers trembled as she dialed the number.

It was true. Galya explained that her mother had been sick for a few weeks and had spent several days in the hospital. The doctors had been unable to help her and had sent her home.

Anguish gripped Tanya's heart. *Why did no one tell me? Why didn't they call and ask me to come home?* She moved about in a daze. *Is Mama really gone?*

The funeral passed in a blur. Tanya was too numb with grief to process what was happening. She plodded behind the casket on the way to the cemetery, grateful for Valentine's steady arm to support her. A fresh layer of snow had fallen, encasing the bare branches of the trees in shimmering white. Everything glistened in the sunlight, but tears hid the beauty from Tanya's puffy eyes.

Sobs ripped her chest as she bent over her mother's still form and kissed her for the last time. She clung to the edge of the casket. "Mama, you can't leave me! Mama! Oh, Mama!"

A cloud of despair descended over Tanya as the winter days dragged on. Whenever she closed her eyes, she would see the face of her mother, bruised and beaten, lying in the casket. At times that picture was replaced by another. In this one, Mama stood with outstretched arms and tears in her eyes, reaching toward her only daughter and granddaughter as the bus took them farther and farther away.

The Reflection in the Mirror

Anguish, remorse, grief, and anger battered Tanya's heart. How she regretted not having talked to her mama that one last time.

Despite having a daughter to love and a husband to care for, Tanya felt alone. Although she had not always gotten along with her mother, she had still loved her and needed her. Mama had been so young. She had not even reached her fiftieth birthday. *Why did she have to die so young? And did she die from a sickness as the doctor said—or was it from those bruises?* Tanya shuddered. Either way, the last weeks of her mother's life could not have been pleasant.

Memories came flooding back. Throughout Tanya's growing-up years, her mother had always been there for her. She had attended every school program and had done all she could to give her children a happy childhood. Some memories brought remorse, like the times Tanya had failed to love and respect her. A deep grief settled over Tanya. Even after the forty days of mourning were over and she quit wearing the black veil, her heart ached in pain.

To drown her anguish, she threw her heart into her work—and turned at times to alcohol. Guilt niggled at her conscience, but she comforted herself by drinking only a little. Cigarettes also relaxed her tight nerves. But always, at the end of the day, nothing had really helped. The darkness seemed to be closing in on her.

Valentine resented the change in his wife, the way grief had aged her. Her eyes were shadowed, her forehead wrinkled, and the light in her eyes had dimmed.

More and more often they clashed. And sometimes their arguments turned into fights. Tanya knew it was best to stay quiet and keep out of Valentine's way, but drink had a way of loosening her tongue and arousing his temper.

One morning as Tanya combed her hair before work, she looked closer at the reflection in the mirror. She shuddered as she saw the likeness of her mother staring back. Never before had she realized how much she looked like her mother. With alarm, she noted the tense lines that creased her forehead, the weary eyes, and yes, there were even bruises. The realization startled her.

As she went to work that day, her thoughts returned to the reflection she had seen in the mirror. *Am I really becoming like my mother?* Tanya remembered how critical she had been when her mother allowed Svetta's death to rob her of the joy of life and her love for others. She remembered how betrayed she had felt when Mama had been too wrapped up in grief to pay her much attention, turning instead to drink for comfort.

And now she was doing the same to her daughter! Would Marina grow up scarred from her neglect?

"Mama, look! A butterfly!" Marina pointed to the flying beauty that had lit on a dandelion that bravely bloomed among the cracks of the sidewalk. She let go of Tanya's hand and scampered ahead, determined to catch it. With a few flaps of its wings, the butterfly soared out of reach.

Marina picked the dandelion and came back to Tanya, giggling and out of breath. "That butterfly ran away from me!" She buried her nose in the dandelion. "Mmm, Mama, it smells good! Smell it!" She held the silky flower up for her mother to sniff.

"You should have left it growing there," Tanya chided. But she could not keep back a smile as she fingered the golden weed. She sniffed the flower. "It smells like spring," she said, squeezing her daughter's hand. "Now we must hurry, or we'll be late for work."

They picked up their pace as they turned at the corner and the daycare came into view. The cloud that had hung over Tanya for so long lifted a little and a ray of hope shone in, melting the cold grief that had gripped her. *I have to go on with life. My family needs me. I must not make the same mistakes my mother made.* Impulsively she planted a kiss on her daughter's forehead.

"Mama, why did you do that?" Marina asked in surprised delight.

"Because I love you. And I'm so glad you're my little girl." Tanya gave Marina a quick squeeze before she opened the door of the daycare.

After two years of working at the daycare, Tanya decided it was time for a different job. Although she had been promoted from domestic care to teacher, the pay was still miserly. She heard about a job offer at a warehouse and applied. She worked there for a month, but the promised paycheck never came. In frustration, she quit and resumed her search.

Valentine continued to pressure her to get a job at a gas station. Finally, desperate for work, Tanya had to eat her words. She applied for a job at the Shell station near their home. Her job description included stocking shelves and filling orders, along with running the cash register.

Working 24-hour shifts was taxing, but there were advantages. Valentine and Tanya juggled their schedule so that one of them was always at home. This way Marina no longer needed to go to daycare. The little girl missed her friends but soon adjusted to staying at home every day.

Since Tanya's father lived alone, Valya felt sorry for him and pressured Tanya to invite him to live with them. Tanya dreaded the thought of living under the same roof as her father, but Valya accused her of being a poor daughter if she did not try to help her papa.

So Mikoli came, bringing all his troubles with him. Not only did Tanya have to live with him, but he got a job at the gas station where she worked. There, out of sight of Valentine or Valya, he tortured his daughter. Tanya no longer wondered how her mama had gotten so many bruises. Her papa's fists were capable of doing much harm, and more often than not, Tanya was the recipient of his blows.

Mikoli knew how to put on a good front, and at first he got along fine with Valya and Valentine, knowing he had to if he wanted to live there. But Tanya was his daughter, so he bossed her around.

Eventually the good front wore away, and Valya saw who he really was. She challenged him for being so mean to his daughter. "Tanya may be your daughter, but she's also my daughter-in-law!" she stormed one day. "And this is my house. I want you to leave—now! And don't ever come back!"

Tanya was relieved to see him go back to his own home. But she had given it an honest try. Nobody could say she had not tried to help her papa.

chapter 23

God's Gift

2008-2009

Marina eagerly anticipated her first day of school. For Tanya it was a different story. Apprehension gripped her heart at the thought of sending her daughter to school. She would have to trust her little girl to strangers. She thought longingly of her own school years and the close-knit little village school in Kryvoshyintsi.

There was a lump in her throat as she thought of Irina Vasilivna, her favorite teacher. After Tanya had flunked first grade, she had been placed in Irina's class. This special teacher had nurtured in her a love of learning. The influence Irina had on her for the next three years trumped that of any other teacher she had. *If only Marina could have her for a teacher as well.*

But Tanya tried not to think about the village. Moving back was not an option. Not only would work be hard to find, but living with Papa would be intolerable.

When the new school year began, little Marina became a first grader. Tanya knew it would not take long for her daughter to make friends. She would love the social life of school.

On the first day, she looked so grown-up in her new school dress, her hair pulled back with a lacy ribbon. Tanya shook her head in wonder. *Can it be that my daughter is a schoolgirl already? It makes me feel old!*

By now the job at the gas station had become a familiar routine. The longer Tanya worked, the more ways she discovered to milk the system. At one time she had been skeptical of how Valentine earned coffee and food, but now she realized how efficient it really was. Many of the customers had gas cards that allowed them to earn points when they bought gas. These points could then be used to buy food from the gas station. Tanya also had a gas card, so if a customer did not want to bother with a card, she could swipe her own card and earn points from the customer's purchase.

Occasionally a customer also gave the cashier a tip or said he did not want to bother with the change. These tips, though often small, could add up to quite a bit by the end of the day.

One day, during a lull in customers, Tanya pulled a pack of dried fish and a bottle of tomato juice off the shelf and paid for it with the points on her card. "I don't know what has gotten into me," she commented to her coworker who sat drinking a cup of coffee. "I don't usually eat these." She pulled several strings of the dried fish from her bag and popped them into her mouth. "For some reason, right now I just crave this stuff."

"Dried fish and tomato juice!" the coworker laughed. "Don't you know what that means?"

Tanya shook her head.

"I'll tell you later," her coworker chuckled, getting up to take care of a customer.

After the customer was gone, Tanya brought up the subject again. "So what is funny about me craving dried fish and tomato juice?"

"You must be pregnant! That's what I always craved when I was expecting. Good luck to you!"

"But I'm not pregnant!" Tanya protested. She laughed nervously. Although she sometimes wished for another child, Valentine had decided long ago that one child was enough. She shook her head. *Surely I am not pregnant.*

She pushed the subject aside and forgot about it. But a few weeks later she felt the all-too-familiar nausea. As the days progressed, she could not deny it—another little one was on the way.

Dread tinged her excitement as she thought of how Valentine would respond.

Tears streamed down Tanya's cheeks as she sat on the edge of the bed. What was she supposed to do? Tanya knew the relationship between her and Valentine had been rocky for the last several months. She had sensed a wall of mistrust between them, but she had not realized it was this bad.

Now Valentine had given her an ultimatum. He said she must choose. It was either him or the baby. His accusations hurt the worst of all. He had accused her of being unfaithful, like Vova's wife, who had disappeared one day, taking little Rostic with her. Later they found out she was living a double life and was seeing another man.

The accusations had flown like daggers to her heart. How could she prove her faithfulness? He said there was only one way: to have an abortion. Sleep eluded Tanya that night as she struggled. Already

God's Gift

she loved the little one she carried. She could not bear the thought of ending the life of her unborn child. But Valentine had said that was the only way she could prove her faithfulness to him.

What will happen if I go against Valentine's wishes? she wondered. *He might kick me out. Then what will happen to Marina? She needs both me and her papa. It's not fair to her if we separate. And where would Marina and I live?*

Morning dawned cold and gray, matching the shadows under Tanya's eyes and the heaviness of her spirit. All night long she had wrestled with Valentine's unreasonable requirement. An abortion would be betraying her unborn child, but there seemed no other way.

But abortions cost money. Carefully Tanya counted the hryvnia in her wallet. There were not nearly enough. She scanned the room, searching in vain for a piece of gold, some money, or something to sell. She shook her head sadly. Nothing she had was worth much.

Suddenly she remembered her sewing machine. She had bought it after she finished studying to be a seamstress, hoping to someday make clothing to sell. That dream had long since died, as sewing had just not been her thing. Although the machine was several years old, it was still in good condition.

She dug it out from under the pile of clothing waiting to be mended. Carefully she set it up on the table and threaded the machine. *I might as well do my mending before I get rid of it,* she thought as she threaded the needle. She mended one of Valentine's shirts and some of her own clothing.

At the bottom of the pile she pulled out a little girl's dress, one Marina had worn as a baby. Tanya's hands trembled. She would not need this dress again. Resolutely she threw it into the trash and went back to her mending. But the tears in her eyes blurred her vision, and her hands trembled so much that she could not continue. Could she really allow her little one to be torn from her and thrown into the trash, just like she had pitched that baby dress?

Every day her love for her little one increased, and Tanya knew putting it off would only make it harder. She didn't talk to anyone about it, but she knew Valentine had told his mother. Tanya wondered if Valya also doubted her faithfulness and would encourage her to have an abortion, but she was afraid to ask.

Tanya bundled up in a large coat and wrapped a woolen scarf tightly about her head. She lifted the sewing machine and stepped out into the blustery November wind.

"Tanya, where are you going with that load?" Valya called after her.

Tanya cast a quick glance at her mother-in-law. "To the pawnshop." She turned so Valya could not see her face. "I need the money."

"Will you be all right, Tanya? Would you like me to go with you?"

Tanya was surprised at the sympathy in Valya's voice. She shook her head. "No, I'll be okay."

Resolutely she faced the wind and marched down the walk. *Will I really be all right?* She hardly thought so. The sewing machine grew heavier with each step, and Tanya was tempted to turn around.

When Tanya left the pawnshop with cash instead of the sewing machine, her arms felt much lighter. But the ache in her heart grew heavier with each step. *How can I do this?*

But it is the only way out. The machine had not been worth as much as she had hoped, but she still had more money in her wallet than she normally carried. And now she was going to give up both her money and the life of her precious child. It seemed so wrong! How could life be so unfair?

The line outside the gynecologist's office was long. Tanya discreetly

God's Gift 177

studied the faces of the other women. Most of them shone with the beauty and love of motherhood, but a few were creased with lines of bitterness and looks of deep sorrow. Tanya knew her own face must look the same.

"How can I help you?" the doctor asked. His voice was gentle and his manner calm.

"I'm here for an abortion," Tanya said, her voice sounding hollow and far away.

"Hmm, I see," the doctor said, studying the woman before him. "Are you sure this is what you want? This is a serious step."

Tanya could not meet his gaze. She nodded and whispered, "Yes, I must."

"Well, I can help you, but I want you to know this is an expensive procedure."

"I have the money," she whispered, opening her wallet. "How much will it cost?"

"Five hundred hryvnia."

Tanya gasped. She had known it would not be cheap, but she had not expected it to be this much—more than a month's wages. "I have only four hundred hryvnia," she said. "Won't you do it for less?"

The doctor shook his head. "I'm sorry, but I cannot back down on my price." He scooted his chair closer to her and said kindly, "Let me tell you something. Don't wait until you have enough money, because by then you will be too far along for an abortion. And don't look for another doctor to do it. Take the money and go buy some groceries. Buy anything you are hungry for. Then go home and take it easy." He looked at her and smiled. "You won't regret it. I promise."

Tanya returned home that afternoon with her arms laden with groceries—and peace in her heart. She worried about Valentine's response, but she knew she had made the right decision. She had tried to do what he asked, but she had been stopped.

Valya met her at the door. "Tanya dear, you did not do it?" she asked as soon as Tanya entered.

Tanya shook her head, chuckling nervously. "No, I didn't have enough money."

Valya wrapped her in a hug. "Oh, I'm so glad! I worried about you all day. I couldn't bear the thought of you losing your baby."

"I didn't want to do it!" Tanya said. "But I wish Valentine would believe me. It is his baby!"

To her relief, Valentine did not kick her out, though he still accused her of being unfaithful. Tanya knew defending herself would be pointless. Only the baby could prove her innocence.

Throughout the long winter and into spring, Tanya continued her job at the gas station. She had decided to work as long as she dared. Even with the child support the government provided, they would need all the money she could earn.

With the arrival of spring, the lilac just outside the front door broke into full bloom. As Tanya inhaled the sweet fragrance, she remembered how the lilac had been an answer to her desperate prayer when Marina had been sick as a baby. Ever since, that lilac bush had symbolized hope. Perhaps everything would be all right.

The first day of June dawned bright and clear. Tanya woke up early with the realization that her baby was on its way. Valentine grudgingly called a taxi. "All this hubbub and expense for a baby," he muttered.

Tanya blinked back her tears.

Valya noticed and squeezed her hand. "Don't worry, Tanya. Everything will be all right. I'm coming with you."

Tanya looked at her in surprise. "Really? You don't have to."

God's Gift

"I want to, and I'll stay with you as long as the doctors let me. I'm eager to meet this new grandbaby of mine."

Tanya turned her face away. At least one person believed her.

Valya was true to her word. She stuck by Tanya all through labor. At times her persistent coaching was wearisome, but Tanya didn't complain. She thought longingly of her mother. She wished she could have another chance to rebuild her relationship with her, but it was too late. Although several years had passed since Mama's death, the ache in Tanya's heart lingered.

"It's a girl! Congratulations!" the doctor said, his voice ringing with triumph. He handed the squalling infant to Tanya.

As Tanya held her baby close, relief and joy flooded her heart. *My baby is here at last!* She shuddered to think how nearly she had ended this baby's life. "Daughter dear, may you always feel loved and wanted. You are truly a gift to me."

Although Tanya was eager to go home, she trembled when she thought of Valentine. Would he accept this little one as his daughter? How she hoped so! She longed for her daughter to be accepted, and she also hoped to be relieved of the false accusations he had hurled at her. As Tanya gazed at the wrinkled red face of her daughter, she whispered, "You must grow up to look like your papa."

At last the day arrived to go home. Valentine treated Tanya civilly, but he hardly glanced at the baby.

Marina was aglow with excitement. "Mama, is this my very own baby sister?" she asked, reaching out a cautious hand to stroke the little cheeks. "May I hold her?"

Tanya watched as Marina gently picked up her little sister. It brought back memories of years ago. She had been nearly Marina's age when her sister Svetta had been born. A sudden longing for her sister swelled within her.

"Mama, why are you crying?" Marina asked, looking at Tanya with puzzled eyes. "This is exciting to finally have a new baby! Don't be sad!"

Tanya smiled and squeezed her hand. "You're right, dear. We must be happy. And I am. I have the two sweetest daughters in the whole world."

Once again, choosing the name was stressful. Tanya and Valentine just could not agree. Tanya was frustrated. Why should Valentine suddenly claim the right to name the baby when he had not even claimed her as his daughter? Then Valya entered the argument. "It is my responsibility to name this child," she declared. "After all, I was with Tanya when she gave birth. I saw this baby before either of you did. I will name her."

There was no use arguing with Valya. She was the lady of the house and always had the last word.

"All right then," Valentine demanded. "What should we name her? She's three weeks old already. It's time we have a name for her."

"Her name is..." Valya paused deliberately. "Bogdonna."

"Bogdonna? Where did you come up with that name?" Valentine asked, his face turning crimson. "That's not a good name!"

"That is her name. I won't have her called by any other. Is she not a gift from God? This name fits her perfectly: *Bogdonna*, God-given."

Tanya blinked back her tears. Was it not God who had given her baby life in the first place and then spared her life when she seemed doomed for an abortion? She smiled weakly. "I think that is a fitting name for our daughter. Don't you agree, Valentine?"

"I guess," Valentine replied grudgingly. "Whatever you say. Why should I care what this baby is called?" He shrugged in feigned indifference.

That night, while the rest of the house was clothed in slumber, Tanya rocked her little daughter. "Bogdonna, you are my gift from God," she whispered. And though the house was dark, she turned her face toward the icon on the wall. "Thank you, God, for the gift of this daughter. May your angels of protection always be over her."

By the end of the summer, Bogdonna grew from a fragile infant into a chubby baby. Her blue eyes shone, and a smile was often sandwiched between her chubby cheeks. She was a happy little girl and soon became the sunshine of the family. The older she got, the more she resembled her papa.

As the realization grew that he had falsely accused Tanya, Valentine felt remorse at how nearly his selfishness and false accusations had ended Bogdonna's life. As she blossomed into a charming lass—and looked more and more like him—she became his favorite.

Valentine determined to be a more faithful husband and a more loving papa. After all, he had a loyal wife and two precious daughters.

chapter 24

The Mysterious Magazine

2009

Trips back to the village always triggered memories. Tanya tried to push them away as she ran her fingers through the rich, dark soil in search of potatoes. Ahead of them, a neighbor guided his horse-drawn plow along the rows, turning over the soil and revealing potatoes of all sizes.

Marina scampered ahead of her parents, picking up the biggest ones. Bogdonna lay in her baby carriage, cooing at the blue sky and sucking her thumb. A lump formed in Tanya's throat. Potato-digging days were family days. She was glad she could come and help Papa harvest his potatoes, but she missed Mama and Svetta. It was her first visit to the village since Bogdonna was born. Mikoli seemed happy to meet his new granddaughter, but he did not gush over her like a grandmother would.

Tanya glanced at Valentine. She was grateful he had agreed to come along, and he actually seemed to be enjoying himself. Potato harvest was about the only time Valentine stepped foot in the garden. The sun shone hot for the end of August, but an occasional breeze cooled the sweat on their brows.

Tanya's hands moved fast as she picked up bucket after bucket of potatoes. Her father would have enough to sell some of them. Her mind traveled back to potato harvests in years gone by. She could still hear Svetta's chatter and smell her mother's borsch that always awaited them after a day of harvest.

Bogdonna's cries interrupted her thoughts. Tanya straightened her back and wiped the sweat from her brow, leaving a smudge of dirt across her forehead. She dusted her hands on her pants and hurried to the stroller.

"Baby dear," she crooned. "Are you hungry?" She bounced the stroller across the garden and toward the house. "Mama will get you a bottle of milk."

Bogdonna stopped whimpering and reached her chubby hands toward her mother. Outside the front door, Tanya lifted a dipper full of water from the bucket and poured it over her hands, scrubbing to get rid of the dark stains of dirt. She dried them on the towel that hung over the fence.

Tanya scooped up Bogdonna and entered the house. She shivered as she glanced around the dim room. The house looked worse every time she came. Empty beer bottles, shells of sunflower seeds, and cigarette butts littered the table and the floor, telltale signs of how Papa spent his days. She balanced her baby in one arm while she cleared off a corner of the table to set down the baby's bottle. She added a scoop of baby formula and poured some warm water from the teakettle.

As Tanya cradled Bogdonna and fed her, she looked around the room.

She wondered how much longer her papa could keep living in these conditions. Suddenly she noticed a magazine lying on the table under some beer bottles. *Strange,* she thought. *I didn't know Papa was a reader.* She pushed the bottles aside and pulled out the magazine and some smaller pamphlets that were under it. She brushed the dust off the magazine and read the title—*Seed of Truth.* "I didn't know Papa is interested in gardening," she murmured as she flipped the magazine open. To her surprise, it was not about gardening at all, but about God and Christians. *Where did he come up with this? Papa has never had anything to do with religion!*

Her curiosity got the best of her, and she began reading. An article titled "Wife of an Alcoholic" grabbed her attention. But what strange advice it gave. She could not imagine treating Valentine kindly when he came home drunk, like the article encouraged. By the time Bogdonna's bottle was empty, Tanya had skimmed through the whole magazine. She shook her head in wonder. *Could anyone actually live like this?*

Bogdonna was sleeping, so Tanya laid her gently in the stroller and pushed her into the shade beside the house. Then she hurried to the join the others in the potato patch.

Valentine scolded her for taking so long, but she laughingly protested that it had taken Bogdonna a while to fall asleep. Her break from picking up potatoes equipped her with more energy, and soon she was picking them up faster than anyone else.

When she found herself working next to her father, she asked the question burning in her mind. "So, Papa, are you becoming a reader?"

"What do you mean?" he snorted. "I don't think there's a book in the entire house!"

Tanya threw a few more potatoes into her bucket before replying. "I just noticed a magazine and some pamphlets lying on the table. Where did they come from?"

Mikoli chuckled. "Oh, those! Yes, I guess I do have a bit of reading

The Mysterious Magazine

material. I got them at the seed meeting this spring. I didn't bother reading them; they'll be great fire starters this winter."

"Seed meetings?" Tanya asked. "What's that?" She could hardly imagine her father attending any classes on agriculture.

Mikoli laughed again. "It must be a long time since you've lived in the village if you don't know what I mean by seed meetings. Every spring those Americans and their people have a meeting at the clubhouse. I'm not sure what they do at the meeting, because I always wait to go till nearly the end. I think they pray and sing and preach. But after the service, they pass out free garden seeds."

"Free garden seeds? Why would anyone do that?" Tanya straightened her back and looked at her papa. "Garden seeds are expensive! What's the catch?"

"I don't know why they do it. But they're free, and they're good quality seeds! I guess it's just because they're rich Americans. It's probably their way of bribing us to come to their meetings and read their literature. Of course, I never read it; I just use it for fire starters. But the seeds come in handy. I think every seed I planted must have come up. I never had such a thick row of carrots before. I even had to thin them."

They worked in silence as Tanya tried to process what Papa had said. She could hardly imagine anyone giving away something as valuable as seeds. And the magazine could not have been cheap to print. Why would people give away stuff like that? Why would Americans come to a poor village like Kryvoshyintsi to start with? It didn't make sense.

"Papa, who are these Americans? What makes them come to Kryvoshyintsi? I can't imagine anyone rich coming to this dumpy little village—much less Americans!"

Mikoli laughed. "Tanya, you really are behind the times! They moved in several years ago. They are believers of some kind and have a house of prayer in Berezyanka. Every Sunday a bus goes through our village and picks up people and takes them to their meetings in Berezyanka. You would be surprised at how many of our people go to their meetings."

Tanya shook her head in amazement. "I can't believe I never heard about this. Who of our people are going to their meetings? Anyone I know?"

"Oh, yes. Luda Yarashuk is one of their faithfuls. And Olya Stepava goes regularly, as does Apetivich and his wife Dosha."

"You mean my former schoolteacher? I can't believe he's interested in Christianity. He was a committed atheist when he taught me in school!"

Mikoli nodded. "I'm not sure what draws them. Probably most of them are going for what they can get, but I have seen a change in some of them. Especially Luda. Remember how lazy she used to be?"

Tanya nodded. "I sure do! She signed up to cook for our class when we went on a trip to the sea. It was just her way of getting a free trip and a chance to boss people around. We were so disgusted!"

"That's what I mean. But look at her now! She works like a horse and keeps her garden in perfect order. But the most amazing thing is the way she gives; she's always taking food to people and helping others. Those Americans have sure taught her a lesson or two."

"Really? She sure must have changed!"

The conversation changed to other topics, but as they rode the bus home the next day, Tanya's thoughts replayed the conversation. *Why didn't I hear about this before? I wonder if these Americans are like the ones at the Baptist church Zhenia attended.*

She remembered her last conversation with Svetta the night before she died, and how she had talked about going to church with their cousin Zhenia. *I wonder if the singing at the Americans' church sounds like angels. That's how Svetta described the singing.*

A yearning grew in Tanya's heart to know more. *Maybe sometime I can learn more about those believers in Kryvoshyintsi.*

chapter 25

Buried in the Barn

2010

Snowflakes twirled and danced as they descended from the sky, covering the landscape in a blanket of down. Smoke curled from the chimneys, lights glowed from the windows, and the village appeared to be wrapped in peace. Mikoli stood at the door of his house, looking expectantly down the road.

In the distance he saw them coming, his drinking buddies. He smiled in satisfaction. His pension had run out weeks ago; the holidays had claimed it all. His friends had also run out of hryvnia. But now the end of the month had arrived, and his working friends had received their paychecks. Tonight the bill would be on them. His hands trembled with excitement.

What else did he have to live for? His wife was gone, buried five years ago. And Svetta, his beloved daughter, had died from a brain tumor. He coughed uneasily as he remembered. Everyone assumed the tumor had been caused by a brick the neighbor boy had thrown, but he knew that was not the only trauma she had received. He hated himself for the way he had acted when drink crazed his body. How could he have beaten his precious daughter like that?

And then there was Tanya, the only family member he had left. She lived in Kyiv with her husband and two daughters. They had not come home this Christmas. He was not surprised. Why should she want to come home? He had not done well at being a loving father to her.

He was a failure, and he knew it. That's why he turned to drinking. To help him forget. To lift his spirits. It always helped for a while, but after the drink wore off, the troubles returned full force—and he was left with a hangover. Did it really help? He was startled for a moment at the question. He rarely allowed himself to think deeply; it just made the pain and the memories worse. But tonight, as his eyes gazed down the road, his mind also traveled down memory's lane.

When had he started drinking? When he had problems? Back when life was good, he had a job as a truck driver for the collective farms. Sometimes the villagers paid him with a bottle of beer, and he began drinking to pass the time. But now he wondered. Was drinking the solution to his problems? Or was it the cause?

He pulled the door shut, as if to block out the memories. Someday he would stop drinking. But not tonight. His cronies were coming and soon the party would begin.

Hours later, the party was still going strong. Raucous laughter bounced off the walls, and the air was blue with cigarette smoke. The men were engrossed in another round of cards. Mikoli studied the face of Meesha, a newcomer. He was merely a youth. Mikoli remembered seeing him at the bar a few times, but he had never learned to know him well. His face, graced with the freshness of young manhood, contrasted sharply with the hard, wizened faces of the others.

Mikoli wondered what had brought Meesha to the party. But he was the perfect guest, having just returned from the city with a generous paycheck. And he supplied more than his share of the drinks. Though Meesha had money, he lacked the skill to keep from losing it in the card game. The more he lost, the angrier he became.

Mikoli was never sure what happened. He remembered the laughter turning into hollering and shouting. And was there fighting too? He could not remember. He must have fallen asleep. What he did remember was waking up hours later. Never would he forget the faces of his buddies as they leered into his face and threatened him. "Be quiet!" they said. "Or you will be next." What did they mean? He could not understand and drifted back to the deep sleep of a drunkard.

The next time he awoke, daylight was streaming through the window. He was still sitting on a chair, his head slouched on the table. Everything felt strangely quiet. He sat there for a moment, trying to remember where he was and what his bad dream had been. Then he remembered: his friends had threatened him to keep quiet. He was sure it had not been a dream, but what had they meant?

He propped up his head and looked around the room. Telltale signs of the party were everywhere. Then he gasped. He was not alone! One man was still in the house. He stumbled to his feet and walked to the other side of the room where the man lay face down on the floor. He gave him a little kick. "Get up, old man!" he slurred. "The party is over!"

The man did not move. Mikoli knelt down beside him and was horrified to find the body as stiff as a board. He turned him onto his side and noticed a pool of blood. The lifeless eyes of young Meesha stared blindly into his face.

Suddenly it came back to him. He remembered the leering faces of the men. The threat to keep quiet or he would be next! Horror swept over him, and he began shaking uncontrollably. What was he supposed to do? He glanced around nervously and went to the door.

Fresh snow had fallen, covering any footprints to the house. He hesitated a moment and then locked the door. He could not risk going outside—not now. But what could he do with the body that lay on his kitchen floor? He continued shaking with uncontrollable shivers, and suddenly it dawned on him that the house was cold. The fire in the stove had burned out hours ago, and the winter wind was seeping through the windows. He started toward the stove to light the fire but suddenly stopped. He must make it look like no one was at home. It was not safe to start a fire now.

He turned back to the bedroom, the room where his daughters used to sleep. He wanted to get as far away as he could from the body in the kitchen. He collapsed on the bed and groaned. What a mess he had gotten himself into! What could he do?

He dared not call the police. If he squealed on his friends, there was no doubt who would be next. He shuddered. He would have to bury the young man. But where? The ground was frozen, probably a meter deep. It had been a hard winter. Mikoli knew he could not do anything as long as it was daylight. He would sleep now, and after dark he would figure out how to solve the problem. He lay down on the bed and fell into a fitful sleep.

When Mikoli awoke again, hours later, night had returned, and a few brave stars twinkled in the sky. By now his senses had returned, and he knew he must hurry. He wondered how long it would be until Meesha was missed. Luckily he was from another village, so they would not think to look for him here. He considered several options but finally decided the best thing to do was to bury the body in the barn. Part of the barn still had a dirt floor. It was packed hard from many years, but it would be better than trying to dig through the frozen dirt outdoors. Besides, the barn would be safer. No one would ever know what happened. He donned his coat and headed for the barn.

Hours later he reentered the house, the deed done. Loose straw covered the mound of dirt in the barn. The hidden grave would be a secret no one would ever know about. But try as he might, Mikoli could not shake the uneasy guilt that nagged him. He could not understand why. It was not his fault that Meesha had been killed. He growled as he thought of the others. How could they do this to him? Weren't they his friends?

Friends indeed! Their words echoed through his mind: *"Be quiet—or you'll be next!"*

chapter 26

The Murderer's Daughter

2010

Tanya was sweeping the floor when her cell phone rang. She propped her broom against the wall and lifted the phone to her ear. "Hello," she said.

"Tanya, is that you?"

"Yes, it's me. How are you, Totya Galya?" Tanya knew Galya rarely called just to talk. It was usually to share news—important news. *What could it be this time?*

"Tanya, you won't believe what happened!" Galya's voice carried a note of excitement—or was it agitation?

"Tell me quickly!" Tanya replied. Her hand trembled as she pressed the phone closer to her ear. "Is Papa doing all right?"

"That's what I'm calling about," Galya said. "He's been arrested! The police arrested him for murder!"

Tanya collapsed into a nearby chair, cold dread filling her heart. "What do you mean? I don't understand!"

"It's true! They found the body buried in the barn!"

"Whose body? What are you talking about?"

"Meesha from Berezyanka. You know, the young man who was recently reported missing."

Tanya shook her head wearily. "No, I don't know anything about this Meesha. Explain yourself!"

Galya launched into her story. "A few weeks ago, we heard that a young man from Berezyanka named Meesha was missing. He worked in Kyiv but often came home over the weekends. People supposed something had happened to him in Kyiv. The police were notified, but they could find no trace of him. He had just disappeared.

"No one seems to know exactly what happened, but last night your papa was drinking with some friends and started bragging about a body he buried in his barn. At first no one took him seriously, as he rarely makes sense when he's drunk. But he kept insisting it's true.

"This morning when the men were sober, they realized there could be some truth to what Mikoli was saying, so they called the police and reported it. Several police officers came out to your papa's place to check things out. They were there for an awfully long time, and when they left, they took your papa with them. He was handcuffed and looked like a regular criminal."

"But I don't understand!" Tanya protested. "He was likely just making up stories while he was drunk. Was that enough to arrest him? Did they have any evidence?"

"They sure did! They found the young man's body buried in the barn! It has been cold enough that he was frozen solid and hadn't even started decaying yet."

"But how do they know Papa killed him?" The lump in Tanya's throat grew until she could hardly swallow. This was like the horror stories she sometimes watched on TV. To think it was happening in her own village and that her own papa was the murderer was too much! "Perhaps Meesha just needed a place to rest and chose Papa's straw pile. Maybe he froze to death! Surely there's some logical explanation!"

"I don't know," Galya replied. "But it scares me to think of living next door to a murderer. If he was bold enough to kill an innocent young man, I wonder what he could do to the rest of us. The whole village is in an uproar. You had better not side with your papa, or folks will be mad at you! You don't want to be identified with a murderer!"

"Thanks for letting me know," Tanya murmured. "I really should go now. I might call you back later." She hung up the phone and sat motionless for a long time.

Was that phone call for real? Or was it just a bad dream? Tanya could hardly believe it was true, yet she was afraid it might be. Questions buzzed around in her mind like a swarm of angry bees. *Surely Papa wouldn't kill anyone just for the pleasure of it. There has to be a mistake somewhere. But how did the dead man end up in his barn?* The awfulness of the whole thing made her stomach churn, and she was afraid she would bring up her lunch.

Tanya knew the strength behind alcohol-powered fists. She had seen it—and felt it. She gently touched the place on her neck. The spot did not hurt anymore, but the memory still did. She had sported many bruises, but that one had been especially painful and had taken a long time to heal. Too well she knew her papa's fists.

But Papa in prison? The thought gnawed at her heart. Despite Papa's fists, his anger, and his addiction to drink, he was still her papa. And deep in her heart, she loved him. She remembered who he used to be—the strong, happy man who loved his children. She remembered him pulling her down the road on the sled, treating them to baked potatoes on Saturday evenings, and taking them mushroom hunting. The thought of him rotting away in prison made her shudder.

She wondered how long it would be until he was sentenced. How many years would he have to be behind bars? Would he survive his confinement?

The slam of the front door roused her from her thoughts. She glanced at the clock and was startled to see how much time had passed. *Marina must be home from school already. I have to prepare supper and tidy up the house.* She shook her head. *I have to forget about Papa for now. I'll find out later if the story is true.*

The story was indeed true, and more news came trickling in over the next days and weeks. Papa was still in prison, awaiting his court case. Unless he could prove himself innocent, he would probably spend years behind bars. Tanya was glad she lived as far away as she did. She could not imagine the stigma she would carry if she lived in the village.

She felt like disowning her father. Why should he bring such shame to her life? Had he not done enough already to make her life hard?

But deep in her heart, other feelings stirred, and when she found out that he was in a prison halfway between Kyiv and Kryvoshyintsi, she determined to visit him.

"Valentine, I'd like to go visit Papa," she announced one evening. "Until his court case, he's at the Bila Tserkva prison. It's only an hour away from us."

Valentine nodded and continued shelling pumpkin seeds.

"Would…?" Tanya hesitated, afraid of his reaction. "Would you consider going with me?"

"You don't know what you are asking!" Valentine thumped the table with his fist. "I spent enough of my life behind bars. I don't plan to ever get close to that place again!"

"Will you at least help me know what to pack and how to go about getting into the prison to visit him?" she pleaded. "You can't imagine how hard this is for me!"

"Listen, I don't want to talk about prison. I don't even want to remember it! Please don't bring it up again!" He stood and brushed a few pumpkin seed shells from his lap. "I need some fresh air." He stepped out of the room and let the door close with a bang.

Tanya propped her head with her hand. It was her duty as a daughter to go visit Papa, but her heart quailed at the thought. Perhaps Valya could help her; she had plenty of experience in that.

Valya was more helpful. She gave Tanya a list of the things she used to send to Valentine. She told her what documents she would need to get in and described in detail what to expect.

With Valya's help, Tanya packed a box with some clothing, food, toilet paper, cigarettes, and other items. *Even if I can't visit him,* she decided, *I can at least pass him this parcel.*

The bus did not go past the prison, so Tanya had to walk the last two kilometers. Her knees weakened as she neared the building. She paused, shifting the heavy package from one arm to the other as she surveyed the dismal scene ahead of her. Barbed wire topped the high cement fences, and a guard watched her from a tower as she neared the big gate. She fumbled in her purse for her documents.

She was tempted to turn around. *No, I must try to visit him,* she resolved. As first one gate and then another was locked behind her, Tanya felt claustrophobic. There was no backing out now. The hassle was worse than she had expected. Both she and the parcel received a thorough inspection. The guard grilled her with questions as he studied her documents.

Finally she stood face to face with Papa. It was love that had brought her here, but the stress of getting into the prison had frazzled her nerves. Mikoli's face filled with wonder as he reached his hands through the bars and squeezed hers.

"Tanya! What brings you here? I didn't expect you to come."

"Yes, Papa, I came. After all, I am your daughter." Seeing the hopelessness of her father's situation hurt more than she had imagined. "I brought you some stuff. They said they'll give it to you later." She studied his face. He had aged so much since she had last seen him. "Are you doing all right?"

He nodded slowly. "You don't believe what they're saying about me, do you? You don't believe I'm a murderer, do you?"

Tanya took a deep breath and looked into his eyes. "I don't know, Papa. What am I supposed to believe? I don't understand why you would do such a thing, but neither can I imagine how a dead body got into the barn. What am I supposed to believe?"

He shook his head and lowered his eyes. "I am a fool. I really am! But I am not a murderer! I was afraid of what they would do to me if I squealed on them, so I kept quiet and buried him in the barn."

"Squealed on whom? I don't understand!" Tanya interrupted.

Mikoli started from the beginning and told his side of the story. His voice was hushed, and Tanya listened in rapt attention. This made more sense.

As Tanya headed home that evening, her heart felt lighter than it had for several weeks. Maybe Papa was not a murderer after all. True, he was to blame. He should not have hidden the body, but maybe he was not as heartless as people thought.

But it would be useless to stick up for him. In fact, it would be more than useless, it would be risky. If what Papa said was true, she would have to be careful. Papa's cronies would not appreciate her revealing their secret. But even if she didn't tell anyone, it lightened her burden to know that she was not the daughter of a murderer.

She would forget about life in the village. As long as Papa was in prison, there was no need to go back. The village could live without her, and she could live without the village.

As winter lingered into spring, tension grew between Valentine and Tanya. Every conversation turned into an argument, and too often the arguments turned into fights. Ignoring each other seemed the best solution. Valentine spent more and more time away from home, and Tanya was almost glad.

The worst times were when Valentine and his brother Vova would bring their friends for a party. Tanya often wished she could take her girls and hide. But where would they go?

Cigarettes were expensive, but at least they helped her frazzled nerves. That and a shot glass of wine. She knew better than to get drunk, but somehow that little drink every morning calmed her nerves and helped her make it through the day.

Tanya had not had a job since Bogdonna was born, and the scarcity of money complicated matters. Any money she had saved up beforehand was long gone—along with the fruits and vegetables that had been stored away last fall. Valentine had a job, but a large portion of his paycheck fed his craze for drink.

Had it not been for Valya's generosity and some child support from the government, they might have starved.

chapter 27

"Save the House!"

2010

"Hi Tanya."

It was neighbor Galya calling again. Tanya was glad that at least one person in the village remembered her, but she had learned to dread these phone calls.

"If you want to keep your house, you'd better claim it!" Galya's voice sounded excited.

"What do you mean?" Tanya asked.

"You know Meesha, the young man your papa murdered?"

Tanya winced. It sounded so wrong. She longed to tell everyone the true story!

"Well, his family is trying to claim your papa's house. They say that since he killed their son, they should be allowed to have his house."

Tanya shook her head. "How can they do that? Is it legal?"

Galya laughed. "It's more legal than murdering someone! If the house is sitting there empty, I don't think anyone can keep them from claiming it. The only way you can stop them is if you come and live in it."

Tanya got off the phone minutes later. *What next?* Quickly she slipped on her boots and carried slop to the goats. It seemed life consisted of one challenge after the next.

What would Valentine say? She doubted if he would be interested in moving to the village. He was a city slicker and wouldn't want to leave his friends.

Maybe she could move without him. What was there to hold her here? She didn't have a job, and sometimes she wondered if she actually had a husband. Maybe this would be a way to escape her problems.

"Neighbor Galya from Kryvoshyintsi called today," Tanya announced as the family sat down to eat their evening meal of cooked buckwheat and gravy.

"Now what?" Valentine asked, his voice sarcastic. "Did Mikoli murder someone else?"

"No, please!" Tanya protested. "She had bad news though. The family of the young man that died is trying to take Papa's house. She said if we don't move in, his relatives will claim it."

As Tanya explained the situation further, Valentine's face grew grave. "We have to stop them. That house is worth a lot of money. We can't just let them take it!"

"Well, what do you suggest?" Tanya asked.

He shook his head. "There's only one option. We have to move there so they know the place is not abandoned. I'd send you by yourself, but that hardly seems safe. Especially if Meesha's family is upset, and they want the house. We won't have to stay there forever, but I think we should go for several months. If we don't like living there, we can always come back."

Tanya nodded, surprised. She had not expected Valentine to get this excited about it. "So what's the first step?" she asked.

"Just pack up and leave! I'm off from work the next two days, so we can leave the first thing tomorrow morning. The place is going to need a lot of cleaning up. I'll go along and help you, but then I need to come back for my next shift at the gas station."

Tanya stood up from the table. "Should I start packing now?" Her voice sounded dazed and distant. This was happening faster than she had imagined. "Are you sure we aren't making too rash a decision? What if just you and I go tomorrow to check out the situation? We can leave the girls here with your mama. That way Marina wouldn't miss school. If we decide to move there, we can come back and get the girls. Or maybe we could wait to move until the school term is over."

"I guess that would work," agreed Valentine. "If we go and start working, the villagers will at least know the house is claimed."

Valentine and Tanya caught the early morning bus. By the time they arrived in the village, the sun was coming up. Valentine glanced at his watch. "What time does the hardware store open? One of the first things we need is a padlock for the front door."

"Not until nine. Why don't we go to the house first? We'll likely need more things from the hardware store."

The house was in worse condition than she had imagined, and the yard was a jumble of dead weeds, bottles, and rubbish. The inside of the house was even worse, with the front door hanging open several centimeters. There were telltale signs of other occupants in the house since Mikoli's arrest—dogs and chickens, perhaps. And by the looks of it, someone had taken advantage of the open door and rifled through the house. They had left the cupboard doors open and the contents strewn about the floor.

Tanya took a deep breath and nearly gagged. It smelled more like a barn than a house. Valentine's jaws were clenched, and his eyes looked grim.

"I'm glad we didn't bring the girls," Tanya said, trying to be positive. "What do you think? Is it worth the work it's going to take?"

"I don't know!" Valentine sighed and pulled out a chair. It was covered with grime. "There's not even a clean place to sit down!" he growled.

"I'm cold!" Tanya said, shivering. She stepped over to the wood stove. The iron door hung crooked from one hinge, and ashes had spilled onto the floor. She found a stick and a bucket and began removing the ashes.

"Here, let me do that," Valentine said. "Then you can start cleaning up the place." He handed her a basin. "You'll have to get water from the well."

Tanya nodded. Obviously Valentine was going to make this work. For a minute she had thought they might catch the next bus back to the city and forget about her childhood home. She glanced up and down the road before exiting the gate. She would eventually meet the villagers, but she would put it off as long as possible. She hurried to the well and soon had a basinful of clear, cold water.

"I'll start in the kitchen," she said when she returned. "That way we can heat some water and make tea. It's chilly in here."

Valentine nodded from where he knelt in front of the stove, still raking out the ashes. "This is my second bucketful," he said, nodding toward the overflowing bucket. "It's a wonder your papa could even make a fire, as full as it was!"

Valentine made several trips to the hardware store and the grocery store. Nails, dish soap, tea, a new padlock, light bulbs—the list of necessities seemed endless. It was evening by the time the fire in the stove had taken the chill out of the air, and the house was stripped of its first layer of grime. Only then did Tanya have time to think about food. She surveyed the bare shelves in the kitchen. The little food they had found was so full of mouse droppings that Tanya had thrown it all out. Perhaps she could find something in the cellar.

Hurrying across the courtyard to the cellar, she felt her way down the steep steps, wishing for a flashlight. After groping her way around the dark cellar, she found a few wrinkled, walnut-sized potatoes and a jar of preserves. When she reached the house, she held up the jar and was pleased to find it was some of the spicy tomato sauce her mother had always made.

She fried the potatoes in oil, along with an onion she had found in the cupboard. The old, greasy frying pan triggered memories of Mama, and a sudden longing for her mother filled her. Valentine and Tanya ate their simple supper in silent exhaustion.

Valentine drained the last of the tea from his cup. "I think I'm ready for bed. It's been a long day!"

Tanya nodded. "I'm exhausted too! Perhaps I can find clean bedding in the cupboards. I don't think I want to sleep on the beds the way they are now."

Valentine grimaced. "Right."

The bedding in the cupboard smelled musty but seemed relatively clean.

Tanya slept fitfully. The mice scampering about felt much more at home than she did. When she finally fell asleep, she had a horrible nightmare of her father hollering and beating someone. She wasn't sure who it was, but then she saw him—a young man lying on the floor, moaning in pain. She awoke with a shudder. *It must have been Meesha, the young man that was killed. Does his spirit haunt the place?* Tanya lay in a cold sweat, wishing for morning. *How can I ever live here?*

Back in Kyiv, Tanya tried to push back the memories of her dream as she sorted through their belongings. They had decided to move after school closed for the year, but she still wondered if they were making the right decision. Valentine had laughed at her dream, saying her imagination was getting the best of her. She hoped he was right. But superstitions did not go away easily. *Is it safe to live there if the house is haunted?*

But then she remembered that every spring the priest went through the village with holy water to sprinkle the houses and draw a cross on the gate. *Surely if the priest sprinkled holy water on our house, no spirits can haunt us.*

Tanya was also worried that Valentine couldn't find a job in the village, but he wasn't concerned. "I have worked hard enough that I deserve a break," he said. "And I'm sure I'll eventually find a job somewhere."

They moved in early July. Marina's eyes shone with excitement as she lugged her own bag of special belongings, along with her schoolbooks.

The first week was a blur of hard work and adjustments. Tanya watched in secret amazement at the change that came over her husband. What made him take responsibility and work so diligently to get the place cleaned up? Was it the sense of responsibility that he felt as the man of the place? Or was it perhaps getting away from his old friends that made the difference?

Maybe we can start a new life in the village.

chapter 28

Bartender Again

2011

If only Papa wouldn't have such a bad reputation. Tanya lifted the bucket of water out of the well and dumped it into her pail. After closing the lid of the well, she grabbed her bucket and started back toward the house. *We've been here eight months, and most of the neighbors still don't want to talk to us. But there's nothing I can do about it.*

She tried to shake off her confusing thoughts as she slipped out of her muddy shoes and entered the house. She poured water into the kettle on the wood stove. "Marina, please bring Bogdonna," she called. She smiled as Marina pranced into the kitchen, bouncing her little sister on her hip.

"Run out and bring in some more wood for the stove while I feed Bogdonna."

Little Bogdonna's face lit up, and she reached out her pudgy arms toward her mama. "Mama, eat, eat?"

"Yes, dear, I'll get you something to eat," Tanya replied, giving her nearly two-year-old daughter a squeeze. "If only I could keep staying at home with you." She spoke more to herself than her daughter. "But I have to start looking for a job. Your papa isn't bringing home much money. Most of his paycheck goes for drink."

Tanya filled a bowl with some oatmeal porridge and set Bogdonna on the stool. "Here, eat your kasha."

The door slammed and Marina came in with her slender arms piled full of wood. "Is this enough, Mama?" she wondered, panting for breath. "I got as much as I could. There's not much out there anymore."

Tanya flashed a grateful smile at her older daughter. "Yes, Marina. Thank you. That was a big load for an eight-year-old to carry. Thank you for being my good helper. Please take Bogdonna back to the bedroom where it's warmer and keep her happy while I make lunch."

The girls retreated to the bedroom. Tanya threw a few more pieces of wood on the fire and began peeling vegetables. *I hoped moving to the village would help Valentine stop drinking. But now he has new drinking buddies and is drinking as much as ever.*

The aroma of borsch soon filled the little kitchen. Tanya set the steaming kettle on the table in the sitting room and called the girls to come. She filled three bowls with the hot soup and sat down with a sigh. "We won't wait on Papa," Tanya replied to Marina's questioning look. "He can eat when he comes home."

Marina grabbed a piece of bread and dipped it into her borsch. Taking a big bite, she smiled. "Mmm, Mama, it's good. But I wish it had meat in it. Can't we at least put in some sour cream?"

"I'm sorry, daughter. Sour cream would be good, but we don't have money for extras. When you are finished eating, put Bogdonna down for her nap. I'm going to go look for a job."

Marina was still finishing her borsch when Tanya pulled on her jacket and prepared to leave. "Take good care of Bogdonna. I'll try to be back before dark. If Papa comes home and isn't feeling well, stay in your room and be as quiet as you can. He doesn't like to hear Bogdonna fussing."

Where should I start? Tanya mused. On impulse, she turned toward Oksana's house, a friend she had known since childhood. Though they had gone to school together, Oksana had been several grades ahead of Tanya, and they had not really connected. But time has a way of diminishing age gaps, and since Tanya's return to the village, Oksana had been her most faithful friend.

"Knock, knock. May I come in?" Tanya called.

"Hello, Tanya," Oksana welcomed. "Take a seat. Would you like some tea?"

"No thanks. I'd love to drink tea with you, but I can't stay long. I have a problem, and I thought you might have some advice for me."

"Sure. What is it? You need more milk for your girls?"

"No, it's not that. We still have some left, and I don't know how I'll ever repay you. You've already done so much for us. But do you know of anyone here in the village who could give me a job?" She paused, half-embarrassed, then continued, "Valentine is back to drinking, and somehow we have to make ends meet."

"I understand," Oksana nodded sympathetically. "What about Bogdonna? Are you sure you're ready to be away from your baby every day?"

"That's the hard part," Tanya said. "But she is almost two, so I suppose she's big enough to go to the village daycare. I have to do something to make money. I can't always be living off my kind neighbor."

"Oh, Tanya. You know I'm glad to help you out," replied Oksana. "Let me think. I can't recall hearing of anyone looking for help. But soon

Bartender Again

people will be working in their gardens, so you might find a short-term job. Maybe you could check with the storekeeper. She might know of someone who could hire you."

Tanya strode toward the village store, her heart aching with an emptiness she could not explain. With a forced smile, she pushed open the door and stepped inside. She was relieved to see that no other customers were in sight. Only Klimenko, the clerk, stood behind the counter.

"Hello. What can I get for you?" she asked. "We're already sold out of bread for the day."

"It's not bread I came for," Tanya answered. "I was wondering if you know of anyone who is looking for a worker? I need a job, and I thought you might have an idea. After all, you get to hear all the village gossip here at the store."

"Yes, I guess I do keep up with the village news." The clerk gave a wry grin. "Is there a certain kind of work you are hoping for? Tell me again what you did in Kyiv."

"Well, the last few years I was working at a gas station," Tanya replied. "Obviously I am not expecting that kind of job here in the village. But I'm willing to do either indoor or outdoor work—anything to provide for my daughters."

"I can't think of anything offhand," the clerk replied. "But I suppose you could check at the café next door. They might be glad for a bartender."

Tanya thanked her and went straight to the bar. The familiar smell of smoke and alcohol filled the dimly lit room. Along with the smell came a rush of repulsive memories from her earlier work in a bar. A sense of guilt niggled, but she pushed it away. *I need to support my daughters,* she comforted herself. *After all, I'm a woman now, not the gullible young girl I was back then. I'll be careful.* She set her jaw and went to find the owner.

Tanya cringed under Ludmilla's scrutinizing gaze and shrewd questions. By the time the interview was over, she was hired.

She got up early every morning. After making breakfast for her family and sending Marina off to school, she pushed the baby carriage to the daycare. At first it pained her heart to leave Bogdonna, but her little girl was a cheerful lass, and it wasn't long until she was a favorite at the daycare.

Marina threw her heart into school. Going to a new school was not easy, but Irina Vasilivna was a kind teacher. She could not help but love young Marina, who was a copy of Tanya when she had been her student years before. After school, Marina walked to the daycare to get Bogdonna. Pushing the baby carriage while carrying a backpack full of books was no small feat for the tender eight-year-old, but Marina was a determined child and took her responsibility seriously.

After eating the food Tanya had prepared in the morning, Marina kept an eye on her little sister while doing her homework. Often the girls would go over to Oksana's house, where they were always welcome. After all, they helped entertain Oksana's own daughter, who was only a few months older than Bogdonna.

At first Tanya hated her job, as it seemed Ludmilla expected her to do the work of three people. On the days when business was slow, it was manageable, but on other days, she ran circles from morning to night—and still could not please her boss. Somehow she was supposed to prepare the food, serve it, and then do all the dishes.

Tanya missed her children, but by the time she came home in the evening, she was so exhausted that she had little time or energy for her daughters.

She soon became more comfortable in the dark surroundings at the bar. Though her conscience bothered her at times, she excused her actions by saying it was for her daughters' sake that she had to work.

Some of the men who patronized the bar freely complimented Tanya on the food she served, the clothes she wore, and how beautiful she was. She enjoyed the attention. Sure, she felt disgusted at them when they became too drunk, but many only drank until they forgot their troubles and became overly friendly.

Valentine rarely talked to his wife unless it was to holler at her for not having his food ready on time. On the rare occasions when he was at home, he was often drunk and disagreeable. The longer Tanya worked at the bar, the more dissatisfied she became with her home life.

When the right man comes along, she decided, *I'm going with him. I'll leave everything behind and start a new life. There is no happiness here in the village. Maybe getting away and starting over with a new man is my answer.*

chapter 29

A New Job

2011

As Tanya slipped into the house, the noise from the TV warned her that Valentine was at home. She hoped he would not be angry at her for coming home this late. Her job at the bar often lasted late into the night, but sometimes it was her own fault that she did not come home sooner. Certain customers had ways of keeping her there longer.

To her surprise, Valentine turned off the TV when she entered the room. "Did you know I got a new job?" he asked.

"Really? Here in the village? Who would hire a drunk like you?" Her voice dripped with scorn.

Valentine glared at her. "In case you're wondering," he spat back, "I didn't tell him I was married to a woman who works at the bar and is the daughter of a murderer."

"Oh, be quiet," she retorted. "So what is this new job you're talking about?"

"Do you remember hearing about those strange believers who moved into our village? They have meetings in the village clubhouse every spring and hand out seeds and literature."

Tanya nodded her head. "Yes, I've heard of them. They're foreigners. But what about it? You're not working for them, are you?"

"Not directly. But the man who gave me a job said his family moved here from southern Ukraine a few years ago to join the faith of these Americans."

"Interesting. They obviously don't know much about our family, or they wouldn't have given you a job. Though we've been here for a while, no one likes us. Why can't people just forget what Papa supposedly did? It's not my fault that he's rotting away in jail." Tanya frowned. "What kind of work does this man have for you? Are they going to make a preacher out of a drunkard?"

"Stop it!" Valentine snapped. "You haven't even given me a chance to explain. I was at home today when this stranger stopped by. His name is Sergei Kotets. He said he needs a strong man to help him with odd jobs around his place and wondered if I'd be interested in working for him. I didn't have anything to lose, so I said I'll try it for a few days."

That night as Tanya was drifting off to sleep, she couldn't help but wonder how long her husband would be able to keep his job. So far he hadn't had much success with jobs. As soon as he got his first paycheck, he got drunk. Then he couldn't work the next day.

The next evening Tanya hurried home from work, eager to hear how Valentine had enjoyed his new job. He was already at home, sitting in his favorite spot by the television. Tanya heated the watery potato soup she had prepared earlier and filled the bowls. "So how was work today?" she asked after they began eating.

Valentine slurped another spoonful of soup before answering. "Not too bad. I chopped wood until it seemed my back would break. But my boss seems nice enough. He invited me to sit down and drink tea with him when he stopped for a rest. They are unique people. The ladies dress even more modestly than the priest's wife. Imagine!" He chuckled. "But I'm exhausted, and I think I'll head to bed." He scooted back his stool and got to his feet. "I need to get some sleep."

Tanya's curiosity almost got the best of her, but she decided not to ask any more questions. It was not worth the risk of getting on the wrong side of her husband. *If he keeps working there, I'll find out more about these believers. Dressed more modestly than the priest's wife? How could that be?*

Tanya was familiar with the priest and his wife. For as long as she could remember, she had lived next door to the village Orthodox cathedral. She often saw the priest and his wife walking down the street. The priest's long black robe and his wife's skirt and covered hair distinguished them from the other villagers. As a child, Tanya had occasionally attended the Orthodox church on holidays. *But surely these believers don't dress like that to work in the garden,* she thought. *I'll have to ask Valentine about that.*

"Tanya," Valentine called a few days later as he stepped into the house. "How would you like to go along with me to work tomorrow? Sergei found out that you work at the bar, and he said I'm going to lose you if you keep working there."

Tanya gave him a look of disgust. But before she could reply, Valentine was talking again. "Sergei said he'd give you a job."

"What kind of work does he have for a lady? Do you really think I'm going to chop wood and dig trenches? I do enough of a man's work at home without having to do it for someone else."

A New Job

"Calm down, Tanya. He's a believer. Of course he won't make you work too hard. Didn't I tell you they have greenhouses? They grow thousands of roses. They're not blooming yet, but Sergei needs help to pull the weeds."

That night Tanya tossed and turned. Part of her was weary of her life as a bartender. Curiosity about the people her husband was working for gnawed at her mind. *But what if I don't like the work? What if these people belong to some dangerous sect?*

I guess I'll try it for one day.

chapter 30

From Slacks to Skirts

2011

"Tanya, are you going with me this morning?" asked Valentine. When she nodded, he grinned and took another slurp of tea before continuing. "I should warn you. Sergei said if you come to work, you need to wear a skirt."

Tanya almost choked on her sandwich. "Me? Wear a skirt? I don't even have one. I haven't worn a skirt since I was a little schoolgirl! Was he serious?"

Valentine chuckled at his wife's incredulous expression. "I think so. But I suppose you can go the way you are. Then you can see what he says."

Tanya called Ludmilla and explained that she couldn't come to work for a day or two. She knew it was risky, but she needed a break from her work anyway. And it would be good for Ludmilla to see how much work she had been doing.

It didn't take long to walk the kilometer to Sergei's house. Tanya shivered with excitement as they neared the large house. *Calm down,* she told herself. *It's just another job. Even though these folks might dress strangely, they're probably just regular people.*

"Good morning!" a cheery voice boomed over the fence. The tall, white-haired man opened the gate and welcomed them in. "Good morning, Valentine. I see you brought your wife along." He looked at Tanya with a smile. "Tell me, what is your name?"

"Tanya," she replied, surprised by the friendly welcome.

"Nice to meet you, Tanya. You have the same name as my wife. I want you to meet her. Come this way." Sergei led the way down the sidewalk to the summer kitchen. "Tanya, come meet our new worker. She has the same beautiful name as you do."

Tanya caught her breath as Sergei's wife stepped outside. *Valentine was right. This lady is more modest than the priest's wife!* Most of her hair was covered by a large white veil, and her one-toned dress reached her ankles.

Sergei's wife smiled. "Hello. My husband told me I might be getting some help today. Welcome. You don't know how glad I am for another pair of hands! Since we started heating the greenhouses, the weeds are running competition with the roses. Let's go straight to the greenhouse, and I'll get you started."

Tanya paid careful attention as Sergei's wife showed her what her job would be for the day. Crawling between the rows of roses, loosening the dirt, and meticulously pulling out all the weeds was far different from being a waitress in the bar. At first Tanya wasn't sure if she liked it. The quietness was almost unnerving. She was used to blaring music and the boisterous laughter of drunks. Even at home, they often had the television running. Here it was so quiet, almost peaceful.

After a few hours of work, Sergei's wife called her to join them in the summer kitchen for a tea break. Tanya stretched her aching back and sank gratefully into the chair that was offered to her. Sergei and Valentine had also stopped their work and had come in for a break.

"Before we eat, let's stand for prayer," Sergei said.

Surprised, Tanya stood up, giving her husband a questioning look. He hadn't told her about this. When Tanya saw that the others had bowed their heads, she quickly bowed hers.

"Father, we thank you for this food before us. Thank you for blessing our work this morning. Bless our workers, Valentine and Tanya. Amen." Tanya was surprised. This was not at all the way the priest prayed. Such simple words. She couldn't help but wonder if it was appropriate.

"Help yourself to the tea and cookies," Sergei urged. "We need to get back to work soon."

After finishing her tea, Tanya resumed her work with more gusto than before. *That break was just what I needed. Wow, these are interesting people. I wasn't expecting a prayer before we eat.* Tanya's thoughts ran as swiftly as her fingers snatched the stubborn weeds. *I hardly know how to describe these people. They seem happy, but it's not happy like people at the bar. Their happiness seems to have more depth. They have a nice house and a good business. Is that why they're happy?*

At lunchtime, Valentine and Tanya sat at the table with Sergei and his wife. "This is my mother Luba," Sergei said, introducing them to the elderly woman filling the bowls. "She lives with us and is our faithful cook."

Baba Luba's face was wreathed in a smile. "It's nice to meet you. I'm glad you could come and work for us today."

Once again they all stood for prayer while Sergei asked a simple blessing on the food. Lunchtime flew by quickly as they chatted while enjoying the tasty buckwheat and gravy. Tanya was amazed at the way Sergei and his family treated her and Valentine with respect. They took an interest in their lives but didn't act nosy.

When their plates were scraped clean and they stood to go back to work, Baba Luba looked at Tanya. "Can you help me clean up the dishes before you go back out to the greenhouse?" Tanya hesitated and glanced at her new boss.

"Sure, you can stay here and help Mama."

Tanya began stacking the dishes. After the others were out the door, Baba Luba cleared her throat. "Tanya," she said, looking her straight in the eye. "Why aren't you wearing a skirt? Didn't Sergei say you should wear one?"

Tanya was startled by the frankness of this frail little lady. "I'm sorry," she said. "Valentine told me I should wear a skirt, but I don't have any. I never wear skirts."

"Oh, I can help you find one," Baba Luba replied.

By the time the dishes were finished and the kitchen tidied, Tanya's mind was whirling. She was glad to return to the quietness of the greenhouse. *Baba Luba said I should dress modestly. What does she mean by that? She also said I should come to church with them on Sunday. But they don't even have church in this village. Why bother going to the neighboring village? Wouldn't it be easier to just go to the Orthodox church across the road from our place? And what did she mean by saying I should repent? Is that the same as making a confession to the priest?*

That evening on her way home from work, Tanya voiced some of her questions to Valentine.

"I've been wondering about the same things," Valentine replied. "They seem like nice people and pay us fair wages. But I get tired of all their talk about God and repenting. The religion we were born in is the religion we will die in. I don't see any reason to go with them to their service. Being Orthodox is good enough for me."

The next morning Tanya tried on the skirt Baba Luba had given her. When she looked in the mirror, she couldn't keep back a giggle. *Why, I look like a regular old babushka. I can't walk through the village looking like this!* Quickly she tucked the skirt back into her bag. *I'll wait to put it on until I get to work.*

The second day at work flew by much like the first. Tanya found working while wearing a skirt to be a challenge. "I keep getting all tangled up in this thing," she complained when Sergei's wife asked her how things were going. "How do you walk between these long rows of roses without your skirt snagging on the thorns? I'm afraid I'm going to break the rose stems. But somehow you do it so gracefully."

Sergei's wife smiled. "I know what you mean. I remember how hard it was for me to get used to wearing skirts when I became a believer. Just be patient. It gets easier."

Tanya looked questioningly at her. "So you weren't born into a believer's family? What made you change?"

Tanya Kotets smiled. "It's a long story, but I'll be glad to tell you about it. Years ago, back when I was thirty…Is that about how old you are, Tanya?" When Tanya nodded, she continued her story. Her fingers flew as she plucked weeds and shared her story.

Tanya also pulled the weeds and loosened the dirt around the tender rose shoots, but she couldn't help but sneak an occasional glance at the storyteller. Her employer's face seemed to radiate something beautiful, but she couldn't quite pinpoint what it was. *Peace? Joy? Maybe it's a combination of the two.*

That night Tanya couldn't fall asleep right away. Although her back ached from her toil and she was exhausted, her mind kept returning to what Tanya Kotets had said: *"I sought happiness, but I couldn't find it in money. There was an ache, a loneliness in my heart, that wouldn't go away. It wasn't until I found Jesus that I experienced true peace and joy."*

Tanya blinked back a tear. *My heart aches too, and I feel so alone. Mama is dead. Papa is in prison. Valentine drinks. And my girls barely need me. They seem to get along just fine when I'm gone.* Tanya buried her head deeper in her pillow and eventually fell asleep.

The rest of the week passed quickly. On Saturday afternoon Sergei told Valentine and Tanya that they could go home early. "Tomorrow is Sunday. If you quit a little early today, you'll have time to prepare for tomorrow. We'll pick you up tomorrow morning around nine o'clock on our way to church. I think you'll enjoy the service."

"He didn't really give us an option, did he?" Tanya asked after they were out of earshot.

"Not really. I guess it won't hurt to go this once." Valentine shrugged his shoulders. "We'll go out of respect. They seem like nice people, and I hate to offend them. Maybe if we go to church with them tomorrow, they'll allow us to keep working for them."

That night Tanya brought down some old boxes from the attic. "What are you doing?" asked Valentine in astonishment. Marina came running to see what was happening.

Tanya grinned sheepishly. "I'm trying to decide what I should wear to church tomorrow. The skirt Baba Luba gave me is too dirty. If everyone else at church is like Baba Luba and Tanya, I'll be the only woman in pants. I thought maybe I could find one of Mama's old skirts."

Tanya opened the box and began sorting through the musty clothing. A surge of memories overwhelmed her as she fingered a faded sweater. "This was Mama's favorite sweater," she told Marina, who stood watching wide-eyed. "She wore it at every holiday." At the bottom of the box, Tanya pulled out a few skirts. "Maybe I can wear one of these."

"Mama, where are you going tomorrow? May I go along?" Marina looked expectantly at her mother.

"Oh, I don't know." Tanya glanced at Valentine. "What do you think? Should we take the children along? Won't they get bored at a church service?"

"Sergei told me to be sure to bring the girls along," Valentine replied. He flashed a smile at his daughter. "He said they have classes especially for the children. I think you might enjoy it."

chapter 31

The Strange Believers

2011

By nine o'clock on Sunday morning, they stood waiting for their ride. Tanya nervously tucked a strand of hair under her bandana.

"Mama, you look funny with Babushka's skirt and that bandana!" Marina said, looking at her mother. "Why are you wearing them?"

"Child, just wait till you see the rest of the ladies at this church. Then you'll understand why I'm wearing them." Under her breath, Tanya muttered to Valentine, "I still don't know why we're doing this. If we really wanted to go to church, we could have just walked across the road to our village church."

"I know what you mean." Valentine rolled his eyes. "But we'll go this once to make Sergei happy."

"You mean Baba Luba," Tanya corrected. "Every single day since I've worked there, she has told me I have to come to church."

Soon a white van pulled up. Sergei hopped out and opened the side door. "Hop in. You can wipe your boots on this rag." He motioned toward a rag lying just inside the door.

Valentine climbed in and then took Bogdonna. Tanya tried to be gracious as she climbed in, but she felt awkward in her skirt. Marina scrambled in last, and Sergei slid the door shut.

As they bumped down the road, Marina whispered to Tanya, "Mama, you were right. These people do dress funny. But what about the little girls? They probably dress just like me, don't they? They wouldn't wear such strange clothes!"

Tanya shrugged and motioned for her daughter to be quiet.

By the time they pulled into the churchyard, Tanya's stomach felt queasy. *Am I carsick, or is it nervousness? I don't think I've ever been this nervous before.*

"You may sit with me," Sergei's wife said. She smiled reassuringly. "And don't be nervous. We're all normal people. Just like you."

Tanya looked around, trying to take in all the action as other families arrived. She was relieved to see some familiar faces when the village bus pulled in and a string of villagers climbed off. *There comes Baba Olya,* she mused as she saw one of her mother's old friends hobbling into church. *I haven't seen her for years.*

Tanya and Marina followed Tanya Kotets into the church. "You may hang your coats here on the right. And the restrooms are on the left," she explained.

Tanya could hardly keep the shock from showing on her face. *Restrooms in a church house! Unbelievable! How irreverent!* When they stepped into the auditorium, Tanya had another surprise. There were rows and rows of benches and chairs. Would they actually sit down during the church service? Never could you do that at an Orthodox service! The walls were bare, with no icons and no candle holders. A simple pulpit stood at the front of the church, and behind it a Bible verse graced the wall.

Tanya sat self-consciously in a row of folding chairs. She squeezed Bogdonna close. "I'm glad I have you to hold," she whispered to the little girl on her lap. "I just hope you'll be quiet. I don't want you to make a distraction during church." Bogdonna replied with a grin, not understanding what her mama said but delighting in the attention.

A bit later Tanya's attention was drawn to the front of the auditorium. To her surprise, she saw two bearded men standing behind the pulpit. *How does this work? Are they both going to speak?* The one man looked too young to be a preacher. He could not have been more than twenty years old.

As the older man began speaking, Tanya leaned forward to try to understand what he was saying. It did not sound like the Old Slavic the priests spoke, but she couldn't understand a word. The older man had barely begun talking when the younger man began.

"I greet you this morning in the name of Jesus." Then, just as quickly, he stopped talking and the older man spoke again, speaking incomprehensible words.

Soon the young man was speaking again. "I'm glad to see all of you here. We give our visitors a special welcome."

Tanya felt her face grow warm. *Is he talking about us? But what is the other man saying?* It didn't make sense.

"Let's stand for prayer," the young man said. They all stood and bowed their heads.

Tanya followed their example and got to her feet, all the while trying to understand what was happening. Suddenly she realized that the older man must be one of the Americans. *He is probably speaking English and the younger man is interpreting.*

The Strange Believers

The ridiculousness of the situation struck her as funny, and she shook with silent laughter. No wonder they needed two men up there! *Maybe that is what the Orthodox churches should do. It sure would be nice if people could understand what the priest is saying.*

"Amen," the whole congregation chorused at the end of the prayer. Tanya whispered it too. She knew that was what prayers often ended with, but she wondered what it meant. She sat down momentarily but then realized that everyone else was still standing. Quickly she stood back up again, shifting Bogdonna in her arms.

Tanya Kotets handed her a white book as someone announced, "Let's sing song number 9." Balancing a book and her chubby daughter proved too challenging, so Tanya handed the book to Marina.

Before Marina had found the number, the congregation began to sing. The music sent shivers up Tanya's back. She had never heard anything like it before. The words were as beautiful as the music.

Oh, how blessed and happy I am. The Lord is my Savior.
He's preparing a place for me in the holy land of heaven.
Praise the Lamb! He died for me on the cross.
Alleluia! Alleluia! Alleluia! Amen![1]

By the time the congregation was singing the fifth verse, Tanya was helping along. Even Marina caught on to the tune and was soon singing with the rest.

The next song was harder to sing, and Tanya struggled to follow along. Finally she gave up and just listened. The voices of the crowd swelled around her in beauty. Then she noticed Tanya Kotets' voice. It rang out in harmony with the rest of the congregation, but it was louder and clearer than any of the others. She cast a quick glance at the

---

[1] Russian song, by an unknown author.

woman standing beside her. Her face shone with a joy that reflected the words she was singing.

Like an angel, Tanya thought, and suddenly memories came flooding back. Memories of the night Svetta died and the singing she had described. Perhaps this is what Svetta had been talking about!

Sudden tears filled Tanya's eyes, and she tried to discreetly wipe them away. How could she have forgotten about what Svetta had said? Maybe these people could tell her more.

Tanya listened to the service with a fresh earnestness. When the children went to Sunday school class, Marina looked shyly after them. Tanya urged her to go, but she remained in her seat. Then a young lady, the teacher of the class, came and invited Marina to go with them. Her warm smile and friendly face wrapped Marina and her mother in a gentle embrace. Marina slid off her seat and quickly followed her to the children's class.

The service lasted longer than Tanya had expected, and Bogdonna became restless and cranky. Crackers distracted her for a while, but soon she was whining again. Tanya looked around nervously. She wondered what the others thought of her noisy child, but no one seemed to be paying any attention.

"You can take her to the nursery," Tanya Kotets whispered, pointing to a door. "There might be some toys in there for her to play with."

The nursery was a small room with a rocker, a single bed, and a box of toys. Tanya stirred through the box and found a toy for Bogdonna to play with. She set her on the floor with the toy and sat down on the edge of the bed. She welcomed the change of position almost as much as Bogdonna. How could these people sit for so long on those hard chairs? Her head ached from trying to understand everything the preacher was saying. What did it all mean? These people talked about God as if He were someone they knew personally. How could they have a close relationship with someone they had never seen?

She scooped up Bogdonna and her toy and returned to her seat in the auditorium. The children had returned from their classes, and the speaker was asking them questions. Tanya watched in amazement as many hands waved in the air, eager to answer the questions. *How do they know that much about the Bible and God?*

The peaceful hush in the church was broken after the preacher closed in prayer and dismissed everyone. A din arose as folks greeted each other and began visiting. *It's like a big family,* Tanya thought, surveying the crowd.

"What did you think of the service?" Sergei's wife asked.

"It was interesting," Tanya replied. "But there was a lot I didn't understand." Her voice ended on an uncertain note.

"That's all right," Tanya Kotets assured her. "I'm sure there were a lot of new things, but you'll get used to it after a while."

Get used to it? Does she think I'll be coming back? Tanya glanced over at Valentine. He was visiting with some of the men. She watched as the American preacher stepped up to him. He had only spoken through an interpreter, but now it looked like he was talking to Valentine.

"Do the Americans know Ukrainian?" Tanya asked Sergei's wife. "It was strange to hear the preaching through an interpreter."

"Oh, yes. Most of them are fluent in Russian. They have an accent, but they can converse just fine."

Valentine and Tanya sat deep in thought as they bounced along the cobblestone road back to Kryvoshyintsi.

"So what did you think?" Valentine asked when they were in the privacy of their house. "Are you glad you went?"

Tanya took off her jacket before replying. "It was interesting; that's for sure!" She filled a kettle with water and set it on the stove. "I'm glad we went this once to see what it is like. But I'm not sure we need to go back."

"Did you see the American preacher talking to me?" Valentine asked. "He preached through an interpreter, but he can actually speak Russian. He has an interesting accent, but he was really friendly."

"It was fascinating to watch everyone relate to each other," Tanya said. She dumped macaroni into the hot water and began heating up the gravy she had made the day before. "They act like one big happy family. I was surprised how many people came to talk to me."

That week at work, Baba Luba again talked to Tanya about her need for repentance. The persistence of the little lady frustrated Tanya, but she could sense the love and concern behind the pressure. As the week crept along, Tanya's thoughts often returned to the church service. They did not discuss it as a family, but Tanya felt an increasing interest to go back and learn more. The love and acceptance she had seen attracted her.

But would they accept her if they realized who she was—that her father was in prison for murder? Or would they reject her like so many others?

The next Sunday only Tanya and the girls went to church. Valentine had a headache and wanted to rest. Tanya suspected his rest would include a trip to the bar, and she was tempted to join him.

Had it not been for Marina, Tanya would not have been brave enough to go back. But Marina had enjoyed the children's class and had made friends with the other little girls after church. Tanya was secretly pleased; she wanted her daughter to grow up with good friends.

As the congregation sang, Tanya could not keep back the tears. Something about the music and the message of the songs gripped her heart.

At the end of the service, the pastor said, "If there is anyone here who is tired of living in sin and would like to repent, you may come to the front."

Tanya leaned forward eagerly. This was what Baba Luba had been talking about. Would the preacher explain what it meant?

"You may kneel here in the front and pray and ask God to forgive your sins," the pastor continued. A hush fell across the congregation as they waited expectantly.

"Do you want to repent?" Tanya Kotets whispered. "You may go to the front and pray."

Tanya shook her head. "Not today."

On the way home, Sergei asked, "So, Tanya, what is keeping you from repenting?" His gaze met hers as he looked in the rearview mirror. "I can tell your soul wants you to. The only way you will find happiness is if you repent of your sins and give your life to Christ."

It was true. There was a longing for something more in Tanya's soul. At times the longing was so intense that it felt like it would swallow her. Would repenting take away that pain? Tanya looked out the window. "Perhaps someday," she said. "But I'm not ready yet."

In the coming days, the burden on Tanya's heart grew heavier. She struggled to sleep at night, burdened by a load of guilt and despair. She had always thought she was a good woman, but now she knew she was a sinner.

She wanted the peace and happiness she saw in the believers, but she was not ready to change her lifestyle. She could not imagine wearing a skirt and a veil all the time, so joining this church was not an option. And she could never stop smoking!

The restless nights and the stress took a toll on her nerves, and she became short-tempered with her husband and daughters.

"Tanya, what's come over you?" Valentine snapped one evening. "Ever since we've met these Americans, you've been hard to get along with. I hoped going to church would change you for the better, not for the worse!"

"As though you are easy to live with," she snapped back. "You're the one who needs to be changed!"

chapter 32

Resurrection Morning

2011

Tanya and her daughters went to church almost every Sunday. Occasionally Valentine would join them. Marina could hardly wait for Easter Sunday, because she would be helping in the children's Sunday school program. She begged Valentine to come along, and he agreed somewhat grudgingly. After all, it was Easter Sunday, a day when most of the villagers attended church.

Everyone at church that morning seemed to be alive with the joy of the day. The songs swelled with triumph. Tanya listened in awe to the beautiful words of "Low in the Grave He Lay." The story became alive to her as she thought of Jesus rising from the grave.

After the first message, the children sang. A lump welled in Tanya's throat as she watched her daughter join the row of girls dressed in beautiful, simple dresses, their joyful faces turned to the crowd. One by one the children stepped to the microphone to recite their poems. Marina stepped forward and said her little poem. The message gripped Tanya's heart.

Tanya sat spellbound as the pastor expounded on the resurrection power. "The God who is able to raise His Son from the dead has power today to raise you from your sins. Never think you've been too great a sinner to come to God. There is victory and power! Today we celebrate the death and resurrection of Jesus." The preacher's voice rang with fervency.

Tanya shifted nervously. It felt like he was preaching right at her.

"With God's help, you can be free from the burdens that weigh you down. You can find forgiveness and freedom through Jesus." Tanya bit her lip and looked out the window. *How can I be free from sin?*

At the end of the service, the pastor gave an invitation for anyone to come forward and repent. Tanya swallowed hard, her heart almost bursting within her. She knew what she needed to do. She needed peace. Her hands trembled as she handed Bogdonna to Marina. "Hold her, please," she whispered.

Her legs were shaking, and she had no strength to stand. She gripped the chair in front of her and tried again. It felt as though the burden of her heart would smother her and keep her from getting up. Finally she rose and walked to the front.

"Do you want to repent of your sins?" the pastor asked.

Tanya nodded. "I have a heavy weight on my soul. I cannot go on like this. I want freedom."

"We will kneel with you while the congregation stands." The pastor and the interpreter knelt beside Tanya. "You may pray first. Ask God to forgive your sins and to wash you in the blood of Jesus. Ask Him to give you a new heart. I'll also pray after you are finished."

Tanya nodded and bowed her head. Tears began running down her cheeks, but she could not say a word.

"Just talk to God as you would talk to your father," the pastor encouraged.

My father? Is God like my father? She shivered in fear. Then she remembered how Sergei always talked to God as though He was right there. *Maybe that is what the preacher meant.*

She took a deep breath and tried again. "Lord, forgive me for my sins." She could see her sins marching before her closed eyes. She shuddered as she realized what a sinner she was. "Forgive me, O God!" she sobbed. "I am such a sinner! Wash me in the blood of Jesus! Come and live in my heart."

A hush hung over the congregation as Tanya called out to God for mercy.

Then the pastor prayed. "Our heavenly Father, we thank you that you have called Tanya to repentance. Thank you for forgiving her sins and accepting her as your daughter. Help her to live a life of victory. Help her to be faithful to you."

After the prayer, the pastor shook Tanya's hand. "God bless you, sister. May you always be true to Him!"

Tanya felt like she could fly as she walked back to her seat. She had never felt so happy and free. The burden was gone!

As she sat down, Tanya Kotets reached over and squeezed her hand. "Praise the Lord!" she whispered.

After the service was over, Sergei hurried over and shook Tanya's hand. "Praise the Lord!" he said, his voice carrying across the church. "Now you are our sister in Christ!"

Others from the church came to offer words of encouragement. Their love and acceptance warmed her heart.

Valentine joined them, smiling nervously. Sergei turned his attention to him. "Valentine, maybe you want to repent today too? Would you like to follow your wife's example and give your heart to the Lord?"

Valentine shook his head. "Someday, but I'm not ready yet. But I am happy for Tanya. I think she made the right choice."

Marina squeezed Tanya's hand. "Mama, does this mean we will always come to church?" she asked.

Tanya smiled. "Probably. Would you like that?"

Marina smiled. "Of course! I have so many nice friends here!"

That night Tanya knelt beside her bed. It felt so strange, so different from praying in front of the icon. But it was what the pastors had told her to do. She just closed her eyes and tried to pray. "Lord, I don't really know how to do this. But I just want to thank you for taking away the load on my heart. Thank you for the peace and joy you have given me. Help me to always be faithful to you. Amen."

When she crawled into bed beside Valentine, her heart was floating. God felt so near, as though she could touch Him. With a happy sigh, she drifted into peaceful dreams.

The next morning Tanya awoke with a start. *Where am I? What happened? Something feels different.* Then she remembered. Yesterday at church she had repented of her sins. The heavy load of sin was gone. She smiled as she got out of bed and prepared for the day.

Sergei had said they wouldn't need to come to work today because it was Easter Monday. He had invited them to join the church picnic. Tanya had never heard of that before. *A church picnic?* These believers were so different from Orthodox Christians. She never knew what to expect.

A cloud of steam rose from the kettle on the stove. Tanya spooned some instant coffee into her mug and poured in the hot water. She added a spoonful of sugar and reached for a cigarette from the pack lying on the table. Coffee and a smoke were part of her morning routine.

Steam curled from her cup of coffee, mingling with the cloud of smoke from her cigarette. As the familiar smells melded together, Tanya took a deep breath. How good it felt to be alive. The heavy weight was gone. She wondered how long this happy feeling could last. Would she actually have to dress like those believers if she wanted to keep her newfound peace?

You have to quit smoking. Surprised, Tanya looked at her cigarette. *Where did that idea come from?* She glanced around the room, but no one was in sight. She put down her cigarette. *Will I really have to give this up?*

She looked at the pack of cigarettes on the table. It was nearly full. Would it matter if she just finished this pack? She picked up the still smoking cigarette and held it to her lips. To her surprise, it had lost its appeal and made her feel guilty. *Strange, I have smoked for years and it never bothered me before.*

Again she put down the cigarette. Could she actually stop smoking? Would she be strong enough to break this habit? How could she calm her nerves without her regular smoke?

But when she held the cigarette in her hand, she could not feel the newfound peace. Resolutely she picked up the box of cigarettes. With a look of determination, she marched to the outhouse and threw all of them, including the lighted one, down the hole.

A strange feeling filled her as she returned to the house. She felt like she could burst with joy. But she was puzzled. *How can I be happy when I have just gotten rid of my cigarettes?*

About midmorning, Tanya heard a commotion out on the street. She looked out the window and was surprised to see a group of people from church. "Valentine, it looks like we have visitors," she called. She quickly pulled a bandana over her hair and slipped into her dress.

"May we sing some Easter songs for you and your neighbors?"

Resurrection Morning

Brother Sasha wondered, looking at Valentine.

Valentine nodded his approval.

"Go tell your neighbors to come and listen too," Brother Sasha said. He gestured toward the houses on down the road.

Valentine looked at Tanya. "You go. They know you better than they know me."

Tanya could feel her face burn. She looked down at her dress. *What will they think if they see me dressed like this and associating with the Americans?* But suddenly she remembered something Sergei had said one day while they were working together. *"What kind of world are we living in? People today are ashamed to dress modestly but not immodestly. And they aren't ashamed to drink and smoke, but they are embarrassed to go to church. They are ashamed of the things they shouldn't be and not ashamed of the things they should be!"*

She would just have to be brave and do it. She ran over to Baba Shura, the lady who lived across the road. Shura looked at her skeptically but said she might come. Tolik, the next-door neighbor, laughed when he saw her. "Who do you think you are, dressed like that? Are you a nun or something? You're too great a sinner for that!"

Tanya tried to smile. "I'm not sure who I am right now. But please come and listen to the believers sing."

A small group of neighbors soon gathered to listen. Tanya could feel their eyes on her, but she tried to ignore them and focus on the words Brother Sasha was saying. He explained Jesus' death and resurrection in such simple words that everyone could understand. Tanya felt joy bubbling within her.

The church picnic was another surprise. After the believers had finished their Easter caroling, they gathered at the church house in Berezyanka. The chairs that usually stood in straight rows on Sunday morning were rearranged. Tables were set up and loaded with food.

Tanya and her great-grandfather Prokip.

Tanya as a little girl, dressed up for Christmas.

Svetta when she was about ten years old.

Valentine and Tanya on their wedding day.

On Valentine and Tanya's wedding day—
with her parents, Mikoli and Natasha.

Tanya and Marina (R), with Vova and Tetyana outside an Orthodox church.

Valya holding Marina.

Mikoli standing in front of his truck holding Marina.

Marina dressed for first grade.

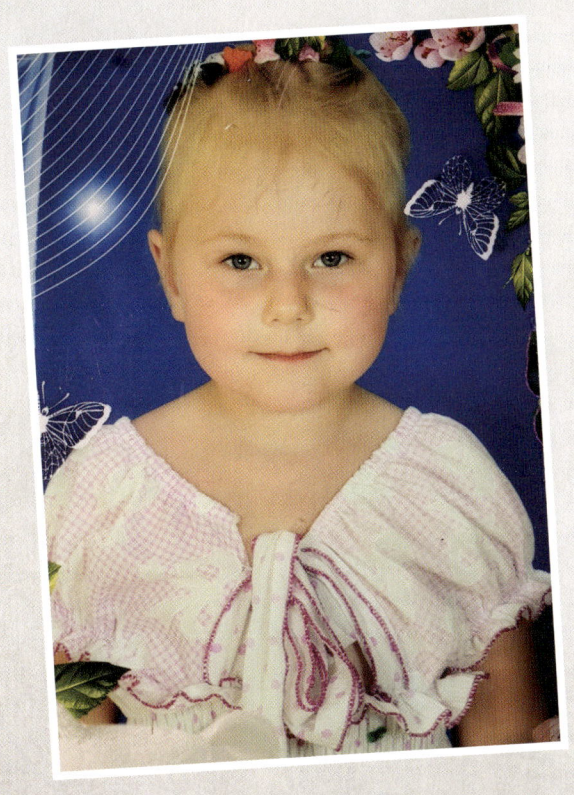

Bogdonna ready for kindergarten.

Connie greeting Tanya on her baptismal day.

A school photo when Tanya was teaching.
Tanya is second from right in the middle row.

With friends at the rain-interrupted birthday party.
(L-R) Tanya holding 7-month-old Anechka, Polina, Lina with her daughter Esther, Alona with her son Victor, and Anya.

Family photo taken the Sunday after Tanya's cancer was discovered.
(L-R) Marina holding Anechka, Valentine, Bogdonna, Tanya.

The church ladies celebrating Tanya's thirty-ninth birthday.

Family photo taken on Tanya's thirty-ninth birthday.
(L-R) Bogdonna, Marina, Tanya, Valentine, Anechka.

Solomia in the little casket made especially for her.

Tanya and Anechka (L), with Anya on
the trip to the Carpathian Mountains.

Before the meal of grilled chicken and other goodies, there was a time for sharing.

"Mama, why are you smiling?" Marina whispered as they sat listening to the singing.

"I was just imagining," Tanya said, suppressing another smile.

"Imagining what?" Marina persisted.

"I was just thinking what it would be like if our family stood up front and sang a song. I doubt if it will ever happen, but the idea makes me laugh."

Marina smiled brightly. "Maybe someday, Mama! That would be fun!"

After dinner, the children and youth gathered outside to play games. When Bogdonna became restless, Tanya took her on a walk. It gave her a chance to observe the games. The youth and children were playing a lively game of prisoner's base, their laughter and shouts ringing through the air. She watched as the girls in their lovely dresses ran and played with as much energy as the boys. She was amazed; their modest dresses did not seem to get in the way.

She noticed Marina playing with another little girl. She watched, amused, as they tried to communicate.

At home that evening, Tanya asked Marina about it. "Who was that girl you were playing with today?"

"That's Michelle; she's American!" Marina said. She smiled as she thought of her new friend. "Her papa is one of the preachers."

"Does she speak Ukrainian?"

Marina laughed. "No, but I'm learning some English. She always tells me 'Come,' and that means she wants me to go with her. Somehow we just understand each other. Look what she gave me today!" Marina held out a sheet of stickers.

"Wow, that was nice of her," Tanya replied.

Little girl treasures, she thought with a smile.

chapter 33

God's Smile of Approval

2011

Spring sunshine poured over the village. The trees exchanged their bridal gowns of lacy blossoms for robes of vibrant green, and tiny sprouts marked rows in the fertile soil of the gardens. Tanya spent hours in her garden, preparing the soil and planting seeds. She was delighted to receive a bag of ten seed packets from the believers, the kind of packets her papa had talked about.

One Friday morning Tanya pushed the baby carriage and Bogdonna to the local market. The market in the village was not nearly as big as the one in town, but it was still a good place to stock up on the week's supply of groceries.

The morning sun drenched the village in its brightness, and Tanya was grateful she had remembered to grab her sunglasses. She had changed from her work clothes into her going-away clothes. Even if she was not going far, it felt good to dress up again.

Sometimes she was surprised at how naturally she had slipped back into village life. Many of her classmates had moved to the city to find jobs, but the older people were still here. Their steps had slowed and more wrinkles were carved in their faces, but they were still the same people they had been when she was a child. The atmosphere was different from the city, where people hardly knew their next-door neighbors. Here everyone knew everything about everyone else. There were no secrets.

Tanya chatted with a babushka in line next to her as she waited at the meat stand to buy a small chunk of pork for their borsch. She made her round among the stands. Fresh radishes. A bag of oatmeal. A bottle of oil. Then she spotted one of the girls from church. "Hello, Anya!" she said, smiling as she pushed the baby carriage closer to the table filled with lovely petunias.

"Good day!" Anya replied, but Tanya noticed a questioning look in her eyes.

"Your flowers are beautiful!" Tanya commented.

"Thank you," Anya replied. She glanced from Tanya to Bogdonna in the stroller. Suddenly her eyes lit up and she laughed. "Oh, Tanya, is it you?"

"Of course!" Tanya replied, looking confused.

"I'm sorry! I didn't recognize you right away. It wasn't until I saw Bogdonna that I realized it's you."

"That's all right." Tanya shifted nervously and ran her hand through her trimmed hair. "I'd better keep going. We'll see you later."

"Yes, I look forward to seeing you on Sunday!" Anya called after her.

As Tanya walked away, her face burned with embarrassment. *It's no wonder she didn't recognize me,* she thought. *I don't look like I do when she sees me at church. I can't keep living a double life. I didn't expect to see her at the market, but I should have known better.* She kicked a pebble along the road. Life was complicated.

Tanya's job at Sergei's varied with the season. Now that the roses were blooming profusely, Tanya's day began early as she helped cut the roses before the morning heat wilted them. Cutting roses gave her the privilege of working with Sergei and Tanya's daughter Lina. A friendship sprouted as they toiled together during the early morning hours. Although Tanya greatly appreciated the job and respected Sergei and his wife, they intimidated her. But Lina was different. She was a few years younger than Tanya and still lived at home with her parents. There was an openness about her that attracted Tanya. Lina knew what she believed, but she never tried to force her beliefs on Tanya.

Sergei had explained to Tanya that she must veil her head now that she had become a Christian. Tanya wanted to please God and do what was right, but she was overwhelmed with all the changes she should make. She began wearing a bandana to work, but she resented it. Especially when the sun beat down on the greenhouse, and it became uncomfortably warm.

One warm day as Tanya walked home from work, she pulled off her veil and tucked it into her bag. It was just too warm to have anything on her head. She had waited until she was far enough down the road so Sergei and Tanya would not see her. She ran her fingers through her hair and smiled. Ah, how good it felt to be free!

She heard a vehicle approaching and stepped to the edge of the road. The van slowed down beside her, and her heart sank when she saw who it was—Sasha Dziuba, a brother from church!

She cringed as he drove past. A sermon could not have hurt more than the disappointment she saw in his eyes. Her face burned. Why did being a Christian have to be so hard? Would she actually have to give up all of her old life in order to be a Christian?

The next morning as Lina and Tanya cut roses together, Tanya told Lina about the incident on the way home from work. "I could see he was disappointed in me," she continued mournfully, "but I just don't know if I can handle the pressure of always having to please everybody."

Lina paused, her clippers in midair. "I think I understand what you're saying. Trying to please everyone is a lot of pressure, especially if you are trying to please your old friends, yourself, and your church family. Perhaps instead of worrying what others think, you should focus instead on God. What would He want you to do?" Lina clipped another rose and added it to the pile on Tanya's arms. "Disappointing God is much worse than disappointing Brother Sasha or anyone else."

Tanya nodded, amazed at the wisdom of her young friend. "You are right. But how can I know if I am disappointing God?"

Lina's clippers moved steadily as she replied, "Pray and ask God for direction. When He is disappointed in us, we won't have peace and joy. But if we walk close to Him and seek His will, it's almost like we can feel Him smiling at us." She straightened her back and smiled. "I still have a lot to learn myself."

That day marked a turning point in Tanya's life. Her heart's desire was to serve Jesus. As she read His Word and spent time each day in prayer, her relationship with God deepened. She treasured the peace and joy she had. At times it would disappear, and she would analyze what she was doing wrong. Slowly her life changed.

It felt like she was trying to swim upstream against a strong current. As soon as she paused to rest, the current took her back to where she had been. Breaking her addiction to cigarettes would have been easier if she could have gotten away from the smell. But as long as Valentine was around, the air was blue with cigarette smoke, tempting her.

The television was another source of trial. After years of watching it daily, breaking the habit was difficult.

Although Valentine was secretly glad for the changes he saw in his wife, it made him uncomfortable. He found a strange pleasure in antagonizing her. He knew she did not want to watch television, so he watched it more than ever—and kept the volume turned on high.

chapter 34

Tough Love

2012

Tanya sat on the bed, a daughter on each side. She treasured this time of day when they read God's Word together. She could hear Valentine out in the kitchen, rummaging through the cupboards. He had come home late. She and the girls had eaten supper several hours ago, but she had left food on the table so he could help himself when he came home. She turned back to the Bible and continued reading.

She was reading the story in the Gospel of John about Jesus calming the storm. "Imagine, girls," she said. "Jesus just told the storm to be quiet! That's hard to comprehend!"

Marina listened wide-eyed. "My teacher told me about that story in Sunday school. But what I can't understand is how Jesus could sleep when there was a storm."

Just then the door opened and Valentine entered, a teacup in his hand. He staggered, leaning against the door frame for support. "Where is the coffee?" he demanded.

Tanya bit her lip to keep back the angry words that threatened to spew forth. Why did he have to interrupt their time of Bible reading?

"In the cupboard where it belongs," she said, turning back to the Bible. She continued reading to the girls, but they were not listening. Their eyes were on their papa.

"Get it for me!" he demanded.

"You can find it yourself," she retorted. "Can't you see I'm busy?"

"You think you are so holy!" he snapped. "I will teach you a thing or two." He hurled the teacup straight at her.

Tanya gasped and ducked her head. The cup just missed her and hit the window with a loud crash. Shards of glass flew everywhere.

"Look what you did!" Tanya tried to keep from screaming. Bogdonna broke into a wail, and even Marina looked like she could cry.

Tanya turned to Marina. "Take Bogdonna into your bedroom and stay there until I tell you to come out. Be careful not to step on the glass!"

As soon as the girls were safely in the next room, Tanya allowed her frustration to spew out on her husband. "How dare you do this? Are you trying to kill me?"

Valentine smirked. "Maybe. What kind of Christian are you anyway to get so upset? I thought you are supposed to be a saint now."

Tanya bit her lip and turned away. Her hands trembled as she picked up the pieces of glass. One piece cut her finger, but it did not hurt half as much as the accusations Valentine had hurled. How could she ever be a good Christian if Valentine acted like this? Was it even worth trying?

"Tanya, you seem rather sad," Baba Luba stated, watching Tanya drain the last drop of tea from her mug. "What's bothering you?"

The others had gone back to work, and only Tanya remained in the kitchen with Baba Luba. Tanya glanced toward the door and hesitated. *Do I really want to tell this woman what is bothering me?*

"I'm all right," she said. She smiled half-heartedly. She could feel Baba Luba's searching eyes piercing through her.

"No, you're not," Luba said gently. "Please tell me what's bothering you."

The softness in her voice touched Tanya. Despite Luba's firm ways, she really did care. Almost before Tanya realized it, she was pouring out her woeful story of the evening before. "I try so hard to do what is right, but Valentine makes it really hard!"

"I know exactly what you mean," Baba Luba said. "My husband also made it hard for me."

Tanya looked up, surprised. She had never thought to ask Baba Luba about her husband.

"As Christian wives, it is up to us to show Christ's love to our husbands no matter how cruel or unreasonable they are."

Tanya noticed the faraway look in Luba's eyes. "I still remember when Vladimir would come home drunk. It was hard. So hard." Luba wiped the tears from her eyes. "But there is no other way. When Valentine comes home drunk, you must love him. You must prepare food for him. If he is too drunk to clean himself up, you must do it. With love, you must feed him, care for him, and put him to bed. It's hard, I know, but it's the only way."

Tanya shook her head. "I don't know if I can do that. I feel like locking him out of the house and telling him not to come home until he is sober!"

"Try love," Luba urged. "I'll be praying for you. With God's help, you can do it."

The opportunity came before Tanya was ready. She had just finished preparing supper that evening when Valentine entered the house, followed by three of his friends. "Supper ready?" he asked.

Tanya cringed as she smelled drink on his breath. "Yes, it is," she replied. "Are you hungry?"

"Yes, and so are the fellows. Give us something to eat!" he demanded.

Tanya took a deep breath and breathed, *Lord, help me!* She smiled at the men. "Welcome. You may find seats in the living room. I'll have supper ready in a few minutes."

With every breath, she begged the Lord for grace. She did not feel a rush of warm love toward her husband, but the bitterness and hatred melted, leaving a trickle of compassion. She saw her husband in a different light—a weak, miserable man in need of a Savior. The same feeling reached the other drunks who had come with Valentine.

She and the girls could eat the leftovers. Carefully she set the table and dished out the food. She hesitated for a moment before cutting the meat and cheese. She had not been planning on serving sandwiches, but perhaps Valentine would like it.

The men sat at the table and began devouring their food. "Bring us some beer," Valentine demanded.

Tanya could feel all eyes on her. "I'm sorry, but I can't do that. But I'll be happy to serve tea."

Valentine growled and muttered something about a disobedient wife. One of the other men protested. "You shouldn't be complaining! My wife would never be this nice. You should be ashamed of yourself."

Tanya acted as if she hadn't heard the remark and continued pouring tea. Then she excused herself to the back bedroom, where the girls were waiting. Her heart felt strangely light as they read the Bible. She could feel Jesus' presence, and His smile of approval warmed her heart.

With God's help, she would show Valentine what it meant to be a real Christian.

chapter 35

Part of the Family

2012

Soon after Tanya had begun attending church regularly, Sergei had encouraged her to ride on the church bus instead of riding with them every Sunday. By then, the rest of the church people had become like family, and Tanya enjoyed the ride. It was a time of rich fellowship. Children, babushkas, and families packed into the hired bus. It was often so full that people had to stand. The bumps on the cobblestone road rattled the little bus.

Sometimes Tanya wondered what the driver must think about the believers he hauled to church every Sunday. Although he rarely came inside the church, he knew a lot about them. He saw them at their best—dressed in Sunday clothes and belting out songs or discussing the sermons as they bumped to and from church. He also saw them at their worst—vying for seats, airing grievances, or sharing village gossip.

It didn't take long for Tanya to realize that the church was not made up of perfect people. As she worked closer with them, she learned to know their faults and failures. She saw their struggles and heard their confessions at church on Sunday. But despite their weaknesses, her appreciation grew. These people showed by example what it means to make restitution, to rise above failures, and to forgive and move on with life.

As Tanya grew in her longing to know God better, she joined instruction class. During the week, she would write down her questions about faith and God, as instruction class gave her the opportunity to ask questions. She also looked forward to the rich discussions each Sunday after the morning service.

At first Tanya had been hopeful that Valentine would also come to Christ, but her hopes had been dashed time and again. Now he seldom came along to church with her, preferring to spend the day with his drinking buddies.

His absence actually made life easier for her. When he was at home, he was often cranky and unreasonable, sleeping off the stupor from his latest party or demanding food and bossing the family around. He had quit working for Sergei and just did odd jobs around the village—jobs that were often paid with a bottle of vodka.

It broke Tanya's heart to see her daughters living with the same kind of father she had grown up with. Yet what could she do? She could not change Valentine. She could only try to be a good mother for her daughters. And she did try, but she hated herself for the times she lost her patience and became frustrated with the children. Time and again she had to ask for forgiveness.

Though Bogdonna was too little to understand, Marina was always willing to forgive. Tanya's heart swelled with love as she thought of her precious daughters. With God's help, she would do her best to raise them in a loving Christian home.

As summer came with intense heat, Tanya diligently cared for the potatoes she had planted. She pulled the weeds and sprayed for the bugs. But the sun beat down on the little plants, and by late July they began to wither. Tanya prayed for rain, but the sky remained clear. An occasional light rain revived her hopes, but since her potatoes were planted on the hillside, the water rushed down the hill and hardly made a difference.

"Are you busy with garden work?" asked Connie, a church sister, one Sunday after the service.

"Kind of," Tanya replied. "I should start digging my potatoes soon. The plants have dried up, so I might as well get started." Tanya glanced around the auditorium to see where her girls were. She didn't want them to miss their bus ride back to the village. "I'm afraid the harvest won't be the greatest. What about you? Do you have a busy week planned?"

Connie nodded. "Yes, a really busy one. We'll be hosting a group of people who are traveling through Ukraine on mission work. They plan to spend several days with us."

"Interesting! Are they relatives?"

"No, they are from America. They're here to visit and encourage believers in Ukraine. Could you use some help to dig your potatoes?"

Tanya looked at her, puzzled. Why was Connie suddenly changing the topic back to the potatoes? She shook her head. "No, I can't afford to hire any help. I'm afraid the harvest will be poor, and I won't have many potatoes to sell."

Connie laughed. "Our visitors don't expect to be paid! They would be glad to help you dig your potatoes for no charge."

"But these people don't even know me!" Tanya protested. "Why would they want to help me dig potatoes?"

"Like I said, they want to encourage the believers in Ukraine. Could they come on Friday?"

Tanya nodded. "I think so. What will be expected of me?"

"If you want to, you could serve them some compote and a snack," Connie replied. "But please don't go to a lot of bother." She smiled. "I'll come and help you."

Tanya arranged for a neighbor to come with his little tractor to plow up the potatoes. To prepare, she sorted through her sacks, mending the ones with holes.

Tanya rose early on Friday morning. She was nervous about serving these American guests. *What if they don't like Ukrainian food?* She had decided to make pizza. She patted a thick crust on her pan and spread a layer of mayonnaise and ketchup over it. Then she layered her toppings: lunch meat, corn, tomatoes, onions, and a bit of cheese. It smelled good as she pulled it from the oven. *I hope the Americans like it.*

The neighbor soon arrived with his tractor and plow. When the sharp plow exposed the harvest of potatoes, Tanya's heart sank when she saw the marble-sized potatoes. Before she had time to blink back her disappointment, a white Sprinter van pulled up and the visitors piled out. She was surprised to see some elderly people among the dozen or so visitors.

By the end of the afternoon, Tanya had forgotten her nervousness and was enjoying the day. Most of the visitors knew little Ukrainian, but smiles and laughter are understood in any language. They worked hard, picking up the potatoes and sorting the few egg-sized ones into bags to sell. The smaller ones went into separate sacks for Tanya's family to eat that winter.

Tanya could see by the visitors' smiles and their simple clothing that they were believers, but the women wore white caps on their heads instead of veils. Tanya supposed that must be what believers in America wear.

After the potatoes had all been picked up, everyone gathered in the yard for a snack. Tanya served plum cherry compote and the pizza she had baked that morning. Connie had brought a large watermelon, which she cut into wedges. A lump rose in Tanya's throat as she looked over the tired, happy crowd. They had worked hard gathering her potatoes. But they had done it with a smile.

"I don't know how to thank you for your help," Tanya said, addressing the crowd. "It would have taken us a long time to do what you did in a couple of hours."

"We are glad if we can bless a sister in Christ," one of the guests replied, smiling. "Your faithfulness to Christ despite your hardships is an example to us."

I still have so much to learn about God, Tanya mused. *How could I have been an example to them?*

"We'll be praying for you," another one said. "We'll pray that your husband will also choose to follow God."

That night Tanya knelt by her bed and let the tears flow. "Thank you, Father, for the privilege of being part of your family." It was strange how she had felt such a kinship with these strangers—people who could barely speak her language. There was a bond of love that made them feel like kinfolk.

What a blessing it is to belong to the family of God!

Part of the Family

chapter 36

The School of God

2012

Tanya's fingers stripped raspberries from the loaded branches in the raspberry patch in front of the house. Although the days were warm, the night air carried a chill that hinted of fall. These raspberries would provide jam for the long winter months. Tanya shivered as she thought of the coming winter. She was grateful for her work at Sergei's greenhouse, but he could not supply her with work in the winter. How would she provide for her precious daughters?

Valentine was gone again. He had gone to Kyiv for a visit several weeks ago and still had not returned. She could not rely on him to meet their needs.

"Good evening, Sister Tanya!"

Tanya looked up, startled. She had been deep in thought and had not noticed anyone coming down the road. Brother Sasha Dziuba and his wife Lyenna stood outside the gate. "Good evening!" Tanya called. "Are you coming here or just walking by?"

"We thought we'd stop by for a visit," Sasha replied. "Unless you're too busy. I see you are hard at work."

"Come in! The raspberries can wait till another day." Tanya scooped up her bowl of sweet rubies and led the way to the house. She set the berries on the table and filled the teakettle with water. By now, Tanya had become accustomed to people stopping by for a visit. It was a part of village life, especially among the believers.

After chatting about the weather and the garden and other everyday matters, Sasha cleared his throat. "Sister Tanya, as you know, in a few weeks school will be starting. I was wondering if you would like to send Marina to our Christian school."

"Oh, I hadn't thought of that!" Tanya exclaimed. "I'm still in instruction class, but I hope to be a member soon. Tell me more about the school."

Sasha smiled. "Well, the Christian school is one reason our family moved here. Children are too precious to be trained by the world. I grew up in a Christian home, with parents who loved God and taught me much about Him. But the teaching I received in school contradicted what my parents taught, and I believed my teachers instead of my parents."

Sasha's eyes held a faraway look, as if he were reliving those days of his childhood. "The results were sad, as I got in with a group of bad friends and ended up in jail. I spent several years behind bars. I don't want my children to go through what I did."

Tanya nodded soberly.

"Although we have a Christian school," Sasha explained, "by law we have to use the public school's curriculum. And every year our students have to take exams at the public school. But we are able to filter the material and teach the students ourselves. It's not easy, but it is worth it."

"Who pays for the schooling?" Tanya wondered, knowing she could not afford educational expenses. "The parents?"

"No, the parents do not have to pay tuition. Have you noticed that the pastor often announces that the offering is going to the school? That's how it is paid for."

Tanya nodded. She had wondered what the offering money went for. Sometimes the preacher said it was for the school and other times for the general fund or special needs.

"So in a sense the parents do pay for the school," Sasha continued, "but they are not required to pay a certain amount."

"I like that idea," Tanya said. "And I want to help too if I can."

"The goal of our school is to teach our children the ways of God, so it's of utmost importance that our teachers are believers. We want our children to learn academics, but that is not our top priority.

"Our teachers are not certified but are our own church people. Last year my wife was one of the teachers." He smiled at Lyenna. "And she'll be teaching again this year, along with our son David."

"How can several teachers teach the whole school?" Tanya asked. "Do they teach all the subjects?"

"Yes, all the main subjects. We plan to ask Anya Hursh to come in two days a week to teach English, and we are still looking for a teacher for the lower grades."

"Interesting! It's hard for me to imagine a school like that! I suppose Marina would enjoy it, but it would be an adjustment. And," she sighed, her forehead furrowed, "I'm not sure what Valentine will say."

Sasha nodded. "I understand. But we also have another request. We still need one more teacher. Would you consider teaching the lower grades?"

What? Did I hear right? Is Sasha asking me to teach school? "I'm not a teacher!" she finally stammered.

"Not yet," he said, smiling. "But I see potential for you to be a good teacher. Do you enjoy children?"

"Well, yes," she admitted. "I worked at a daycare for a while in Kyiv, but that is different from teaching school."

"I've seen how God has worked in your life, and we are honored to count you as a sister in Christ. You've been a blessing to our church, and I think you could be a blessing to our school as well." He paused. "And another thing to think about—it would provide an income during the winter months. So think about it and pray about it. You don't have to decide today."

Before Sasha and Lyenna left, Sasha led in prayer, asking God's blessing on Tanya and her family and praying that God would show her His will.

The longer Tanya thought about it, the more the idea grew on her. It felt like an answer to prayer. She needed to support her family, and this would give her the added blessing of working with other believers. She agreed to try it.

On the first day of the school term, everyone pitched in with cleaning the school, setting up desks, and sorting through the books. Tanya noticed that the books they received from the public school had changed since she was a student. They no longer held any traces of Lenin, Stalin, or communism.

The school building was an old village house that had been turned into school quarters. Tanya was given the first classroom, the walk-through room. She wondered how she could keep her students studying when the other three teachers and their students had to walk through her room to get to their classrooms.

As she tried to prepare for the day, Tanya stuck her head into Lyenna's classroom. "Sister Lyenna, are there any teacher's guides for these books? Or answer keys?"

Lyenna laughed. "I'm sorry, but there are not. You will have to teach without them. It makes it tough, but at least we don't have to worry about the students peeking in the answer key!"

Tanya's head was swirling by the end of the first day. Sasha had come and led in devotions and had gone over the school rules.

Eventually Tanya got into the rhythm of school. She enjoyed interacting with her students and co-teachers. The highlight of the school day was the tea break at 11:30 when the teachers took turns providing a snack. When Tanya's turn came, she often baked a pizza. The thick crusts helped make up for the narrow slices each child received.

Twice a week Anya came to school to teach English class, and she soon became a trusted friend. Though Anya was more than ten years younger than Tanya, the two became fast friends. During the quiet moments before the children arrived at school, they found time to visit and encourage each other in the Lord.

The whirl of busyness often overwhelmed Tanya. After the children were dismissed at 2:00, she hurried to the greenhouses to work for several hours before heading home. Evenings were filled to the brim as she tried to keep up with her household work. By the time the day was over, she was exhausted—both physically and mentally.

Winter finally arrived, and the work ended at the greenhouse. Although Tanya missed the paycheck, she knew she needed the break. Her children did too. Bogdonna, who spent her days at the daycare, thrived on more quality time with Mama. She had grown into a stocky three-year-old. Her bright smile and blue eyes were a copy of Svetta's. Sometimes Tanya called her Svetta by mistake.

As the months rolled by, Tanya realized more and more the challenges of being a teacher. Besides knowing the material well enough to explain it, there were other problems. One of her students seemed unable to comprehend even the simplest math facts. Tanya tried every way she could think of to explain math concepts to this child, but they seemed to make no headway. In desperation, Tanya went to visit Irina Vasilivna, her teacher of old.

"You are a teacher?" Irina exclaimed. "The way you struggled in school, I never imagined you would be a teacher!" She laughed. "But some of the best teachers are those who had to work hard in school. It makes them more sympathetic with students who struggle."

After visiting with Irina, Tanya felt renewed enthusiasm. Her former teacher had given her some practical pointers and had encouraged her to not give up.

But there was another problem that Tanya did not know how to deal with. One student had a severe attitude problem. One day it reached a climax.

"You are a bad teacher!" the stubborn student stormed. "I don't like you!"

Tanya was shocked at the outburst. Although she knew the boy was rebellious, she had not expected this—not in a Christian school! Even in public schools, children were not allowed to talk like this.

"Sister Lyenna is a much better teacher than you!" he continued.

Tanya cringed. How was she supposed to respond to this outburst? She breathed a prayer for wisdom. "I'm sorry you think I'm not a good teacher," she said. A brave smile hid the frustration mounting within her. "Sister Lyenna has years of experience, so of course she's a better teacher than I am. This is my first year, and I have a lot to learn. Hopefully with time I can be a better teacher." She smiled. "Now let's get back to our lessons."

But by the time Tanya reached home that evening, her head throbbed and her nerves were taut. *Why am I teaching?* she wondered. *Is it worth the stress and hassle? Maybe I really am a bad teacher. Maybe the children hear their parents saying the same thing. Should I quit?*

She tried to forget about her problems over the weekend. But Monday morning arrived and with it came doubts and discouragement. She went to school early to study. As she sat at her desk, a tear of discouragement slid down her cheek. How could she continue to teach with this kind of attitude in her room? Perhaps she was a failure.

The door creaked on its hinges. Surprised, Tanya looked up to see her troublesome student and his father enter the room. The student hung his head and shuffled his feet.

"Good morning, Sister Tanya. My son would like to tell you something," the father said.

The sheepish student raised his head and mumbled, "I'm sorry I said mean things to you on Friday. You are actually a good teacher."

Tanya felt tears sting her eyes. "I'll gladly forgive you," she said. She felt like giving him a hug, but she knew he would not appreciate it. "If I do my best to be a good teacher, and you do your best to be a good student, I think we can have a good school year," she told him.

He nodded and gave her a shy smile.

"Thank you, Sister Tanya, for all you are doing for our school," the boy's father said. "I was very disappointed when I found out what my son had said. Please let us know if you have any more problems. We want to help you."

Tanya nodded. "Thank you. I appreciate that!"

The School of God

chapter 37

Answered Through Pumpkin Seeds

2013

Winter wrapped its cold claws around the little village house. Tanya shivered as she threw a few more pieces of wood into the stove. She blew on the coals, coaxing the fire to burn brighter.

She sat down weakly on the bed. *Where is my energy?* Even the simplest tasks seemed to wring the strength from her.

Marina stirred under the covers.

"It's time for you to get up," Tanya said. She nudged her daughter and tried to smile. "You don't want to be late for school."

Marina rubbed the sleep from her eyes and stared at her housecoat-clad mother. "But you're not dressed yet either!" she exclaimed. "You'll be late too!"

"I'm not going to school today," Tanya said. "I'm not feeling well."

"But, Mama, who will teach your classes?"

"I don't know. I'll call Sister Lyenna and see what she says." Tanya stirred the last of the oatmeal into the boiling water for breakfast.

Marina took one bite and wrinkled her nose. "Ugh, this stuff needs sugar!" She reached for the sugar bowl, but Tanya stopped her.

"Careful, dear. That's the last of our sugar. Use only a little."

Marina studied the sugar bowl. It was nearly empty. She sprinkled a little on her porridge. "Mama, may I have some bread and jam with my tea?"

Tanya shook her head. "I'm sorry, dear, but we don't have any bread."

"Maybe I can go to the store after school and buy some," Marina suggested.

"Perhaps," Tanya said, but her voice sounded flat.

Tanya watched from the window as Marina, bundled in her winter coat and scarf, plodded through the snow. The tears that had been pooling in her eyes all morning slipped unnoticed down her cheeks. Marina was so small and frail for her age. She needed more to eat.

The sharp pain in her stomach caused her to gasp. She sat down on the chair and leaned her head against the wall. "Lord," she prayed, "please help me." She had prayed these words so often that they had become a refrain that played constantly in her mind. She had felt the pain for a while, and it was getting worse. She had to see a doctor.

But there was no money. She had used the last hryvnia to buy a loaf of bread. Now the bread was gone, and so was the money. It would be another two weeks before she received her next paycheck for teaching. They would not starve until then, but they might have to do without bread or meat. It would not be the first time.

At least Valentine was not here to complain. Several months had passed since he was at home. Most days Tanya did not mind that he was in Kyiv, living at his mother's house. Life was simpler when he was gone.

She could make the food stretch until the end of the month, but that would not solve her problem of needing money to go to the doctor. She fell to her knees and poured out her problems in prayer. Even when no more words came, Tanya continued kneeling in God's presence. When she rose, peace filled her heart. God would make a way.

Tanya was still mulling over their lack of money as she stripped the milk from the goat. Suddenly she stopped in surprise. Maybe this was her answer. She could sell the goat! Then she would have enough money to go to the doctor and also buy some groceries! Quickly she finished milking the goat and headed for the house. She would call that man from town who bought animals for the meat factory.

Tanya's heart felt heavy as she put down the phone. The price the man had offered was less than she had hoped. Had he sensed her desperation for money and used it to his advantage?

As Tanya placed the jar of milk on the table, she began to have second thoughts. The milk was not much, but at least it gave her daughters a bit of calcium every day. *Should I really sell the goat?* She shook her head. *No, I won't back out now. We need the money. Tomorrow the man will come and buy the goat.*

The next day Tanya kept her ears tuned for the sound of the truck coming for the goat. About midmorning she heard a honking horn and a voice over a loudspeaker. She slipped on her coat and hurried outside, hoping it was the man to buy the goat. As the vehicle drew nearer, she heard words coming over the loudspeaker: "Buying feathers, pumpkin seeds, and nuts! Buying feathers, pumpkin seeds, and nuts!"

She shook her head. It was not the goat buyer after all. She turned to go inside, the words "feathers, pumpkin seeds, and nuts" still ringing in her ears. Suddenly she stopped and ran back toward the road, waving for the driver to stop. "I have pumpkin seeds," she said eagerly. "I'll bring them out."

Answered Through Pumpkin Seeds

She hurried into the house and found the bundle of pumpkin seeds wrapped in newspaper. She had collected the seeds from her pumpkins last fall. Pumpkin seeds were Valentine's favorite, and she had saved them for him. But now he was gone, and she had no idea when he would return.

The driver weighed the packet of seeds and handed Tanya the money—thirty hryvnia. Inside the house, Tanya fell on her knees with tears of thanksgiving rolling down her cheeks. God had provided enough money for a bus fare to town and a loaf of bread.

Tanya was exhausted when she came home from church the next day. As she fumbled in her coat pocket for her keys, a piece of paper dropped to the ground. She bent down to pick it up. She gasped. *A hundred-hryvnia bill! Where did this come from?*

For the second time that week, Tanya knelt by her bed with tears of gratitude. God always made a way. Sometimes He used pumpkin seeds, and other times He used caring friends. She prayed that He would bless and reward the anonymous giver.

The man never did show up to buy the goat. Tanya was grateful; God knew her children needed the milk. He had provided a way to keep the goat and still pay for the medicine the doctor prescribed for her a few days later.

chapter 38

Oh, Happy Day

April 13, 2013

The sun was just peeking over the horizon when Tanya's alarm rang. She knelt by her bed and committed the day to the Lord. She felt a tingle of excitement. Today was her baptismal day—the day she would seal her commitment to God with water baptism. Yesterday she had met with the preachers and the bishop that had come from America especially for this.

She slipped into her new dress, a light blue one that shimmered in the morning light. Most of her dresses were secondhand, but this one had been sewn especially for her. It fit perfectly. Tanya looked in the mirror and smiled. Not even the happiness of her wedding day was as great as the joy she felt today.

When the bus arrived at church, Tanya hurried to find Dina and

Lashonda, the other applicants for baptism. Their faces reflected her own excitement and nervousness. They sat together in the front row of chairs. As the congregation sang "Oh, Happy Day," Tanya thought her heart would burst with the joy that pulsated within.

When it was time for testimonies, Tanya shared hers first: "God reached out and saved me, for I was at the very edge of hell. I was working at the local bar, and my marriage was falling apart. I don't know where I would be if Jesus hadn't reached out and brought me to Him." Her voice trembled with excitement and nervousness at first, but she gained confidence as the words began to flow. "I'm so thankful that He saved me, and that today I can become part of a Christian church family. A family that supports me and cares about me…"

When Brother Art asked her the vows, her voice rang out clearly. "I do." She bowed her head as the bishop laid his hands on her head. "I baptize you in the name of the Father, the Son, and the Holy Ghost." Tears of joy mingled with the water that trickled down her face.

As the bishop moved on to the next applicant, Tanya's head remained bowed as she breathed a silent dedication prayer. *Lord, no matter what happens, I will be true to you. Thank you for accepting me as your daughter. Thank you, Jesus! Thank you!*

"Hurry, girls, or we'll miss the bus!" Tanya urged. "Marina, run ahead and tell the bus driver to wait."

As Marina scampered ahead, Tanya grabbed Bogdonna's hand and pulled her along. "Mama, carry me!" Bogdonna pleaded.

Tanya shook her head. "You're a big girl, Bogdonna. You'll soon be four! Mama can't carry you."

When Tanya reached the highway, she looked toward the Dziuba home where the church bus always stopped to pick up people. Sure enough, it was there and most of the people were already aboard.

By the time Tanya reached the bus, her face was flushed and her leg throbbing. She sank gratefully into the seat by the window and lifted Bogdonna to her lap. Marina slid into the seat beside her.

Tanya pulled Marina close and whispered, "Don't tell your friends what happened this morning, all right?"

Marina nodded soberly. "It would make Papa even more upset, wouldn't it?" Her big eyes looked deep into her mother's.

"Yes." Tanya squeezed Marina's hand and turned her face toward the window. She closed her eyes and begged for strength to make it through the day.

"Good morning, Sister Tanya! How are you?" Babushka Ria asked.

Tanya forced a smile and said, "Praise the Lord, we're doing all right. And how are you?"

"As good as can be expected for an old lady like me," Ria chuckled. "Where's Valentine?"

"At home," Tanya answered. "He was not in the mood for church today." She turned and looked out the window. She didn't want to think about Valentine right now, but her throbbing leg and aching heart would not let her forget. *Help me, Lord. Give me strength for today. Help me forgive. Help me, Lord!*

It felt like every breath was a prayer, but sometimes she wondered if God even heard. Where had God been this morning when she needed Him so much? She blinked back her tears and pasted a smile on her face. *I must stay strong for my children's sake.*

Tanya stood with the congregation as they sang the opening song, but she could not concentrate. In her mind, she could see Valentine towering over her with clenched fists. Her body still ached from the impact of his fists, but her heart ached even more. *Why do my children have to see such misery?*

When the song leader announced the second song, Tanya numbly turned to it. Her thoughts were still replaying the scenes of the morning, and she hardly noticed when the congregation began singing. But suddenly the words penetrated through the fog and entered Tanya's heart.

Does Jesus care when my heart is pained
Too deeply for mirth and song;
As the burdens press, and the cares distress,
And the way grows weary and long?

O yes, He cares, I know He cares!
His heart is touched with my grief;
When the days are weary, the long nights dreary,
I know my Savior cares.[1]

Tanya could no longer hold back the tears. The words were the cry of her heart. In desperation, she slipped past the girls and hurried to the kitchen at the back of the church. She was grateful to find it empty. She sat down and leaned her head on the table. *Does Jesus truly care?* The tears she had been holding back came forth in a torrent.

She heard the door open but didn't look up to see who entered.

"Tanya dear, are you all right?"

Tanya could hear the loving concern in the voice. She lifted her head and smiled bravely as Connie pulled up a chair beside her. "I'll be all right," she whispered. "It's just that this song touched my heart. Sometimes I wonder if Jesus truly cares."

Connie nodded and squeezed her hand. The two sat in comfortable silence as the congregation continued to sing.

"I saw you limping," Connie said when the last notes of the song had died away. "What happened?"

---

[1] "Does Jesus Care?" by Frank E. Graeff (1901).

Tanya closed her eyes for a brief second and swallowed hard. "Valentine wanted me to go buy him cigarettes, but I refused. It made him angry, and he beat me up."

A look of horror washed over Connie's face. "Oh, Tanya, that's awful! I'm so sorry!"

Tanya shrugged her shoulders. "I think I did the right thing. I just wish the children would not have seen it. Marina was scared that he was going to kill me, so she grabbed my phone and tried to call the police. That only made Valentine more upset. He turned on Marina and would have hurt her too, but she got away from him. He was so angry that he broke my phone."

"Oh, Tanya! That's terrible!" Tears shone in Connie's eyes.

"Please don't tell the others what happened," Tanya pleaded. "It will only make things worse if Valentine finds out I've been talking to people."

Connie nodded slowly. "I see what you mean, but I don't want this to happen again!"

"Me neither!" Tanya agreed. She winced as she stood. "Just keep praying for us. That is the biggest help. Pray that Valentine would repent. I have faith that he will someday."

As Tanya returned to her seat in the auditorium, her heart felt lighter. Sharing the burden with a sister had helped.

No matter what happened, she knew deep in her heart that Jesus did care.

chapter 39

The Resurrection Power

2014

*E*aster Sunday dawned bright and glorious. Tanya's heart swelled with joy as the family walked to the highway to catch the bus. Today marked three years that she had given her heart to the Lord. She marveled at the way God had provided for her family during that time.

She glanced at her husband and smiled. "It sure is a beautiful day. Easter is my favorite holiday!"

He smiled back and nodded. "Yes, it is a beautiful day. It would be perfect to go fishing."

"Perhaps you can go after church," she said. "Unless you want to go with me and the girls to visit my relatives in Tsapiivka."

He shrugged. "I'll see how I feel after lunch."

The last two Easters, Tanya and the girls had spent Sunday afternoon visiting her relatives in the neighboring village. None of them were believers, but they had learned to respect Tanya. She marveled at how open they were.

Brother Wayne Hursh preached a message on the power of the resurrection. "The power that raised Jesus from the grave is also strong enough to raise you from your sins. On your own you can't do it, but through Jesus you can find power to live in victory!" Brother Wayne's eyes filled with tears as he looked across the crowd. "If you are burdened with sin, come to Jesus and He will help you!"

At the end of the service, Brother Abner asked if anyone wanted to repent. Tanya stole a quick glance at Valentine. She had noticed that he had been listening attentively during the service. Silence fell across the auditorium as Brother Abner waited.

"Lord, please give Valentine the courage to do it!" Tanya breathed, her head bowed in prayer. She did not notice the slight rustle as Valentine made his way to the front of the congregation.

"I want to repent!"

The words startled Tanya from her prayer. Valentine stood before the congregation, shoulders slumped, head hanging.

"I'm tired of trying to live a good life in my own strength. I've been trying to get my life in shape before I come to God, but it's not working. No matter how hard I try, I can't stop smoking. I need God's help!" His voice was thick with emotion. "I want to ask God to forgive me. I want Him to live in my heart and give me His resurrection power!"

As Valentine fell to his knees, the congregation stood. In brokenness, Valentine confessed his sins and asked the Lord to change him.

Joy surged through Tanya's heart. "Thank you, Lord! Thank you!" she whispered again and again.

As the family walked home from the bus stop, Tanya squeezed Valentine's hand. "God bless you, dear!" she whispered. "You don't know how happy I am! I believe God will help you find victory!" Tears of joy shone in her eyes.

Valentine nodded. "With God's help, I want to be a different man. If it wasn't for you, I would not be where I am now." He swallowed hard. "I know I've been a mean husband, but you kept loving and forgiving me. Thank you, dear!"

After a hasty lunch, the family walked to Tsapiivka. It was a long walk, and Bogdonna was tuckered out long before they arrived.

Uncle Sergei and Aunt Elena welcomed the family warmly. "We were hoping you would come!" Aunt Elena said. "We even saved some of our special holiday dinner to eat with you."

"Would you like something to drink?" Uncle Sergei asked. He looked at Tanya with a question in his eyes. It was a holiday and everyone was expected to offer alcohol to their guests. He knew Tanya's feelings about it and what a beast it turned Valentine into. But as a host, he felt obligated to offer.

"The girls and I will be glad for some water or juice," Tanya said, inwardly pleading for God to give Valentine strength. She glanced at him with a look that said, "I believe in you! You can be strong!"

Valentine hesitated, then smiled broadly. "I think a drink of juice would be just the thing for me too!"

The tension in the air eased, and once again joy bubbled within Tanya. God had helped her husband win this victory.

"Will you sing some Easter songs for us?" Aunt Elena wondered as they ate together. "I remember how you did that the last time you were here."

Tanya nodded. "We would be happy to sing some Easter songs. The girls learned some new ones in children's class, and they also learned some poems." She smiled at her daughters. "Do you think you can recite them?"

The afternoon and evening passed quickly. As they walked home in the twilight, Tanya thought her heart would burst with joy. God had saved her family, and now they were able to serve Him together!

Valentine stepped closer to Tanya's side as they slowed their pace, allowing Marina and Bogdonna to walk ahead. "I threw the rest of my cigarettes away," he said in an undertone. "I'm determined, with God's help, to find victory."

"I believe you can do it!" she said. "It won't be easy, but I'll stand by you. With God's help, you can be victorious!"

chapter 40

War!

2014

"Come, girls. Let's read the Bible and pray together before we go to bed," Tanya said.

Marina pulled the door shut, but the noise of the TV still carried into the room. Valentine was home, and so was the noise. Sometimes Valentine truly seemed to want to do what was right, but lately things had gotten worse again. More and more often, his presence brought noise, frustration, and stress.

"Will you read a story from the *Seed of Truth?*" Bogdonna asked, holding out a magazine.

Tanya smiled, glad her daughters enjoyed the magazine as much as she did. "Sure, I think we have time for a story tonight. But first let me read from the Bible."

She enjoyed this evening time with her daughters. Bogdonna was too young to understand everything, but Tanya marveled at Marina's insight. Though she was only eleven, she had a keen interest in the Scriptures, and Tanya enjoyed discussing the Bible stories with her. This evening their Bible reading was from Matthew 24. The girls listened as Tanya read.

"Mama, is there going to be war?" Marina asked when Tanya finished reading.

"What makes you ask that?" Tanya asked her wide-eyed daughter.

"Well, you read something about wars and rumors of wars, and I remembered what I saw in town today. Several big army trucks drove past, and someone said they are on their way to fight!"

"They probably are," Tanya replied, nodding her head sadly. "I heard that Russia wants to control part of our country. If that happens, there might be war. But you don't need to be afraid." She smiled encouragingly at her daughters. "It says here that he that endureth to the end shall be saved. God will keep us safe, and we can trust Him."

They knelt for prayer and asked for God's protection through the night. "And help there not to be war in Ukraine," Marina added. "Help Russia not to steal our land!"

After tucking the girls into bed, Tanya slipped into the bedroom. She expected to find Valentine asleep, as she no longer heard the blaring of the television. Instead, she found him sitting in the kitchen, puffing on a cigarette.

She poured a cup of tea and sat down across from him.

"It doesn't look good," he said.

"What doesn't?" Tanya asked, surprised by the heaviness in his voice.

"The situation our country is in," he replied. "I was watching the news tonight. It doesn't look good at all. Russia is determined to claim part of Ukraine."

"Do you think there will be war?" Tanya asked, fear creeping into her voice.

"Very likely. We won't give up our independence that easily."

Sleep eluded Tanya that night as she tossed and turned. *Will war come to Ukraine? Will it reach us?* She finally turned her worries into prayer and fell into a troubled sleep.

As days and weeks passed, the war clouds thickened. The hum of army trucks could often be heard as convoys of soldiers and trucks headed east to where some fighting was taking place. Because Russia was claiming some industrial areas in eastern Ukraine, certain grocery products became unavailable. Russia also overtook some of the electric stations, causing a shortage of electricity. Every morning and evening, the electricity went off for several hours.

The threat of a draft became reality one sultry day in August when army officials came to the village with a list of seventy-five men who needed to register to fight. In a village of only three hundred homes, this was a high percentage and affected everyone.

Valentine broke the news to Tanya when she came in from picking tomatoes in the garden. "They've issued a draft," he said, his voice husky. "The army officials brought a list of seventy-five men from our village who need to register."

"Do you think you'll be called?" Tanya asked, looking at her husband.

Unusual seriousness lined his face. "No, I don't think so. They won't accept me because I was in prison. That is to my advantage now. But I was talking to Sasha, and it could really affect his family."

Tanya nodded soberly. "Three of their sons would be eligible, right?"

Valentine nodded. "They are talking about leaving. They want to flee the country before the boys are drafted."

"The Dziubas are leaving?" Tanya gasped. "I can't imagine church without them! Surely they won't do that! We need them!"

Valentine nodded. "I don't know if they actually will, but Sasha wondered if we could take care of their house and greenhouses if they leave."

"You mean they are that serious? What did you tell him?"

"What could I say? I told him we would do our best to help them. But I can't imagine them leaving now, with the flowers in the greenhouse just starting to bloom and the tomatoes in full production."

But nothing was dearer to Sasha than the souls of his children, so two days later he and his family left for Poland. That quickly, Valentine and Tanya found themselves managers of the Dziubas' greenhouse business.

Everything happened so fast that Tanya wondered if it was actually true. It was strange to walk into their friends' house and take up residence. It felt as though they were imposing on their privacy. Surely any moment Sasha or Lyenna would walk in and wonder what they were doing in their house.

The responsibility weighed heavily on their shoulders. Tanya had been a gardener for years, but caring for a greenhouse full of tomatoes was a different story. Occasionally they could call one of the Dziubas for advice, but international calls were expensive. Tanya was grateful for others in the church who had greenhouses. They were always happy to share advice on what sprays to use for bugs or disease.

Living in a house with indoor plumbing was a new experience, and Tanya was amazed at how nice it was to have running water. But when the first electric bill arrived, she realized how much it cost to have hot water. After that, they only turned on the water heater on Saturdays so they could have warm baths.

Even with the additional time-saving conveniences, Tanya never had enough hours in a day to reach around. Besides the added responsibility of caring for the Dziubas' property, she still had her own garden and canning to tend to.

At first Valentine often found excuses to go back home to watch television, but as time went on, he became too busy for that. There was a spring in his step and a gleam in his eyes that Tanya had never seen before. He worked from morning till night and fell into bed exhausted.

When school started, Tanya resumed her place as a teacher. The changes of the past month had rocked the school. Sasha, the school director, was gone, and so were her co-teachers and some students. In addition to learning to know three new co-teachers, two new families planned to send their children to school. In this whirlwind of change, Tanya held tightly to her Father's hand.

Tanya was concerned about the environment Bogdonna was in at the daycare, so she pulled her out and brought her along to school. One of the new teachers also had a five-year-old daughter that she brought along to school, so the two little girls kept each other company while their mothers taught.

By October, the hundreds of chrysanthemums in the Dziubas' garden were turning rich shades of burgundy, gold, and rust. Every Saturday, Valentine and Tanya hired a taxi to take the flowers to town to sell at the market. Tanya quickly learned to recognize the regular shoppers, and Valentine turned out to be a persuasive salesman.

As Valentine worked in the greenhouse and cared for the plants, he began to think of the future. Maybe he could have his own greenhouse. He enjoyed the work and worked longer hours than ever before.

And as he worked, he dreamed.

chapter 41

The Smoking Battle

2015

While unrest and fighting continued in the eastern part of the country, life in Kryvoshyintsi returned to normal and the fear of war gradually subsided. After living in Europe for a year, Sasha and his family returned home.

The Kosenko family moved back to their little house. It felt crowded after living in the Dziubas' spacious house, but Tanya was happy to be home. It had been a good experience, but she was relieved to hand the responsibilities back. She missed the indoor plumbing more than anything else. The inconvenience of cranking water from the well and using an outhouse was worse than she had remembered. Perhaps someday they could afford the luxury of indoor plumbing.

For Valentine, the adjustment was harder. "I wish we could have our own greenhouse," he said one evening as they picked sweet corn to sell. "I'm glad we have this corn to sell, but we need more than that to live." He threw another ear of corn into his sack.

"Perhaps someday we can do that," Tanya said, wiping the perspiration from her brow. "Are you going to try to get a job again, or what are you planning?" She pulled her sack of corn farther down the row.

"I don't know. I wish I could build my own greenhouse, but we don't have enough money."

A week later Valentine was sitting at the table, studying a stack of papers in front of him. He looked up and smiled when Tanya entered the room.

"I think I have it mostly figured out," he said. "Could you look over it to make sure I didn't miss anything?"

Tanya took the paper from Valentine and sat on the stool next to him. It had seemed almost too good to be true when Brother Wayne had come to them last night with an offer to help them start their own small greenhouse. Tanya knew he worked for a mission, but she didn't know much about it before the visit with Wayne and Connie.

"Christian Aid Ministries has a program to help families start their own businesses," Wayne had explained. "Believers in America donate money to help people support themselves. You did a great job with Sasha's greenhouses while they were gone. Have you ever considered building one of your own?"

It was a direct answer to prayer. Together Valentine and Tanya prepared the business plan, figuring how much the greenhouse would cost. Then they added up the cost of the seeds, pots, a wood stove, and a load of firewood. "It takes more to get started than I thought it would," Valentine remarked.

"I just hope our application will be accepted," Tanya said.

"Me too." Valentine hung his head. He knew Tanya was likely remembering what Wayne had told them—that Christian Aid Ministries usually helped only families where both the husband and wife were church members. But Wayne thought they might make an exception for them. Valentine hated himself for not being a true Christian. He wanted to do what was right, but he just did not have the strength. "I'll be bitterly disappointed if this doesn't go through," he sighed.

"So will I," Tanya replied. "But I keep reminding myself that we really don't deserve it; it is a gift. And if we do receive help, we have a responsibility to pass the blessing on to others."

Valentine nodded. "By the way," he said, "I'm getting rid of the TV. That was one of the questions on the application. I hardly watch it anyway, so I decided we'd be better off without it."

Tanya swallowed the lump in her throat and smiled. "Wonderful! We won't miss the thing!" Finally, after all these years, there would be no television in the Kosenko home. God was working in her husband.

"Our application has been accepted!" Valentine's eyes gleamed with excitement as he stepped inside the house. He brushed the snow from his boots and set them by the stove to dry.

"Praise the Lord!" Tanya breathed. "I was starting to worry that we wouldn't get accepted. Or that it would be too late for this spring!"

Valentine immediately began preparations for his greenhouse. After he bought the metal, a local welder helped him build the arches. The winter weather made it challenging to work outside, but not even the frigid cold could put a damper on Valentine's enthusiasm.

One day when Valentine was outside working alone, finishing the greenhouse, he was humming a little tune. Suddenly he stopped, startled. What was that song he was humming? It was a song they had sung at church the other Sunday: *"Trust and obey, for there's no other way to be happy in Jesus, but to trust and obey."* The words came to him in a flood.

As he looked around at the nearly completed greenhouse, sudden tears filled his eyes. The ladder he was standing on wobbled a bit, and he nearly lost his balance. He reached out a hand to steady himself, then climbed slowly down the ladder. He felt overwhelmed by the blessings that surrounded him. Here he was, a poor village man who could hardly support his family, yet someone had sacrificed to help him build a greenhouse.

His shoulders shook with sobs as he fell on his knees, weeping and praying. "Lord, I'm not worthy of this kindness! You have given me so much. Forgive me, Lord, for not serving you with my whole heart. Help me be the husband and father my wife and children deserve!"

"Tanya, I'm done smoking!" Valentine announced abruptly as they were eating supper that night. Bogdonna paused in the middle of taking a bite and looked wide-eyed at her papa.

"Really?" Tanya's voice held a tinge of doubt. "What makes you say that?"

"I was out working in the greenhouse…" Valentine sought for words to tell them of his special experience. By the time he finished talking, tears glistened in all their eyes. "I want to be a good papa for you," he said brokenly, looking at his daughters. "Can you forgive me for the times I was mean?"

The girls nodded soberly. This was not the way they were used to hearing Papa talk.

The next few days were tough. Valentine tried to smother his craving for cigarettes by working hard and spending long days in the greenhouse. He was determined to remain strong, to not give in to his craving. But every fiber in his body screamed for nicotine.

He was miserable, and so was the rest of the family. Everything irritated him, and he resented himself for being so touchy.

Tanya spent much time in prayer, imploring the Lord for grace and courage to be sweet and begging Him to help Valentine become free from his addiction.

Every day Valentine hoped the battle would become easier, but it became harder and harder. A week passed, and Valentine thought he would go crazy if he waited another minute for a cigarette. After he had hollered at the children and snapped at his wife, he pulled on his coat to go outside. *I'm more of a brute without my cigarettes than with them,* he thought disgustedly.

"Where are you going?" Tanya asked, looking up from where she was washing the supper dishes.

"On a walk," he snapped. "It's too noisy and stuffy in here."

Tanya watched as he walked down the path and turned toward the store. *Lord, have mercy on him,* she prayed. *Have mercy on us all. This battle is too intense. Give grace, Lord. Help him find victory!*

She rinsed the last dish and dumped the dirty dishwater outside, her eyes straining into the darkness. *Where did he go?* Groaning in her spirit, she entered the house and knelt by her bed. Tears slipped silently down her cheeks as she interceded for her husband.

The Smoking Battle

Valentine growled as he stepped into a puddle. He should have thought to bring a flashlight along. He didn't know where he was going—he just had to go. His steps led him to the store. By this time his whole body was screaming for a cigarette, and he could no longer think clearly. He fumbled at the door of the store, but it was locked. He should have known the stores would be closed by now. When he tried the second store, it was locked too. Now what?

He paused as he thought of his wife and children at home. "I'm doing this for their sakes," he muttered under his breath. "I can't be a good papa as long as I am so miserable." Up ahead was the bar. Yes, a light still glowed. He hesitated. Did he really want to go in there?

He walked into the dimly lit bar and went straight to the counter. "I'd like a pack of cigarettes," he said. The smell of the bar brought back a flood of emotions.

"I'm sorry," the bartender said. "We're out of cigarettes. What would you like to drink?"

Valentine gripped the edge of the counter. This was ridiculous! How could the bar have no cigarettes?

"I didn't come for a drink," he said sourly. "All I need is cigarettes!"

He scanned the room and noticed a man sitting in the corner. The telltale glow of a cigarette caught his attention. Valentine walked over to the man.

"Hey, can you give a man a cigarette?" he asked, trying not to sound too desperate. "I really need one."

A wicked grin played on the man's lips. "I'd be glad to help you, but I can't. This is my last one." He held the smoking stick in Valentine's direction. "And I'm not about to give it up!" He laughed, and Valentine turned away and headed out the door.

Once outside, he paused as his eyes adjusted to the darkness. "Valentine, I want to give you victory," a voice in his conscience said.

"I'm here to help you. Let me give you the courage to win this battle."

Tears filled Valentine's eyes as he started homeward. "Thank you, Lord, for keeping me from smoking tonight. Help me find strength in you. Help me be victorious."

He entered the house a few minutes later and found Tanya still kneeling by the bed. She got up when he entered and gave him a questioning smile.

"Thank you for praying," he said, his voice husky. "I learned tonight that God is serious about not wanting me to smoke. He is strong. Even stronger than my addiction to cigarettes."

chapter 42

Released

2017

"You may gather in groups for prayer," the moderator announced after taking the prayer requests. It was Tuesday evening, and the believers had gathered for their regular prayer meeting. Tanya and a few other sisters made their way to the church kitchen.

"Please keep praying for my papa," Tanya said. "In a few months he will be released from prison. I should be glad, but I am worried. Though I love my papa, he has a very hard character. I don't think it's possible for both him and Valentine to live in one house." Her forehead creased in worry. "Since we're living in Papa's house, we will likely have to move when he is released. I'm not sure what will happen."

"Where would you go?" one sister asked in concern.

"I don't know. I suppose we could always go back to Kyiv and live with Valentine's mother, but none of us wants that. Let's pray that Papa will repent, and that God will show us what to do."

The sisters knelt in prayer and poured out their longings to God. Tanya looked forward to these weekly prayer meetings. Praying with her sisters in Christ always strengthened her faith and gave her courage to keep on.

Every time Tanya sent a parcel to her papa, she struggled. He wanted her to send cigarettes, but she could not make herself do it. Instead, she sent him tea, sugar, and other products.

She wondered if he ever read the literature she sent. Surely with all the time he had on his hands, he would read at least some of it. Or perhaps share it with the other inmates. Every time Tanya sent him a package, she wondered if she was wasting her time and money. But he was her papa, and she wanted to support him.

Tanya dreaded the thought of moving. Though the house still belonged to Papa, they had been fixing up the place. They had planted fruit trees and built a greenhouse. They had dreams for this place they called home. She was hoping someday they could install indoor plumbing.

The scent of fried potatoes floated through the open doorway. Tanya turned her face away and tried not to gag. Morning sickness was getting the best of her again, but she smiled a happy smile. After years of wishing for another child, God was answering her prayers. Another little one was on the way.

The girls were excited about the thought of having a baby. Marina gladly took over the cooking responsibilities so Tanya could spend more time outside. Bogdonna also tried to help with the work.

Valentine seemed pleased at the prospect of having another child, as he had long hoped for a son to carry on the family name. But to him, work was still more important than anything else. Tanya dared not take it easy when he was around.

Valentine had changed in the past few years, and Tanya now no longer carried the burden of providing for her daughters' needs alone. She had enjoyed the four years she spent in the classroom, but she was thankful that she could now stay at home and work alongside her husband in the greenhouse.

The cucumbers were producing well this spring. Already the tender plants were higher than her head. Because of the cool spring, the cucumber price stayed high, and Tanya was amazed how they had covered their costs and continued to make money.

Valentine's victory over smoking also gave Tanya courage. She rejoiced that God was giving him strength to control his craving for cigarettes. If only he could also find victory over his temper.

Spring eased into summer, and the sun beat down mercilessly. Their little house with its thick mud walls soaked up a lot of heat, making it feel like an oven. Perhaps it was the pregnancy that made the heat harder to bear.

One day while selling cucumbers at the market, Tanya's phone rang. She studied the unfamiliar number and handed the phone to her husband. Lately a credit card company had been calling. She would let Valentine talk to them.

"Hello," Valentine said, his voice steady and firm. Tanya's eyes twinkled. The credit card company would learn their lesson this time.

"What?" Valentine's face twisted in agony. "When? What happened?"

Something was wrong; Tanya could tell by his voice. A hundred possibilities flashed through her mind. *My children. My house. My neighbors. My church family. What could it be?*

"Yes, I am his son-in-law. His daughter Tanya is my wife."

Papa? Has something happened to him?

"Sure, I will tell her to call you back. Thank you." Valentine ended the phone call.

Tanya waited for him to speak, a sickening dread filling her heart. "I'm sorry, Tanya," he said. "Your papa died last night. They said he had a stroke."

Papa dead? It can't be. She had just talked to him a week ago. Papa had called to wish her a happy birthday and had asked her to send him another package. Just three days ago she had sent him a letter and a package. Likely he had not even received it yet.

"Now what?" she choked.

"You are supposed to call them back to figure out the details."

Tanya squeezed her eyes shut and took a deep breath. Her chin quivered as she returned the phone call. "Hello," a man's voice answered. "Are you Kosenko Tatianna Mikolievna?"

"Yes, I am," Tanya said.

"And Mikoli Dmitruk is your father?"

"Yes," she murmured. This felt so wrong. Could it actually be happening to her?

"Your father died last night. If you would like to bury him, you may come pick up his body. Otherwise, we'll take care of it."

"We'll come get the body," she replied, her voice unnatural and distant. "Can we come tomorrow?"

"No. Because of the government holiday tomorrow, the morgue won't be open until Monday."

"Oh!" Tanya swallowed hard. *Three days? In this summer heat?*

There was nothing to do but wait. It gave Valentine and Tanya a few days to clean their house and yard for the funeral.

Early on Monday morning, Brother Abner came to pick up Valentine and Tanya to head for the prison.

"Come with me," a guard ordered after they had completed the paperwork. "You need to identify the body."

Tanya followed him to the morgue, all the while begging God for strength. She blinked as she stepped inside—the dim, cool interior a sharp contrast to the sunshine outside. There he lay in the open casket—her papa. Gone. Tanya could hardly believe it. Her heart churned in pain and grief. All hope of a restored relationship with her father was gone. Worse yet was not knowing where Papa's soul was. Had he realized he was dying? Had he called out for mercy? Maybe all her prayers and care had not been wasted. A glimmer of hope flickered in her heart.

There was also a bit of relief. She had been pleading with God to help them know what to do when Papa was released from prison. She had never guessed that God would answer in this way. Perhaps it was best. Tanya wiped her forehead.

"It's him," she whispered to the guard.

They loaded the casket into the van and began the journey home. The tears Tanya held back finally broke forth as they pulled up to the house. Church people and many other villagers had already gathered, and chairs had been set up in the courtyard.

Tanya swallowed hard. She could not help but think of the other funerals that had been held in this yard. She could still picture Svetta's funeral as though it had happened yesterday. She remembered the anguished grief of laying her sister to rest. Mama's funeral had been hard too. She had felt so alone, so out of it. But this time, as she looked around the crowd, she felt the support of her church family.

The brothers from church preached powerful messages, urging people to repent and prepare for eternity. Tanya looked over the crowd. Many of her papa's drinking buddies were there. She studied their faces and wondered which ones had been with her papa that awful night when young Meesha was killed. *Lord,* she prayed, *please speak to the lives of these people! Don't let Papa's death be in vain.*

After the burial, Tanya sank into a chair at one of the tables in their yard. A sister from church brought her a drink of compote. The cold juice refreshed her, and she smiled wearily. "I should help the ladies set out the food," she said.

"Don't you worry about it. It's all taken care of. You just take care of yourself and your little one!"

To the disappointment of some of the villagers, no alcohol was served at the funeral. Tanya overheard some of them muttering about it. She bit back the words she felt like saying: *It's because of that cursed drink that Papa ended up in jail! And if drink hadn't ruined his life, he would probably still be with us.*

chapter 43

A Lost Battle

2017

The summer days slipped by, each one full and busy. Papa's funeral sapped Tanya's strength, and for days afterward she had no energy. She would have pushed herself harder, but she was worried about her unborn child. The doctor also seemed concerned and told her to take it easy. That was hard, especially when work stared at her from every corner.

She welcomed the arrival of fall and cooler temperatures. By the time October came with its cold nights and sunny days, most of the canning was done, and Tanya was counting the weeks to her due date.

One Sunday morning while the family was eating breakfast, Valentine's phone rang. He pulled it out and frowned. "Mama's calling. I don't feel like talking to her this early in the morning." He silenced it and they resumed eating breakfast and talking about their plans for the day. Only a minute or two later, his phone rang again. He growled as he silenced it. Then Tanya's phone began ringing.

"Good luck to you," Valentine said. "You can talk to her if you wish. I don't want to."

Tanya hesitated a moment. Right now she didn't feel like talking to her either. "Hello!" she answered with forced cheerfulness.

She could not understand what Valya was saying. She put the phone on speaker so Valentine could listen. It sounded like Valya was sobbing.

"What's the matter, Mama?" Tanya asked. "Are you all right?"

The sobbing only increased.

"Mama! What's wrong?" Valentine hollered into the phone. "I can't understand you when you are crying like that!"

"Vova! Vova's gone!"

Between sobs, Valya told them that Vova had died. He had been sick for a while. His kidneys were not working right, and he had been quite miserable the last few days. "Last night he got drunk again. He begged me to bring him some alcohol because he couldn't go buy it himself—he was that sick. I finally brought it to him, hoping it would calm him down. This morning when I went to check on him, he was gone!" Valya began sobbing again.

Valentine's face paled, and his head slumped onto the table. "My brother!" he moaned. "Oh, my brother!"

"Come! You must come to help me prepare for the funeral!" Valya pleaded. "I can't do this alone."

Valentine promised to come as soon as he could. Tanya felt like she should be there too, but she knew in her condition it was not wise. With her baby's due date only three weeks away, it was a risk she did not want to take.

But Tanya worried about Valentine. Would he be strong enough to resist the drinking and partying at the funeral? "Should one of the girls go along?" Tanya asked hesitantly. "Maybe it would help to comfort your mother."

Valentine studied his daughters for a moment. "Sure, I'll take Marina with me. She can help clean the house and get it ready for the funeral."

Marina nodded and blinked back tears. She didn't want to go, but she knew she didn't have a choice in the matter. "How long will we be gone?" she asked. "I don't like missing school."

Later, when Tanya and Marina were alone in the kitchen, Tanya hugged her daughter. "I'm proud of you for going, dear. Papa needs you to help him remember to be a man. I'm afraid if he goes by himself, he will start drinking. I'll be praying for you!"

Valentine and Marina left that very afternoon. Filled with worry, Tanya watched them leave. She thought of Vova. *He wasn't even forty years old. What a shame that he died so young.* Memories of the past washed over her like an ocean wave. She remembered how Vova's wife, Tetyana, had become her good friend and how they had done things together. Would she be at the funeral? Would she bring Rostic? They had walked out of Vova's life years ago, and Tanya had not seen them since.

The next three days stretched long as Tanya waited on Valentine and Marina to return home. Time and again, she interceded for her loved ones. Finally they returned. As Tanya met them at the door, she noticed the smell of smoke clinging to Valentine's clothes. Her heart sank, but then she noticed the same smell when she hugged Marina. *Perhaps the smell is just from being at Valya's house,* she reassured herself. *No one can come out of that house without smelling like smoke.*

But she was wrong. Later that night, Valentine went outside. When he stayed outside for a while, Tanya went looking for him. She found him in the greenhouse, smoking. She felt like running to him and pulling the cigarette away, but she knew that would be asking for trouble.

Instead, she quietly returned to the house and fell on her knees beside her bed. "O God, have mercy on us!" she prayed. "Please help Valentine through this time of grief!"

The heavy burden on her heart lifted a little as she knelt in God's presence. She seemed to hear God whisper, "I care, my child. I can help him find victory. But only if he wants it."

chapter 44

A Gift of Grace

2017-2018

Tanya held her baby close, blinking back tears of happiness and exhaustion. Her little one was finally here! It was a girl—a precious, beautiful daughter. It was November 13, 2017.

The past two weeks had been long and hard. Because of complications, the doctors had kept her in the hospital on bed rest. She hated waiting, resting, and hospitals. It was only the love for her unborn child that kept her there.

If Valentine was disappointed that it was another girl, he did not make it obvious. Tanya watched him gingerly pick up his daughter. "It's been so long, I almost forgot how to do this," he said, chuckling nervously. "My little Anya," he murmured. "You are beautiful!" He looked questioningly at Tanya. "Are you still all right with that name?"

Tanya smiled. "Of course. I love that name. If that is the name you want, that is who she will be!"

For both of the other girls, they had argued about the name. Tanya had decided right from the start that this time she would let Valentine name the baby. To her surprise, he had chosen Anya. Tanya was pleased. Not only did it rhyme with her own name, but it was also the name of one of her close friends. But the meaning of the name is what Tanya liked most of all: "grace." Little Anya was truly a gift of God's grace. For years, Tanya had longed for more children. This baby was an answer to prayer.

Tanya leaned back onto her pillow, her eyes closed. *O God!* she prayed. *Little Anya is truly a reminder of your grace. It is your grace that gave me this child, and I commit her to you. Thank you, O God.*

Anechka, as little Anya was fondly called, brought sunshine to the family. Even Valentine seemed touched by her precious innocence and adored her. Ever since his brother's funeral, he had picked up his old habit of smoking. He hated himself for it, but he seemed powerless to stop.

Sunday was Tanya's favorite day of the week. Not only was it a break from the never-ending work, but it was a day of spiritual nourishment and fellowship with friends. "I feel like a wilted flower by the end of each week," she told a friend after church one Sunday. "But church always refreshes me. It keeps me going through the week."

Occasionally, by the time Sunday rolled around, Tanya found herself too exhausted to even attend church. Then she would send the rest of the family off to church and spend the morning in solitude. She savored the sacred quietness of a Sunday morning spent alone at the feet of her Master.

One Sunday afternoon Marina seemed extra subdued, and Tanya

wondered what was bothering her daughter. That evening while Bogdonna and Anechka were playing in the bedroom, Marina found a chance to talk to her parents. "Did you hear Brother Abner announce that a new instruction class is starting?" she asked, looking hesitantly at her parents.

Tanya nodded encouragingly.

"Well, I've been thinking about it. Do you think I'm ready for that?"

"Oh, Marina, I would be so happy if you would do that!" Tanya said. "I've been blessed to see God at work in your life ever since you repented." She turned to Valentine. "What do you think about it?"

He sat deep in thought. "You know, Marina," he finally said, "I would be happy if you went to instruction class. And maybe I'll join you."

Tanya and Marina looked at him in surprise.

"I know I'm not the man God wants me to be. Maybe going to instruction class would help me find victory."

Tears glistened in the eyes of mother and daughter. Perhaps there was hope for their home. Perhaps Papa really wanted to do what was right.

When Marina and Valentine joined instruction class, Tanya rejoiced to see both of them growing in their walk with the Lord. But Valentine still struggled with smoking. On Christmas, when the preacher gave an opportunity for repentance and testimonies, Valentine once again confessed his sin. He seemed truly broken and wanted to do what was right. But all too soon he was back to smoking. He seemed to blame his failure on God. "I don't know why God doesn't give me victory," he complained. "I try to stop, but I just can't."

The preachers pleaded with him and offered to do whatever it takes to help him. "We'll fast and pray with you, Valentine. But you must learn to hate sin."

But Valentine could not find the strength to quit. He kept smoking even though he knew it was a great waste of money and a detriment to his health and family. When the weather was mild, he went outside to smoke. But if it was cold, he found it easiest to stay inside. The whole house reeked of cigarettes.

March arrived, and though there were occasional glimpses of spring, winter seemed determined to hang on as long as possible. In the fall, they had planted hundreds of hyacinths and tulips in pots in the cellar. Later Tanya had helped Valentine bring them to the greenhouse, and by now everything was pulsing with new life.

They were raising flowers for Women's Day on March 8, so they were kept busy packaging and selling them. By the time Women's Day was over, the whole family was exhausted. But it had been a profitable venture, and Tanya knew they would be raising flower bulbs again next year.

Marina was baptized the last Sunday in March. Tanya thought her heart would burst with joy as she watched her daughter stand in front and share her testimony. She wished Valentine could also be baptized, but he was far from taking that step. While he looked good on Sundays, she knew the real man at home. Her heart ached for him, knowing he hated himself for his weakness. Daily she interceded for his soul and begged the Lord to help her be a humble, submissive wife. It was so hard to know where her place was.

Several weeks later the church celebrated Christ's resurrection. Tanya's thoughts traveled back to the Easter service seven years earlier when she had given her life to God. After the Sunday school, when the children shared their songs and the moderator opened the time for others to share, the Kosenko family went forward. Valentine carried Anechka, and Marina and Bogdonna stood close to their parents.

Tanya's hands trembled as she held the songbook. This was the day she had been dreaming of for years. Hesitantly she started the song, and the rest of the family joined in.

> *Hope is always with me, in joy and in sorrow.*
> *Hope helps me find victory in the battle of sin.*
> *My hope is in God. My hope is in Christ,*
> *For He is the only way to everlasting life.*[1]

It was a song the children had learned at Bible camp, but the words captured her heart as well.

Yes, she would hold on to hope. Hope that her husband would someday be a victorious Christian. Hope that someday life would be easier.

Tanya smiled as she pushed the stroller down the street. Anya had called and said she was planning a special supper for a few friends who had summer birthdays. *What a blessing friends are!* she mused.

Anechka cooed, happy to be out on a stroll with her mama. The stroller raised a cloud of dust in the air. For weeks, they had been praying for rain. Everything had a wilted, glazed look. *Just the way I feel sometimes,* Tanya thought. *Perhaps an evening with friends will perk me up.*

Although it was evening, the sun still shone hot. Days in June seemed never-ending. A burst of wind swirled the dust on the road ahead of her, and Tanya glanced up at the sky. She was startled to see a dark cloud billowing. "Perhaps we'll get some rain tonight," she told Anechka.

Once she reached the Hursh farm, she joined the rest of the ladies in the little woods near the house. "This is really neat!" Tanya said. "I didn't

---

[1] Ukrainian song, by an unknown author.

A Gift of Grace

know you had such a great picnic spot. It feels so nice and secluded!"

The trees closed in around them, creating a canopy overhead. Tanya looked around her circle of friends—Anya and her mother Connie, Lina, and two newer friends, Alona and Polina. Tanya's heart welled in gratitude for the gift of these women's friendship.

Just as the women had finished prayer, Anton, one of the Hursh boys, broke into the clearing. "I'm sorry to interrupt your supper," he said, "but I came to help you carry your things into the house. It's going to rain."

The women looked around. "I don't see any storm," Anya protested. "Do you really think we need to go in?"

He nodded. "The sooner the better—or you'll get wet. Here, I'll help you carry the table." Anton grabbed one end of the table and Anya took the other. The ladies grabbed their babies and whatever else they could carry and began hurrying toward the house. As they left the shelter of the woods, the wind threatened to blow away the table and the food. The heavens that had been closed for weeks suddenly opened and sheets of rain began to fall. The women hurried to the house, laughing and grabbing for the dishes the wind tossed into the air.

Within a few minutes, the table was set up inside the house, and the women resumed their supper. The food was slightly dusty, but the unexpected storm had only added to the adventure of the evening.

Lina had bouquets of roses for the three birthday ladies, and Anya had little gifts for each one. The evening passed swiftly as they laughed and talked and shared their hearts.

"This evening together is so inspiring," Tanya said, looking around the table. "I can't begin to compare it to the parties I used to have with my friends years ago. Back then I thought it wouldn't be a party if there was no strong drink. What a blessing it is to have friends like you."

"It's a blessing for me as well," Alona added. "Often I get so bogged down with my work that I forget to count my blessings and enjoy life."

It was still pouring down rain when the ladies were ready to go, so Connie took them home in the van. "This was such a refreshing evening!" Tanya sighed in satisfaction. "The fellowship for my soul was just as refreshing as the rain is for the parched gardens. Thank you so much!"

chapter 45

The Shock

2018

Tanya shivered as she stepped onto the bus. The brisk morning air hinted of fall. Tanya scanned the bus for an empty seat. With a smile of thanks, she sank into the seat offered her. A smile played on her lips. *A year ago, when I was doing prenatal blood work, I didn't dream I would be doing it again in just a year.* Tanya's eyes shone at the thought of another little one joining their family.

As the bus puttered out of the village, Tanya's heart warmed as she thought of her family. Little Anechka had still been sleeping when Tanya slipped out of the house. Marina would keep an eye on her and would likely have lunch ready by the time she returned. And Bogdonna would be shadowing her papa when she returned home from school, helping with the greenhouse work.

For years, Tanya had longed for more children. Then, after many disappointments, God had given them Anechka. And now another one was on the way. Tanya's heart was overwhelmed with gratitude. *Lord, you have blessed me far more than I deserve, and now you have surprised us again. O Lord, bless this little one. Thank you for the privilege of being a mother.*

The bus screeched to a stop, and Tanya was brought back to reality. She followed the other passengers off the bus and hurried to the clinic.

Dr. Adamivna was known as the crankiest gynecologist in the local hospital, but at least she stayed on schedule. Tanya was soon seated in her office, answering the normal questions. Although the doctor frowned, Tanya sensed a hint of gentleness behind her rough exterior. Why else would she keep working when she could be retired?

The checkup seemed to take longer than usual. "Wait here a bit," Dr. Adamivna said. "I need a second opinion." Tanya was baffled by the expression on the doctor's face as she strode out of the room.

The minutes crawled by, and eventually Dr. Adamivna returned with another lady doctor. When Tanya saw their sober faces, a cold dart of fear pierced her heart. Together the two doctors examined her. Tanya's thoughts raced. *What could be wrong?* She couldn't catch the muffled words of the doctors.

When the examination was over, Dr. Adamivna sat down across from her. "Tanya," she said, peering over her spectacles, "we have found a problem. You have a fast-growing tumor." She paused to let the news sink in. "In all my years of practice, I have never seen anything like this that hasn't been cancerous. You need to get it checked out immediately."

Bewilderment and shock clogged Tanya's thoughts. Finally she stammered, "Are—are you sure?"

Dr. Adamivna nodded grimly. "I wish I was mistaken. But something is wrong. I will refer you to a hospital in Bila Tserkva. Maybe they can help you." She turned back to her desk and filled out a referral.

Tanya sat in stunned silence. *Tumor. Cancer.* The words screamed through her mind. *It can't be. Never. Why, Lord?*

The doctor handed her a stack of papers. "Here are your records and a referral for the Bila Tserkva hospital. Go as soon as you can."

Tanya clutched the papers and stood to leave. She leaned against the door frame, drained of strength. It took a few moments before she found the courage to whisper the question that was burning in her heart. "But what about the baby?"

The doctor continued filling out forms at her desk. "The baby?" She cast a quick glance at Tanya before replying. "Abort it! That's the only way you are going to live."

Tanya stared mutely at the doctor. But Dr. Adamivna was engrossed in her work and paid her no more attention. Tanya turned and numbly headed down the long hospital corridor.

In a daze, she trudged to the bus stop and caught the first bus home—her grocery list still in her purse. She wanted to wake up and find out this was only a nightmare. Each bump on the road added to her throbbing headache. She moaned, and a tear trickled down her cheek. *Be strong. You can't cry here,* she told herself. Never had it seemed to take so long to drive the few kilometers from town to Kryvoshyintsi.

Finally the bus came to a stop at the village center. Still clutching her papers, Tanya stepped off. She glanced around, relieved to see no familiar faces.

Marina looked up in surprise when Tanya entered the kitchen minutes later. "Mama, you're back early. But where are the groceries? I wanted sour cream for the borsch I'm making for lunch."

Tanya tried to smile. "I'm sorry, dear. I wasn't feeling well, so I didn't stop at the market. I guess we'll just have to eat borsch without sour cream."

The Shock

Concern filled Marina's eyes. "Maybe you should lie down until dinnertime."

Tanya nodded gratefully. "Thank you," she whispered.

In the privacy of her bedroom, Tanya let her pent-up emotions flow. She wrapped herself in a blanket, but even its warmth didn't ease the coldness that filled her heart. Tears slid down her face. *No! No! It can't be true!* In sheer weariness, she drifted off to sleep.

"Mama! Mama!" The cheery voice of Anechka awoke Tanya with a start. For a moment she was confused. The bright sunlight streaming in the window told her it was the middle of the day. *But why am I in bed?* Then she remembered. *The doctor. A tumor. Cancer. Abortion.* It all came back like a flash, and fear and dread gripped her heart. "Lord, help me," she whispered.

"Mama!" Again Tanya heard her little girl calling for her. *Lord, my family needs me. Help me be strong for their sake.* With a quiet peace settling into her heart, Tanya joined her family around the kitchen table.

Little Anechka's face wreathed into a smile. Tanya took her from Valentine and smiled appreciatively at Marina. "Lunch smells good."

The small family stood for prayer, and Valentine offered a blessing on the food.

As Marina filled the bowls with steaming soup, Valentine turned to his wife. "Marina said you weren't feeling the best this morning. How are you feeling now?"

Tanya smiled bravely. "I had a refreshing nap and feel better than when I came home." She paused, wondering how to continue. "But I had a stressful morning. The doctors are pretty concerned about me."

When Valentine raised his eyebrows in question, Tanya continued. "Look at these papers." She retrieved the papers from the bedroom.

Valentine took the papers and began scanning them. Marina peered over his shoulder. As he read, he shook his head in disbelief.

Marina was the first to talk. "Mama! It says something about a tumor. You must have gotten the wrong papers. Surely it's not talking about you!"

Valentine said nothing. He just sat staring out the window. Finally he looked at Tanya. When he saw the quiver in her lip and the tears in her eyes, his own eyes pooled with tears. "Is this true?" His voice wasn't much more than a whisper. "How can this be?"

The rest of the day passed in a blur as Tanya went about her household duties. She fed little Anechka her bottle, rocked her to sleep, and prepared a tasty supper for her family. But while she worked, her mind was racing in high gear. *Maybe the doctors made a mistake. Could it be that Dr. Adamivna just wanted to test me? But no, the other doctor agreed.* Again and again she committed it to God.

I wonder what Alona would say. Her friend was a nurse and always had good advice. Whether it was how to treat ailing plants in the greenhouse or what medicine to give a sick child, Tanya could be sure to find a caring heart and sound advice from Alona. *I'll call her.*

Soon Tanya found herself pouring out her heart to her friend. "The doctor thinks the tumor is likely cancerous..." Her voice broke.

Alona's voice rang through the phone. "Who was the doctor that checked you? Was it Dr. Adamivna?"

"Yes."

"Well, I wouldn't be too worried then," Alona replied. "She has told other women they have cancer and been wrong. Did she do any tests?"

"No, but another doctor agreed that something is wrong. They are sending me to the Bila Tserkva City Hospital for tests."

"Until you have the test results, I wouldn't believe what Dr. Adamivna says. But I think you should get it checked out. There are some excellent

The Shock

doctors at that hospital. I worked there years ago. Take courage. No matter what happens, God will be with you. And if you need help, let me know. I'm here for you."

As Tanya resumed her household duties, she felt a sense of peace. Maybe Alona was right. It wouldn't be the first time Dr. Adamivna had misdiagnosed someone.

Surely everything would turn out all right.

chapter 46

Abortion?

2018

Abortion? The very word numbed Tanya's heart. Surely that was not an option. *Lord, you have helped us out of an abortion before. We're counting on you to do it again.*

Tanya glanced at Marina, who was resting her head against the bus window. How glad she was that she didn't need to make this trip to the Bila Tserkva hospital alone. She wished Valentine had come along, but the greenhouse needed his attention. Besides, hospitals and doctors had never been Valentine's thing. Just the sight of blood turned his stomach.

Marina's calm, collected nature reflected that of her mother's. A smile played on Tanya's lips as she thought about her firstborn. A more responsible, hardworking young lady could not be found in the village.

But it was her spiritual stability that blessed Tanya most of all. How she treasured the bond they shared.

After the hour-long bus ride, Tanya and Marina walked the last few blocks to the hospital. Tanya sighed as she climbed the steps and entered the dimly lit hall. "I'm glad you're with me, Marina. I could have come by myself, but it's a comfort to have you along."

Marina nodded. "I wouldn't want to go by myself either, Mama." With a shiver, she added, "It's chilly in here. I don't believe they started the heating system yet."

"Probably not. It's only October."

After examining Tanya's papers, the receptionist directed her to a doctor's office on the fourth floor. By the time Tanya had trudged up the flights of steps, she was panting and out of breath. "Are you all waiting in line?" Tanya asked, looking in amazement at the group of people standing outside the doctor's office.

"Yes, I'm last in line. You can stand behind me," answered a middle-aged lady. "You can identify a good doctor by the line of people outside his door," she added wryly.

Tanya took her place in line. The people around her wore sad, anguished looks. Some were mere skeletons, their bald heads evidence of being ravished by chemo. Heaviness filled the air. *Lord, what am I doing with these people? This is so disheartening! Help me, Lord!*

After waiting in line for nearly three hours, Tanya's turn finally came. She greeted the doctor with a nervous smile and took the proffered seat. She tried to sound calm as she explained her situation.

"I was sent here by the Skvira hospital because of complications with my pregnancy."

"Let me see your papers," the doctor said.

Tanya handed him the stack of papers and tried to read his expression as he studied it. Finally he looked at her. "It does look like you are having serious complications. I'll see what I can do to help you. But first we need some blood tests. The lab is down on the first floor."

Many minutes and several blood tests later, Tanya and Marina once again entered the doctor's office. *Surely he'll say everything is all right,* Tanya told herself again and again.

When the doctor returned to his seat, he looked her in the eye. "Tatianna Mikolievna," he said, addressing her by her formal name, "you do indeed have a tumor growing next to the uterus. It must be fast-growing, because it's already the size of a fist." He jotted a few things on his paper. "I won't know if it is cancerous or not until we get your results back tomorrow. But either way, you will need surgery."

Thousands of questions pounded Tanya's brain, screaming for answers. But there was one that caused her mother-heart more agony than all the rest. She took a deep breath before asking, "What about the baby?"

The doctor sighed. "The best thing to do is to have an abortion. You are only twenty weeks along." Before Tanya could protest, he continued, "As fast as your tumor is growing, there's no chance of you carrying your baby full term. Besides, this tumor is probably cancerous, and any kind of treatment will harm the baby. It's either your life or the baby's."

Tanya shook her head to get rid of the fog that clouded her mind. "Where do we go from here?" she finally asked. "What is the next step?"

"We'll have you stay here at the hospital until tomorrow. I want to see the results of the tests we did this morning, and I'd like to do some additional testing. You can stay in one of the hospital rooms. Maybe we can give you a vitamin boost through an IV."

So far Marina had wordlessly stuck to her mother's side. Now she reached over and squeezed her hand. "What about me, Mama?" Her voice was barely above a whisper. "Am I supposed to stay here too?"

Tanya shrugged. "I don't know. It's already getting dark outside. I don't want you to travel home alone…"

"You may return to the waiting room until I reserve a hospital bed for you," the doctor said, looking at Tanya. "It would probably be best if your daughter went home. There is no room for her here—unless she sleeps on the concrete floor." He gave a sardonic chuckle.

Just thinking of the damp, cool hospital rooms made Tanya shiver. But much more frightening was the thought of Marina finding her way home alone through the city.

Tanya was relieved to find the waiting room empty. Gratefully she sank into a stiff-backed chair and rested her head on her hands.

"Mama, what are we going to do? Do I really have to go home alone?"

Tanya didn't look up right away. Finally she said, "I don't know, Marina. I just don't know. Right now I'm in shock. I can't think clearly." She sat in silence for a few minutes. "Maybe you could call Papa and see what he thinks. Tell him what the doctor said." She pulled out her phone and handed it to Marina.

Soon Marina was telling her papa what the doctor had said. Tanya tried to listen, but everything seemed far away, as though through layers of fog. *Lord, help me,* she prayed. *I need you.* Through the haze in her mind, Tanya kept breathing that prayer: *Lord, help me.*

"Mama." Marina waited to continue until she had Tanya's attention. "Papa said Brother Wayne just called. He had some business in Bila Tserkva today and thought Papa might need a ride home."

"So you can go home with him?" asked Tanya, relief in her voice.

"Yes, Papa said he'll call Brother Wayne and ask him to pick me up. Then Papa plans to come to the hospital tomorrow while I take care of the girls."

A few hours later, Tanya eased into the hospital bed. Although the bed wasn't as comfortable as the one at home, it felt wonderful to lie down. The stress of the day and the exertion of climbing the many flights of stairs caused her whole body to ache in sheer weariness.

A kind nurse brought her a cup of hot tea and a cup of bland porridge. The sight of food made Tanya nauseous, but she forced herself to eat a few bites, knowing she would need strength for the days ahead. The steaming tea warmed her from the inside out. As Tanya lay in bed, she tried to tune out the noise of the television and her roommates.

Lord, I need you. Please help me. Again and again Tanya breathed those words, too weary to sort out the confusing events of the past few days.

It was a long time before she drifted off to sleep.

chapter 47

"You Know the Way"

2018

The words from the hymnbook blurred as tears filled Tanya's eyes. She gave up trying to sing and allowed the tears to flow as the beautiful words and melody of the song washed over her aching heart.

> Lord, you know all the winds that blow and frighten,
> The storms of life your orders still obey.
> And even though my burdens may not lighten,
> Still I'm at peace, because you know the way.[1]

Tanya's gaze rested on the church family around her. *What a wonderful place to be, surrounded by my dear family.* Ever since she had

---

[1] "You Know the Way," by Hedwig von Redern (1866-1935).

begun attending church, she had looked forward to Sundays when she could join her brothers and sisters in Christ. She drew strength from the inspiring messages, the encouraging songs, and the fellowship with other Christians. Today she felt especially grateful to be at church. Was it only four days ago that she had received the shocking news of her cancer?

Tanya's thoughts were brought back to the service as she heard her name. What was Brother Abner saying?

"We're especially glad to have Sister Tanya Kosenko with us. As most of you have heard, she found out this past week that she has a cancerous tumor. We plan to have an anointing service for her at her home this afternoon. We know that God can heal her if it is His will. Let's keep her in our prayers. Let's pray most of all that God's name would be glorified."

Once again, tears surfaced in Tanya's eyes. Sister Luda, sitting next to her, reached over and squeezed her hand, as if to say, "I care."

Then Brother James stood to preach the message. He spoke with firm conviction of the blessing of children. "Each child is a deposit of God Himself. Empires fall, houses crumble, cattle die, and machinery rusts away. But a child lives on into eternity."

Brother James's voice rang confidently over the auditorium. His words were like water for Tanya's parched soul. "Too many children are unwanted and considered a bother. Do we realize what a blessing children are?"

Deep in her heart, Tanya knew that children were a gift from God and that abortion was sin. But over and over the doctors had told her the only way for her to survive was to have an abortion. Their laughter and ridicule when she tried to explain that abortion was not an option still echoed in her ears. Doubts had crept in, and at times her own thoughts scared her. Now, as Brother James shared Scripture verses, she felt her confidence returning. *No matter what happens, I must give my little one a chance to live.*

"Sometimes it's hard. My heart goes out to the Kosenko family right now and the decisions they have to make." Brother James's voice broke. "What right do we have to decide if a child lives or dies? God is the One who gives life. It is not in our hands to decide when to end that life." Brother James's voice was gentle.

As the congregation knelt for prayer, tears glistened in many eyes as the worshipers of the Berezyanka church thought of Tanya and what her baby's life might mean to her.

When the time opened for testimonies and confessions, Tanya was quick to stand to her feet. "I want to thank God for the words of encouragement He gave me today. I don't know what the future holds for me or my little one. But I—I…" Tears threatened to choke her. "I will do all I can so my baby can live. Even if I die, I know I can trust God and my church family to care for my children. My greatest desire is that my baby would live." She wanted to say more, but tears were streaming down her face. "Pray for me," she whispered, then she sat back down.

Brother Abner's voice was thick with emotion. "We will be praying, Sister Tanya."

Then Valentine stood to his feet. "I appreciate the message we heard today—that children are a gift from God. I have faith that God can do a miracle for our family. I am trusting Him to heal my wife and give life to our little one."

After the service, Tanya found herself surrounded by sisters. Their words of encouragement did much to boost her spirits. She glanced across the room and was touched to see Valentine encircled by caring brothers. How blessed she felt to be part of a caring church family.

All too soon the church bus was ready to leave. As the bus bumped its way over the cobblestones to Kryvoshyintsi, the children and youth sang. Tanya observed her daughters joining in the singing. Even little Anechka bounced up and down on her papa's lap, delighting in the music.

Outside, the sky was clear blue, with golden leaves dancing in the breeze. The sun's rays melted the bite of autumn. In the bus, Tanya was surrounded by the singing and companionship of fellow believers. It brought peace to her heart. No matter what happened, God knew the way.

Weeks went by, and the weather lost its autumn glory. The sun rarely showed its warmth through the thick layer of clouds, and the bare trees shivered in the cold wind. Oozing mud clung to boots, just like the dread that tried to cling to Tanya's heart.

"You will just have to wait at home. There's nothing we can do for you if you're not interested in doing an abortion," the doctors told Tanya. "All the treatments would be harmful to the baby. After the baby is born, we can help you, but for now you just have to wait."

Valentine and Tanya checked into various hospitals, but the answer was always the same: "Come back when you are farther along. Then we can take the baby early and do surgery."

At the Regional Clinical Hospital in Kyiv, one of the cancer doctors expressed his concern. "Your tumor could rupture at any time. If that happens, you will lose the baby and hemorrhage to death. You should stay at the hospital so we can help you if that happens."

Tanya didn't relish the idea of spending weeks at the hospital in Kyiv away from her family, especially if she was not doing any treatments. She decided to wait it out at home as long as she could. Cancer and the many "what ifs" filled her mind, making it hard to focus on her work.

She determined to treasure each moment she had with her precious children instead of dwelling on the many things that could go wrong.

Marina had long been anticipating Youth Bible School during the first week of November. But now, because of her mother's sickness, Marina wondered if she should go. Tanya assured her they would be fine and that she should go while she had the chance. They decided to make plans to go to the hospital soon after Marina returned home.

Little Anechka was nearing her first birthday. Tanya's heart thrilled as she watched her little daughter take her first unsteady steps. Often at night while Tanya rocked her, tears would silently slide down her cheeks. *Who will take care of Anechka while I'm gone?* Overcome with emotion, she held her little girl close.

It was late Friday night when Marina returned home from Bible School. Tanya's bags were packed for her planned trip to the hospital Monday morning. As the little family lingered around the breakfast table Saturday morning, Marina was overflowing with stories from Bible School.

Tanya couldn't help but wish she could push "pause" on this special time. Her gaze rested on each one—her husband Valentine, bouncing ebullient Anechka on his knee; Marina, her face shining with the vibrancy of young womanhood; and Bogdonna, whose clear blue eyes reflected her feelings. How could she leave them?

Sunday morning arrived, and Tanya treasured the privilege of going to church again as a family. Brother Abner talked about how life consists of little things. How it's the little things that make life special. Tanya added her own list of little things she would miss: Anechka's little fingers grasping her hand, mealtime with her family, sprouting plants in the greenhouse, and fellowship with her church family. Her heart quickened, and a smile played on her lips as she thought of another very little, precious thing. How she looked forward to the day she could hold her little one in her arms.

Monday morning came all too soon. Dawn was just beginning to break across the dark sky when Tanya kissed her daughters goodbye. "Be strong, Marina. Take good care of your little sisters." Tanya held her oldest daughter close. "I'm glad I can count on you."

Bogdonna threw her arms around her mama's neck. "Mama, I'm going to miss you!"

"I'll miss you too, dear. Be brave. Be sure to help Marina all you can when you get home from school. Study hard and do your best."

Tanya planted a gentle kiss on her baby's forehead. Anechka cooed and reached for her mama.

"Tomorrow is your birthday, Anechka." Tanya's voice broke as she squeezed her daughter's pudgy hand. "You will be one year old. Mama won't be here to celebrate it, but she loves you with all her heart."

As the van left the village and picked up speed, Tanya leaned her head against the seat. Tears squeezed through her closed eyelids and splotched her dress, but she did not bother wiping them away. The van took her farther and farther from her dear daughters, from her home, and from her church family.

Looking back hurt too much, but looking forward was even worse. She felt trapped in a dark tunnel. What was ahead for her and her little one?

chapter 48

Now Where?

2018

As the van bounced toward Kyiv, Tanya leaned her head wearily on Valentine's shoulder. How grateful she was that Brother Abner had offered to take them. Traveling in his van was much more comfortable than riding on the bus.

"Where do you want me to take you?" Abner asked as they neared the edge of Kyiv.

Valentine looked at Tanya. "To my mother's place. We'll drop our luggage off there, and then we can find our own way to the hospital."

"Are you sure you don't want me to wait and then take you to the hospital?" Abner asked.

"I think we'll be fine. Thank you, though."

Valya welcomed her son and daughter-in-law into her home and insisted they stay for tea and a bite to eat before they leave. "How are the children doing?" she wondered. "Oh, how I love them—my dear little granddaughters." She sniffed and wiped a tear. "This is so hard. Why is God allowing this?"

"Mama." Tanya's soft voice calmed her mother-in-law's nerves. "God will be here for us. We need to trust Him. The Bible says everything works together for good to those who love God."

"It says that in the Bible? I'm trying to learn more about God, but there's so much to learn."

Tanya smiled. God was at work in her mother-in-law's life. Soon after Vova's death, Valya had begun attending church in Kyiv. She had committed her life to God, and a few months ago she had been baptized. Some days Tanya could hardly believe it was true.

After finishing their tea, Valentine and Tanya were in a hurry to be on their way. "Mama," Valentine said, "I think we will leave Tanya's luggage here until we know for sure where she will be staying. We're hoping to be admitted to the Kyiv Regional Clinical Hospital. That's where the cancer doctor said we should stay in case the tumor ruptures."

Valentine and Tanya squeezed onto the already full bus. There was no room to sit, so Tanya clung to Valentine's arm to keep her balance during the frequent starts and stops. Tanya was relieved when they finally arrived at the hospital.

Tanya was hoping to see Doctor Kriachok, who had been sympathetic when he examined her earlier, but he was on vacation. The lady at the front desk directed them to another cancer doctor. Tanya entered his office with trepidation. She disliked meeting new doctors, but Valentine's presence helped steady her mind and her nerves.

"I brought my wife here today to see if there's an opening in the hospital," Valentine told him. "Doctor Kriachok is working on our case."

Tanya couldn't help but feel proud of her husband. He hated being in hospitals even more than she did, and yet here he was, sticking by her in her illness.

"Let me see your papers," the doctor said. He showed little emotion as he scanned Tanya's medical records. "I see you have a cancerous tumor. But why are you not treating it?" He looked at Tanya with steel blue eyes.

Once again Valentine came to her rescue. "We don't want to do anything that would harm the baby."

"I see. So you want to do nothing. The baby may live, but you will die. Is that really what you want? More motherless children for the government to care for?"

"No, doctor, that is not what we want," Tanya replied. She had seen the flicker of anger in Valentine's eyes and hoped she could keep it from bursting into flame.

"You are a foolish woman. Do you not understand the kind of cancer you have? It is growing rapidly. If you have an abortion and then have surgery to remove the tumor, you have a good chance of surviving. You may not even need chemotherapy. But if you wait, the cancer will spread and you will likely die before your child reaches his first birthday. Is that really what you want?"

Tanya struggled to steady the tremor in her voice. "Abortion is not an option for us. We are believers. Our lives are in God's hands. So is the life of our little one. An abortion would make us guilty of murder."

The doctor stared at her for a long minute. "I never saw such a crazy person," he muttered. Getting to his feet, he handed the papers back to Valentine. "I can't do anything for you," he said. "The only place I can advise you to go is the Kyiv Medical Institute. Maybe they can help you." He opened his office door, making it clear they were to leave.

As they exited the hospital, the overcast sky seemed to reflect the heaviness of their hearts. "I'm sorry, Valentine," Tanya whispered. "I'm sorry I'm causing so many problems."

"Tanya, it's not you that is the problem—it's these doctors! I feel so angry that I wish I could bomb this whole building!" He clenched his fists.

Tanya shuddered. "Don't get upset, dear. Being angry won't help anything."

They walked on in silence, deep in thought and oblivious to the crowds around them. As they neared the bus stop, Tanya asked, "Valentine, do you know how to get to the Medical Institute? I think we should try that. Anything would be better than the doctor we just saw."

Valentine let out a deep sigh. "I guess we can try, but it feels hopeless. No one gets into that hospital without big money or at least some connection. We have neither."

"We could still try," she said.

"Okay, I know the general location of the hospital. We'll catch a bus headed that way and then ask for directions."

Once again Tanya found herself on a crowded bus. She was grateful when someone offered her a seat. She leaned her head against the seat in front of her and rested her weary eyes. *Lord, please give me strength. And help Valentine remain calm.*

They had no problem getting directions to the Medical Institute. Everyone they asked seemed eager to help them. "You're going to the Medical Institute? Good! You couldn't ask for a better hospital," said one passerby. Hope sprouted in Tanya's heart. *Maybe I can find the help I need.*

But an hour later Valentine and Tanya left the hospital with dashed hopes. "We should have known we couldn't get in without big money or connections," Valentine growled.

"It seems no one wants to help me." A tear slipped down Tanya's cheek. "I don't feel like trying anymore. Let me just go home and die."

"Be brave, dear." Valentine tried to sound calm despite his rising frustration. "Let's try the Israeli Cancer Clinic. Maybe they can help us."

"But that's a private hospital. We'll never be able to afford that."

"Let's just check it out," Valentine insisted. "The buses are crammed with people, so maybe we should try the metro."

As they went down into the depths of the earth, Tanya muttered, "Look at all these people. It doesn't look much better than the bus."

Sure enough, when the subway train stopped, a wall of people rushed in. Valentine grabbed Tanya by the arm for fear of losing her in the crowd. They squeezed into the little remaining standing room. As the metro surged forward, Tanya gave a grim smile. "I don't think I could fall if I wanted to; we're crowded in so tightly." She held on to Valentine and leaned her head on his shoulder.

Suddenly Valentine realized that Tanya was leaning quite heavily against him. "Tanya, are you all right?" he asked urgently.

She slowly shook her head, barely opening her eyes. "No," she whispered. "I can hardly breathe. I think I'm going to faint." As her head slumped over, it was all Valentine could do to keep her on her feet.

Panic gripped his heart. He yelled for someone to pull the emergency stop button, and someone dialed for the ambulance. As they screeched to a stop, Valentine struggled to get Tanya off the metro. The seconds seemed like hours as he waited for help. He was weak with relief when he saw medical personnel rushing in their direction. A doctor checked Tanya's pulse. "We need to get this lady out into fresh air as fast as we can. I believe she passed out because of lack of oxygen."

Together they worked to get Tanya up the elevator. As they helped her sit down on a city bench, Tanya looked about, trying to figure out her surroundings. "Where am I? What happened?" Her voice sounded slurred and distant.

When the doctor saw that Tanya's condition had stabilized, he turned to Valentine. "Are you crazy? Do you want to kill your wife? It's pure foolishness for you to make her travel on the metro in her condition. What kind of husband are you anyway?"

Valentine listened to the accusations, the heat rising under his collar. Trying to keep his voice steady, he replied, "I'm doing my best to care for her. I came along to help her."

"Humph," the doctor snorted. "If you really loved her, you would hire a taxi to take her to the hospital."

Valentine didn't reply, but determination shone in his eyes. After the ambulance pulled away, he sat down beside his wife and took her hand. "Tanya, you know I love you, right?" When she nodded, he continued, "I'm sorry I suggested going on the metro. Do you think you'll be all right?"

"It's okay," she replied. "I just wish I wouldn't be such a wimp. I don't know what's wrong with me. With the crowd pressing around me, I suddenly couldn't get my breath. The next thing I knew, the doctor was checking me out. I guess I passed out." She paused to catch her breath. "I'll be all right. I just feel weak and tired."

"But I think the doctor was right," Valentine said. "We'll get a taxi to take us home."

Tanya shook her head. "No, that's expensive!"

"Some people are worth spending money on," he replied, squeezing her hand. "We've had enough hospital experiences for one day. Let's go back to Mama's house and try again later."

The trip back seemed to take no time at all. The taxi sped through the city, and almost before she knew it, Tanya was tucked into bed. Her body screamed with exhaustion and weariness. The doctors' heartless words echoed endlessly through her fatigued mind. As she lay in bed, the dam of emotions she had suppressed for so long burst open.

"O God, why was I ever born?" she cried. "My life has been nothing but trouble. I don't think I can go on another day. Just take me home, Lord. I'm tired of seeing these heartless doctors. O God, is there no one who can help me?"

The nauseating smell of cigarette smoke drifted into the bedroom, causing another torrent of tears. "Lord, this is too much for Valentine to bear. He is turning to his cigarettes for comfort. O God, why do you feel so far away? We need you!"

chapter 49

"Lord, Lead Us"

2018

"Thank you, Mama, for the breakfast." Valentine scraped the last bit of buckwheat from his plate. "We must be leaving."

"Could we have prayer first?" Tanya asked. "I dread another day of going from doctor to doctor and hospital to hospital."

The three knelt together and prayed. Tears streamed down their cheeks as they begged God to show them the way and guide them to the right doctors. Time seemed to stand still as they prayed for strength and wisdom.

As Tanya listened to her husband and mother-in-law pleading on her behalf, she was again amazed at the change in their lives. A few years ago, this was where they had drunk alcohol. This room held memories of countless arguments and fights. Now they were kneeling on holy ground. God's presence filled the room.

Nearly an hour passed before they rose from their knees. A deep peace settled into Tanya's heart. No matter what they faced, Christ stood by her side.

They had decided to try again at the Regional Clinical Hospital. "Do you think we will find any answers today?" Tanya asked. She looked hopefully at her husband as they stood at the bus stop.

"I don't know. I hope so. We've been here in Kyiv almost a week. It's high time I get back to the children."

"I know. I dread the thought of you leaving, but I know they need you even more than I do."

Hope sparked in Tanya's heart as she entered the doctor's office. She did not recognize the doctor; perhaps he would be nicer than the earlier ones. Tanya's hands trembled as she gave him her paperwork.

The silence grew thick as the doctor studied it. Finally he spoke. "I see this is not the first time you have tried to get into this hospital. And it's your own fault that we haven't accepted you." The sneer in his voice cut through Tanya's heart. "You refuse to have an abortion, showing that you care little about your life. So why should we bother helping you? You are an ungrateful, stubborn woman!"

The pool of tears in Tanya's eyes overflowed.

"You are crazy," the doctor continued. "Go home and have your baby in the Skvira hospital. Then you can die with the child!" His face grew red in frustration as his heartless words pierced Tanya to the core.

When she trembled, Valentine reached out a hand to steady her. She spoke not a word, but her heart cried out, *Lord, have mercy on me! Where do I go now?* With tears blinding her eyes, she stumbled toward the door.

"Where are you going?" the doctor demanded. "I didn't excuse you yet. Do you want help, or don't you?"

Before Valentine or Tanya had a chance to answer, the doctor scribbled something on a piece of paper. "You may stay here one week," he said, handing her the paper. "Then we will decide what to do with you."

Tanya drew in a shaky breath as Valentine reached for the paper and said, "Thank you, doctor." Valentine's voice did not betray the relief he felt, but Tanya could read it in his eyes. He squeezed her hand and together they walked out of the office.

Will I ever get used to being in the hospital? Tanya asked herself as she spent another lonely day in her hospital room. Nearly a week had gone by since the doctor had admitted her to the hospital. *Am I just wasting my time?* So far the doctors had not really done anything. But every day a doctor would stick his head into the room and ask how she was feeling.

Her answer was always the same: "I'm feeling fine."

Then, without another word, the doctor would leave.

Frustration clawed at Tanya's heart, and worry threatened to devour her. Was there anything more she should be doing? Her thoughts went to Dr. Davidiva, whom she had heard much about. Dr. Davidiva was a specialist at the Medical Institute who had helped many cancer patients and expectant mothers. *If only we could get in touch with her.*

Tanya spent many hours talking on the phone. She loved when Marina called to ask how to cook something. And every day Valentine called her. Even though she felt far removed from her family and church friends, she could connect with them through her phone.

Three other women shared the room with Tanya. The ladies passed many hours visiting. Tanya did not want to add stress to her roommates, so she shared little about her sickness. Instead, she talked about her family and friends.

"Excuse me, Tanya," one of them said one evening.

Tanya looked up. "Yes, Lidiya?"

"Why are you in the hospital? I've been here three days, and I haven't seen you getting any treatment."

A slight smile flitted over Tanya's face. "I can see why you are wondering. It does seem rather strange." Breathing a prayer for wisdom, she gave her a short version of the complications she was facing.

Lidiya listened, wide-eyed. "But you should be in the Medical Institute, not here!"

"You're right," Tanya agreed. "But they won't let me in because I'm not from this area."

"And you are still so positive and cheerful? How can you be that way?"

"It's only because of God." Tanya's face shone with peace and joy. "He gives me grace, and I know it's all in His hands."

"Tanya, I admire you!" Lidiya shook her head in amazement. "Do you know what? I have an acquaintance who works at the Medical Institute. She is the anesthetist for Dr. Davidiva."

"Dr. Davidiva?" Tanya restrained the excitement bubbling in her heart. "We've been wishing we could see Dr. Davidiva. Do you think your friend could connect us with her?"

"Maybe. I'll find out." Pulling out her phone, Lidiya messaged her acquaintance, telling her about Tanya's need to see Dr. Davidiva. Almost immediately she received a reply: "I'm doing surgery now. I'll call back later."

Finally, two hours later, Lidiya's phone rang. "It's the anesthetist," she said as she answered the phone. A minute later she laid down the phone and smiled triumphantly at Tanya. "You have an appointment with Dr. Davidiva on Wednesday at 12:00."

Tanya squelched the urge to jump up and down on the bed. "Praise the Lord!" she exclaimed. Tears of gratefulness filled her eyes. "God still does miracles!"

She phoned Valentine, and he too rejoiced at the exciting turn of events. He made plans to go along to her appointment with Dr. Davidiva.

On Wednesday morning, as Valentine and Tanya were leaving the hospital to go to the Medical Institute, a nurse stopped them. "Where do you think you're going?" she demanded.

"I have an appointment with Dr. Davidiva at the Medical Institute," Tanya replied. She tried to sound confident, but her voice trembled.

"There's no chance of you being accepted in that hospital," the nurse sneered. "You tried it before. You're just wasting your time!"

"We are going anyway," said Valentine calmly.

When they arrived at the Medical Institute, they were told they would have to wait because Dr. Davidiva was doing an emergency surgery.

Several hours later they were ushered into Dr. Davidiva's office. Her starched white coat presented an air of professionalism, while her kind face reflected a sincere interest in her patients. "Tatianna Mikolievna, I'm glad to meet you." She gave them a welcoming smile. "And this must be your husband?" She nodded toward Valentine. "Thank you for coming along. Please be seated."

Tanya felt a tingle of excitement and hope as Dr. Davidiva skimmed over her papers. Finally the doctor looked at her and smiled. "Tell me about your situation. I am eager to see what we can do for you."

As Tanya shared the journey of the two months since she had been diagnosed with cancer, Dr. Davidiva listened closely, at times jotting notes or comparing Tanya's story with her records.

"Tatianna, there is hope for both you and your little one," she encouraged. "Your situation is rare indeed, but it is not hopeless."

Tanya shifted in her chair, hope swelling her heart.

"I wish you could have come to me sooner," the doctor continued.

"When your tumor was first discovered, it was still small enough that we could have operated on it even during your pregnancy. You could have carried your baby full term, and all would likely have been fine.

"But now your tumor is too big to do that. What we'll do is admit you to our hospital and keep close tabs on you and your baby. As soon as the baby's lungs are fully developed, we can do a Caesarean. Then we will immediately do surgery to remove your tumor. If everything goes well, both you and your child will be fine. I admire you for wanting to keep the baby. You are a God-fearing woman. God will help you."

When they stepped out of the office, Tanya fell into Valentine's arms, crying. Suddenly the door opened and Dr. Davidiva stepped out.

"Please don't cry," she said gently. "Everything will be all right."

Tanya smiled through her tears. "We're crying from joy. Your kindness and help mean so much to us. We can't thank you enough!"

"It's a privilege." Dr. Davidiva's soft voice and smile echoed her sincerity. She returned to her office.

The pent-up emotion and stress from the past weeks poured out in tears of relief. God had answered their prayers!

chapter 50

"What Next, Lord?"

2018

Marina tried to be brave, but the load she carried weighed heavily on her young shoulders. She checked to make sure Anechka was still sleeping, then she touched her little sister's forehead. It seemed warm. Too warm. She tried to shake the worry from her mind.

Slipping into her outdoor boots, Marina donned her coat and grabbed the water buckets. She trudged through the snow toward the well. The path she had shoveled open yesterday was already blowing shut. The gray sky and the gusts of snow did nothing to perk her spirits. Although the buckets were heavy, Marina did not complain. It was nothing compared to the weight on her heart.

I don't mind the work as much as the emotional strain. If only I knew what the outcome will be. Her mind traveled to the upcoming surgery. *Oh, how I hope everything will be all right! I feel so alone.* She glanced at her watch. *Oh, Bogdonna will soon come home from school. Maybe she can watch Anechka while I work in the greenhouse.*

Marina set her buckets full of water just inside the door. She paused to listen if Anechka was crying. The house was still wrapped in quietness, so she hurried to the woodshed for a load of wood. Concern etched her face as she saw the diminishing pile. And winter had only begun.

It was not the first time the Kosenko family was running low on resources. In fact, Marina remembered many times when there wasn't even enough to buy bread. But in the last few years, things had been going better. Papa had quit drinking and worked hard to make a living for his family.

Marina set her armload of wood in the entrance and hurried inside to warm her hands. Hearing little Anechka whimpering, she hastened to her little sister and gently lifted her from the crib. Another coughing fit racked her small frame. Again Marina felt Anechka's forehead. *I'm afraid she has a fever. Oh, what shall I do?* Tears pooled in her eyes and threatened to spill over. *If only Mama were here to take care of her!*

Just then Marina heard someone at the door. "It's just me," their neighbor Oksana called, brushing the snow off her boots. "How are you today?" Quietly she entered the kitchen. "You look worried, Marina. Is everything all right?"

Marina bit her lip to keep from crying. What a relief to see Oksana! "I am worried about Anechka," she said, brushing away the tear that insisted on sliding down her cheek. "She keeps coughing, and I don't know what to do."

Concern filled Oksana's eyes. "Does she have a fever?"

Marina shrugged her shoulders. "I don't know. I tried checking her temperature, but she won't let me. She just cries and pushes the thermometer away. But I think her forehead feels warm."

Oksana reached for Anechka and felt her forehead. "Yes, she does feel warm. I wonder if we shouldn't call the doctor." She pulled her cell phone from her pocket and stepped into the next room.

A few minutes later, she returned. "I talked to Dr. Srudmillo. He said he would stop in to check on her. I'll stay here until he comes."

Oksana picked up Anechka and held her close. "You dear little girl. You miss your mama, don't you?"

Anechka's only reply was, "Mama. Mama."

A tear stood in Oksana's eye. "Have you talked to your mom today, Marina? How's she feeling about the surgery tomorrow?"

Marina shook her head. "I don't like thinking about the surgery. But I talked to Mama, and she seemed in good spirits. Of course, she's worried about the surgery—and especially about the baby. I think she's just ready to have it over with. But, Oksana," Marina paused and looked into the kind eyes of her neighbor, "do you really think the baby will be all right? Isn't it too soon to take the baby?"

"I know what you mean, Marina. It's easy to worry. But we need to trust the doctors. The longer your mama has to wait, the more the cancer can spread. And remember, the last test showed that the baby's lungs were sufficiently developed. If she can breathe on her own, she's not too tiny to be born."

Marina nodded. "I guess I worry too much. I want to trust God, but it isn't easy!"

Another coughing fit interrupted their conversation. Oksana held the little girl close and rubbed her back. "You're a brave girl," she crooned. "The doctor is coming soon. Maybe he can help you feel better."

The sound of stomping boots caught Marina's attention, and she hurried to the door. "Oh, Bogdonna, it's you! I thought maybe the doctor was here."

"The doctor?" Bogdonna queried. "Why is the doctor coming?" She looked anxiously at her big sister. She finished stomping the snow off her boots and entered the warm kitchen. "Are you sick?"

"No, it's Anechka. I think she has a fever. She just coughs and coughs."

Bogdonna shook her head. "It seems sickness is all we have right now. I hope she's not getting the measles."

A knock at the door interrupted their conversation. Marina welcomed Dr. Srudmillo, and he set his satchel on the chair and proceeded to check out Anechka. He was a man of few words, but everyone in the village knew that behind his quiet mask was a gentle, caring heart. Carefully he listened to Anechka's chest, took her temperature, and looked into her ears and mouth.

Finally he looked at Marina. "Your little sister isn't very sick. She has a mild case of pneumonia, or maybe even whooping cough. She has a fever, but it's not very high. She could go to the hospital, but she might be just as comfortable at home."

Oksana, who had been a silent observer, now shared her mind. "Are you sure she shouldn't go to the hospital? Both of her parents are gone, and it's a large responsibility for young Marina to take care of her."

"Good idea," Dr. Srudmillo answered. "Why don't I write out a referral for Anechka to go to the Skvira hospital?"

Almost before Marina realized what was happening, Oksana was making arrangements for Bogdonna to stay at her house until Marina and Anechka returned home. Marina was relieved to let someone else make decisions for her. The stress and exhaustion were wearing her down. It was all she could do to keep from breaking into tears.

Marina stuffed some clothes and a few toys into a bag to take along to the hospital. Oksana offered to look after the house and feed the animals. Marina tried to be brave as she called a family from church and told them what was happening. Relief filled her heart when they offered to take her and Anechka to the hospital.

A few hours later, Marina found herself in a hospital room with her little sister. Suppertime came and went, but Marina had no appetite for the fruit, yogurt, and other goodies Oksana had added to the meager hospital fare. Nurses popped in at times to check on Anechka.

Concern for her little sister, worry for her mama, and apprehension for her unborn sibling gnawed at her heart. Never in her life had Marina felt so lonely.

chapter 51

Solomia

2018

The night sky was still thick with darkness when Tanya awoke. Today was the day she had been looking forward to and yet dreading for so long.

"My precious baby," she whispered, caressing her abdomen. "Are you ready to enter this big, scary world?" She shuddered. "I hope we aren't making a mistake!"

Tanya felt the flutter of her baby kicking, as though to assure her that she was ready and eager to meet the world.

The doctors had been keeping close tabs on Tanya and her unborn child. Tanya was thankful that the atmosphere at the Medical Institute was much different from the Regional Clinical Hospital.

"Solomia." Tanya whispered the name reverently. "Perhaps soon I can hold you in my arms!"

She turned her thoughts to prayer and committed the day to God's keeping. After the last test, the doctors had agreed it was time to do surgery. The baby's lungs were fully developed.

The darkness outside melted as the faint light of morning tinted the sky. The hospital door opened, and a nurse walked in. "Your husband is here to see you," she said, her voice soft, trying not to disturb the other patients in the room.

Tanya slid into her slippers and wrapped her fuzzy housecoat more tightly around herself. Somehow the December wind had followed the nurse into the room. She padded down the hall to the entrance where Valentine sat.

"Good morning," she said, easing into the chair beside his. "Today's the day."

Valentine nodded, his eyes full of concern. "Are you ready?"

Tanya shrugged her shoulders. The lump in her throat kept her from saying more.

Valentine reached for her hand and they sat in silence.

"How are the girls?" Tanya finally asked.

Valentine's forehead creased, but then he smiled. "They're all right. Marina said Oksana visited them last evening."

Tanya smiled. She could have known that Oksana would look after her girls. Between Oksana and the church families, they would be taken care of.

"I'll stay here until you go for surgery," Valentine said, "but then I think I'll go back to Mama's house to wait. I can't be with you anyway, and the doctor thought the surgery would take most of the morning, right?"

Tanya nodded. "Yes, that's what they said. I just hope the baby will be okay!"

Valentine smiled. "It will be all right. We waited until the doctors said it was safe for the baby to be born. They said waiting longer would be risky for both you and the baby."

Tanya knew what Valentine said was true. In the two months since the tumor had been discovered, it had grown rapidly.

A nurse stepped into the room. "It's time," she said, glancing at her watch. "The surgeon will be here soon."

"It will be all right," Valentine whispered, squeezing her hand. "Remember, everyone is praying for you."

Tanya nodded as she got up to follow the nurse.

The bright lights above the operating table shone into Tanya's face. She squeezed her eyes shut and tried to concentrate on what the doctor was saying. Dr. Davidiva was in charge of the team that would do the Caesarean, and her husband was part of the team that would then remove the tumor.

"You'll be awake for the Caesarean," Dr. Davidiva explained, "but then they'll put you to sleep for the rest of the operation." Her voice was kind and reassuring. "We trust God will help us with this surgery. Without Him we could do nothing. He is the One who gives life and healing."

Tanya nodded, grateful for the gift of believing doctors. She was overwhelmed as she saw all the nurses and doctors who would help with her surgery. She could feel the prayers of her church family as they interceded for her.

Time seemed to stand still as the doctors prepped her for surgery. As her eyes adjusted to the bright lights, she noticed that she could watch what the doctors were doing by looking at the reflection in the light above her. The discovery pleased her. She watched closely, eager for the first glimpse of her little girl.

Suddenly she gasped. There, in the reflection of the light, she saw her baby girl! She turned her head and caught a glimpse as a nurse sped the baby away to an incubator.

"Congratulations, Tanya!" Dr. Davidiva said, smiling. "You have a beautiful daughter!"

"But she's so tiny! Will she be all right?" Tanya wondered. She had known her baby would be small, but she had not imagined her to be this tiny!

"Yes, she is just fine!" Dr. Davidiva assured. "I've delivered smaller ones that pulled through. She'll make it! And so will you." Dr. Davidiva patted her hand reassuringly. "Now just relax and go to sleep. The other team will take over now."

Tanya was too tired to keep her eyes open or concentrate on what the doctor was saying. She sighed in satisfaction as she thought of her little one safe in the incubator. *Even if I don't make it, my baby will live.*

Marina sighed as she put down her phone. "I was hoping Papa would have news about Mama," she told her friends Lashonda and Dina, who had come to spend the morning with her at the hospital.

Anechka looked up from where she was playing with her teddy. "Mama?" Her eyes shone questioningly.

"No, that wasn't Mama." Marina caressed her sister's forehead. "It was Papa. He wanted to know if his little girl was feeling better."

Anechka smiled, oblivious to the seriousness of the moment.

"So he didn't have any news yet?" Dina wondered.

Marina shook her head. "No, but we should hear something soon. They started surgery at 8:00 this morning, and it's noon already." She was grateful for her friends. Their presence gave her courage through

Tanya

the long hours of waiting.

Anechka had slept better last night, so perhaps the nebulizer treatments were making a difference. She was not coughing as much either. Hopefully they could soon go home!

"Dinnertime!" a nurse announced, rolling a cart of food down the hall. She handed Marina a bowl of soup.

The soup consisted of a watery broth with little chunks of potato. "This is enough to feed a bird, but that's all!" Marina laughed. The other girls joined in. It felt good to laugh. The suspense of the morning had all the girls on edge.

"It's good we brought food with us," Lashonda said, pulling out their packed lunches. Before eating, the girls prayed together, each taking a turn to intercede for the burdens heavy on their minds.

Suddenly Marina's phone vibrated in her pocket. "Papa's calling!" she said. Quickly she pressed the phone to her ear.

"The baby's here!" The bad connection on the phone could not hide the excitement in Papa's voice.

"Is everything okay?" Marina wondered. Her heart thumped rapidly.

"Yes, she's just fine. She's breathing on her own and seems to be doing great."

"What about Mama?" Marina wondered.

"She's still in surgery. The doctor said he'll call me when he's finished."

Marina smiled at her friends as she put the phone away. "Little Solomia is here!" Joy shone through the tears in her eyes. "Praise the Lord, everything is all right!"

***

Tanya groaned as she struggled to open her eyes. *Where am I, and why does everything hurt? Is it a dream?* She shivered. *Where is that cold air coming from?*

"How are you feeling?" The words startled her. She had not realized anyone was around. She turned her head toward the sound and saw a nurse standing by her bed.

"Where am I?" Tanya wondered. "What happened?"

"You had surgery," the nurse said.

Suddenly everything came flooding back. "My baby! Is my baby all right?"

"Oh, yes. She's doing just fine. You have the sweetest little girl."

"Take me to her! I want to hold her!" Tanya begged, trying to sit up. She fell back weakly onto the pillow.

"Just a minute," the nurse said, stepping nearer. "You just had major surgery. You can't go anywhere right now. As soon as you regain your strength, you can see her."

Tanya nodded and closed her eyes. She felt like she could go right back to sleep.

The next twenty-four hours were an endless nightmare of weariness and pain. Tanya drifted in and out of sleep, at times trembling with cold or soaking in sweat. The incision began to bleed, and Tanya thought she would hemorrhage to death.

She had been given a private room in the intensive care unit. Tanya knew she should be grateful for the privacy, but the solitude of the room got to her. She was sure she would die alone.

She longed for someone to sit by her side—to hold her hand and pray with her. Valentine had gone back home to the girls. It was probably for the best, but it made her lonely. He had promised to come back on Monday.

By the evening of the second day, Tanya's condition had stabilized somewhat. She was jarred from her sleep by the vibrating of her phone. It was a neighbor lady. "How are you feeling?" she asked.

Tanya struggled to find the right words. "Better than yesterday, I guess."

"How's Anechka?" the lady wondered. "Do you think she can soon come home from the hospital?"

"You mean Solomia?"

"No, Anechka. It's too bad she had to get sick while you were gone. Do you think she has the whooping cough?"

"I don't know," Tanya answered, her mind racing. *Anechka sick and in the hospital? Why didn't anyone tell me?*

"Thank you for calling," she managed to say. "Goodbye."

Tears brimmed in her eyes and trickled down her cheeks. *Anechka sick! What next?* Her heart ached for her little girl. It also ached for Marina, who was no doubt with Anechka in the hospital. *And what about Bogdonna? How is she handling this? No wonder Valentine went home for the weekend! The girls needed him!*

Then she thought of little Solomia, the precious daughter she had not yet met. How she longed to hold her baby daughter!

The doctor had given her a good report on Solomia. She was tiny, weighing only 1.09 kilograms,[1] but she seemed to be doing fine. The doctor promised Tanya that she could see her soon.

The night stretched long and dark as Tanya drifted in and out of sleep. She felt utterly weak and spent. "Lord, please be near me!" she cried. "I need your strength and healing touch. So do my daughters! Care for us, Lord!"

Suddenly, in the midst of the darkness, she saw a nail-scarred hand reaching out. And there, in the palm of the hand, she recognized herself. Anechka was there too—and a tiny baby she knew must be Solomia.

Tears streamed down her eyes as the picture faded, but the warmth remained. She could sense a soft voice saying, "I am holding you, my child. I am also holding your daughters. Trust me."

---

[1] About 2¼ pounds.

chapter 52

Safe in the Arms of Jesus

2018

Tanya propped herself up in bed. Feeling a bit stronger, she had been transferred out of the ICU into a regular room. She was grateful. The ICU room had been chilly and had felt like a prison cell.

Three days had passed, and Tanya was more and more eager to meet her little daughter. The doctor was pleased with Tanya's progress and told her that maybe by tomorrow she could sit in the wheelchair, and they could take her to see her baby.

The door slowly opened and Valentine stepped inside. His face lit up when he saw Tanya sitting up in bed. "Tanya, my dear!" he said, stepping to her bedside. He reached for her hands and held them for a long moment. "How are you?"

"Better, I think. How are the girls?"

"Which of the girls?" he asked, a sparkle in his eye. "I have something to show you." He flipped open his phone and showed her a picture. "That's our little girl!"

Tanya's hands trembled as she took the phone from him and gazed at the picture. It was blurry—either from her tears or the poor quality of the photo—but the baby was beautiful.

"She's so perfect!" she breathed in awe. "So tiny, but so perfect!"

Valentine smiled. "She might be tiny, but she's a strong little mite. I was allowed to hold her little hand, and she wrapped it right around my finger. She has a good grip for as tiny as she is!"

"I can hardly wait to see her!" Tanya said. "How are the rest of the girls doing? Is Anechka any better?"

Valentine nodded. "Yes, she is. Praise God. It looks like she can come home this evening."

"Praise the Lord," Tanya murmured. Suddenly she was exhausted. Gingerly she lay back down, groaning softly. Every movement brought pain. "I'll be okay," she whispered. "It'll just take time."

Valentine nodded soberly. "I'm afraid it will take longer than we wish." He glanced at his watch. "I really should be going and let you get your rest. I'll stop by again this evening."

"Thank you," Tanya said. Her gaze followed him to the doorway. She smiled as she closed her eyes. She would rest now and do all she could to regain her strength. Somewhere in this hospital was her baby—and she could hardly wait to hold this precious child in her arms.

Tanya stirred from her sleep. She sensed someone beside her. She turned her head and saw Valentine. He was sitting on the chair by her bed. From the slump of his shoulders and the haggard look on his face, she knew something was wrong.

Tanya

"What happened?" she asked hoarsely, trying to sit up.

Valentine bit his lip and looked out the window.

"Tell me! What's wrong?"

He reached for her hand. "I'm sorry, Tanya, but…" He paused, unable to go on. An endless stream of questions rushed through Tanya's mind, possibilities of what could have happened.

"Solomia's gone."

Tanya shook her head. "What do you mean?" Her eyes blinked rapidly.

"She died. The doctor just called me. He said I should tell you."

"How? Why? I thought she was doing fine! What happened?"

"I don't know." Valentine shook his head and continued staring out the window.

A doctor entered, a sober look on his face. "I give you my sympathy," he said.

"What happened?" Tanya demanded.

The doctor shook his head sadly. "I don't know. We did not expect this. She was doing so well. Her heart just suddenly stopped beating, and she was gone. We tried everything, but we could not revive her. I'm sorry." A tear glistened in his eye and his voice carried a tone of defeat. "I am so sorry. There was nothing we could do."

Tanya pinched herself to make sure she was awake. Surely this was all just a bad dream, a nightmare, and she would soon wake up and see her baby.

"Can I see her?" she asked. Perhaps then she could believe it.

The doctor shook his head. "Not now. She's already in the morgue." He looked at Valentine. "Do you want to claim the body, or would you like us to dispose of it?"

"I don't know. We haven't discussed it yet." Valentine looked at Tanya. "What do you think?"

Tanya thought she would faint with grief. How could it be that her little one for whom she had been willing to give her life was gone? She shook her head. "I don't know. Do we have to decide now?"

The doctor shook his head. "No, take your time." He turned to leave, but paused at the door. "I'm really sorry this happened. It's a shock to all of us."

Just then a nurse walked in. "It's time for your medicine, Tanya. Here, swallow this." She handed the cup to Tanya.

"Already?" Tanya asked. "I thought I get my pain relievers closer to bedtime." She puckered her lips as she swallowed the last drops of the medicine. "What was that nasty stuff?"

"Just something to help you relax and feel better," the nurse replied. "It might make you tired, but that's all right. Your body needs to rest."

Tanya nodded, suddenly overwhelmed with exhaustion. "I am tired, but…" Her voice trailed off. Suddenly she lifted herself up on her elbow. "That was a tranquilizer she gave me!" she sputtered. She could hold back her tears no longer. "Are they afraid I'll go crazy? Is that why she gave it to me?"

Memories marched through Tanya's mind—memories of Mama wailing at Svetta's grave, hysterical with grief. Now she understood her mother's pain, the heartbreak of losing a child. She sank back onto the pillow as everything became foggy.

"I can't stay awake," she muttered, her words slurring together. In a few moments, she slipped away from the grief and pain into the bliss of sleep.

When she awoke several hours later, darkness had descended on the city and Valentine was gone. Tanya wondered if it had all been just a bad dream. Surely Valentine would come any minute for his evening visit.

She would tell him about her nightmare. He would laugh and assure her everything was fine and that tomorrow she could see her baby.

She lay there for a long while, her mind foggy. Then her phone beeped. It was a message from one of the church sisters. She read, "Tanya dear, we are praying for you. May God hold you close during this time."

The message didn't say anything about Solomia. Had that just been a bad dream? Her phone vibrated again, and Tanya groaned when she saw it was Valya calling.

"Tanya! Oh, Tanya! The baby! Why did she have to die?"

From the hysterical crying on the phone, Tanya knew it had not been just a nightmare. She bit her lip. Her nerves did not need this outburst.

"Mama, look. We are all sad! But right now I can't handle this. We can talk some other time when you are calm." She hung up the phone and stared at the ceiling. *Why did this happen? What went wrong? Did we make a mistake in allowing the doctor to go ahead? Maybe we should have waited longer.* Questions and pain bombarded Tanya's mind. She felt a cloud of fog and despair settling into her brain. Nothing made sense anymore.

She drifted into a restless sleep, dreaming of babies whimpering and mothers crying—of graves and grief.

After Valentine left the hospital, he caught the first bus back to Kryvoshyintsi. He dreaded breaking the news to the girls, but he hoped to get back in time so they could hear it directly from him. Marina had told him earlier in the day that Anechka would be released from the hospital. He was glad. They needed to be together as a family at a time like this.

The news had reached the girls before Valentine arrived home. He sensed their sorrow the moment he stepped indoors. He saw grief written on their faces but felt unable to comfort them.

The ministers and their wives soon arrived to show their comfort and support. "What are you thinking about a funeral?" one of them asked.

Valentine sighed. "I don't know. Do you think we should even have a funeral? Will anyone come? No one knows Solomia. It might be simplest to just have a private family burial."

"Your grief is our grief," one of the ministers said. "We have all been praying for Solomia, and even though we haven't met her, she is special to us."

Together they made funeral plans. Brother Abner offered to take Valentine to pick up the body. Brother James said he would build a little casket.

Sister Robin offered to sew a tiny dress, and Marlene and Connie said they would organize the funeral meal. Valentine was grateful for everyone's help and support, but he kept thinking of his wife in the hospital.

The funeral was held two days later in the Kosenkos' courtyard. Despite the chilling wind and mounds of snow, a surprising number of neighbors and relatives gathered to show their support and sympathy. Some of them had never been at a church service before.

Little Solomia looked so peaceful and angelic in her soft white dress. A hint of a smile graced her lips. She looked too tiny and fragile to be lying in a casket and exposed to the brutal wind.

Brother Wayne preached the funeral message. "To us it seems Solomia's life was too short; she lived only three short days. But because of her, we are gathered here. Her life speaks to us and reminds us that life is uncertain. We are thankful that Solomia is safe in heaven with our Lord, the One who loves little children. Where would you and I be if our lives had ended today?"

As the congregation sang, many wiped tears from their eyes. It was a holy, somber occasion. Solomia's death touched many hearts.

At the graveside, Valentine and Marina stood together beside the casket for the final viewing. Bogdonna had stayed at the house with Anechka, who was still too frail to be out in the cold. Valentine felt so alone standing at his daughter's grave. If only Tanya could be here, and they could grieve together!

Little Solomia was buried between the graves of Tanya's mother and her sister.

After the burial, Valentine spoke. "Thank you for coming to walk with us as we carried our tiny daughter the last mile. Actually, she's not really my daughter, but God's daughter. Before she was even born, we committed her to God. He gave her to us for only a few days. Now He has taken her home."

Tears rolled down his face, and he could say no more.

chapter 53

Pain Is Never Wasted

2019

Three weeks later, Tanya came home from the hospital. She had missed New Year's Day but was grateful she could be at home for Christmas on January 7.

Her recovery was slow and painful. Doubts and grief plagued her. *Why did God claim Solomia's life when I was ready to die to give her life? Maybe we should have listened to the doctors' advice and done an abortion.* Tanya was suddenly horrified at her thoughts. *No, that would have been wrong.*

Tanya had hoped the surgery would take care of the cancer, but it hadn't. It had spread, and the doctors were unable to remove all of it. They recommended further treatment.

"You must start treatment as soon as possible," the doctors urged.

As they researched various treatment options, they finally settled on a hospital in Belarus that offered a hyperthermia treatment in which cancer cells were killed by heating the body to 104°F. This treatment was more natural and less harsh on the body than radiation or chemo.

Tanya had never traveled out of the country before, and the trip looked scary. She was grateful when one of the young sisters from church, Leah Dziuba, offered to travel with her. The Dziuba family had acquaintances in Belarus and had arranged lodging with believers who lived near the hospital.

As Tanya prepared for the trip, she felt a glimmer of hope. Perhaps this treatment would help her. Maybe she would get a second chance at life.

The hospital in Belarus was nicer than any Tanya had ever seen in Ukraine. But on the second day there, she had a bitter disappointment. The hyperthermia treatment the hospital specialized in would not work because of the plastic implant Tanya had received when the doctors removed the tumor. Instead, the Belarusian doctors encouraged her to do radiation treatments for six weeks, starting as soon as possible.

After talking with Valentine, Tanya felt ready to go ahead with the treatments. But the cost looked overwhelming. Where would they ever find $5,000 to pay for it?

That evening Tanya wept when she got off the phone with the ministers. They had promised that the church would help with the hospital bills. They were also supporting her with prayer and fasting. Their kindness and support overwhelmed her. She was not alone on this journey.

Leah was a big help in figuring out the bus system, buying groceries, and providing moral support. But by the end of the first week, Tanya had settled in and was fine with the idea of Leah returning home. "I don't know what I would have done without you," she said. "Thanks again for coming along."

Tanya was grateful for the lodging she had with a widowed mother and her daughter. They both worked, so Tanya was often alone during the day.

The radiation treatment robbed her of her appetite and energy, and most of the time she was content to rest. But spending hours alone was hard, and her thoughts often wandered to her family in Ukraine. How she missed them. Phone calls were expensive, and Tanya didn't want to waste money. But it was her only way to stay connected to her family.

The final two weeks of Tanya's radiation treatments dragged by, and at last she was free to go home. Valentine traveled to Belarus to accompany her home.

"I recommend you do a few more treatments in Kyiv," the doctor advised. "But then I think you should be good to go. You should do regular blood work to make sure everything is fine, but at this point, your cancer is in remission."

His words were almost too good to be true!

Tanya looked around her at the brothers and sisters in church, her eyes misting with tears. So much had happened in the four months since she had last worshiped with the believers. It had been hard and painful, yet she had felt their love and presence all along.

When the opportunity was given for people to share testimonies, Tanya was the first on her feet. Tears shone in many eyes as she shared her journey through grief. "Through it all, God has not failed me, and I can feel His presence right now. I like the words of the 'Pain Is Never Wasted' poem in the little scrapbook you made for me. It tells me that God always knows what He is doing."

Pain is never without gain;
Hearts are never hurt in vain.
Sorrow sometimes fills your days;
God will honor one who prays…

Whether you will walk through waste,
Fire, or storm, note God's great grace:
Though much sorrow you may fend,
God will hold you to the end.

Pain is never without gain;
Hearts are never hurt in vain.
Every tear you ever cry,
God will use to beautify.

Tanya slowly regained her strength. For several weeks after returning from Belarus, she continued radiation treatments in Kyiv, and every six weeks she went to the hospital in Skvira for blood work. So far everything had come back clear, and her cancer appeared to be in remission.

After staring death in its face, Tanya cherished every breath. It was a privilege to spend time with her family and to cook and clean and work in the garden. She treasured church services and time spent with friends. Every day was a gift.

Her heart ached for others suffering similar sicknesses. Everywhere she went, she took gospel tracts with her. Nothing brought her more joy than sharing encouragement with others. When Masha Klimenko, the village storekeeper, was diagnosed with cancer, Tanya could feel her pain. In the weeks following Masha's surgery, when she fell into discouragement, Tanya reached out to her. Again and again God brought people into Tanya's life who needed encouragement.

One evening Tanya's classmates got together at the village school for a reunion. Twenty years had passed since they had graduated, and life had taken them in many directions. A few of her classmates still lived in Kryvoshyintsi, as did most of her teachers.

Tanya almost did not go. She knew she would not fit into the group. Besides, she was still not feeling strong. It would be easier to stay at home.

But when Irina Vasilivna, the teacher who had coached Tanya through her first few years of school, called to give her a special invitation, Tanya knew she must go. She wondered if her schoolmates would even recognize her. Would they have anything in common?

Tanya felt like a white raven. Her friends were dressed in classy clothes, their ages hidden behind a shield of makeup. Some even had their hair dyed. Tanya noticed their long, painted fingernails, and for a moment she wished she could hide her work-worn hands. But just as suddenly, she realized how blessed she was to have work-worn hands.

Lord, give me grace and strength, she begged. *Help me be a witness for you!* With a calm smile, she joined the circle of laughing, chattering folks. The conversation hushed for a moment, and Tanya's hands felt clammy with sweat as all eyes turned upon her. "Good to see all of you!" she greeted them. She turned to the woman closest to her. "Natasha, how have you been? It's been so long!" Soon the conversation resumed as lively as before.

The evening passed quickly, and Tanya enjoyed it more than she had imagined. Her classmates and teachers seemed genuinely glad to have her there. After supper, everyone took turns sharing about his or her life, family, and work. Tanya listened in amazement. There were doctors, farmers, and even a few teachers in the group.

When it was Tanya's turn to speak, all eyes were upon her. She had prayed that God would help her be a witness at the reunion, and she knew that now was her chance. She told them briefly about her life, about how she had moved back to the village and found the Lord. She told them about her cancer journey, about the death of little Solomia, and how she thanked God for every new day. "Without God, I don't know how I would have survived the grief and sickness. But God has been faithful. He is the One who gives me fulfillment in life."

At the end of her testimony, she recited the poem "Pain Is Never Wasted," which had become her mantra. By the time Tanya reached the end of the poem, tears smudged the eye shadow of more than one classmate. But the tears that shone in Tanya's eyes were tears of joy. Once again God had used her cancer journey as an opportunity to witness.

After the formal part came the drinking and dancing. Tanya quickly excused herself; she had been there long enough. It was time to get back home to her family. Her heart overflowed as she walked home. God had been so gracious to her. She would not trade her place with any of her classmates. How blessed she was to be part of God's family!

chapter 54

Limitless Love

2020

Anechka's blue eyes looked pleadingly at Tanya. "Mama, hold me?" she lisped.

Tanya winced as she lifted two-year-old Anechka to her lap. She planted a kiss on the silky blond hair.

"Yes, Mama can hold you for a little." Tanya squeezed her daughter closer. "But then Mama needs to go out to the greenhouse and work." She felt her baby's forehead. "I'm afraid you have a fever, baby dear. Let Mama check your temperature." She slid the thermometer under Anechka's arm.

Anechka whimpered as the cool thermometer touched her feverish body. "A shot?"

"No, dear. Mama's not giving you a shot. Just Mama gets shots." Tanya smiled wryly. A two-year-old shouldn't have to worry about shots. But shots were a part of daily life for their family. For the past few weeks, every evening Valentine had to give Tanya a shot. But even with the strong pain medicine, the sharp pain in Tanya's back was almost unbearable.

The thermometer beeped, and Tanya peered at the numbers. "Hmm, you do have a fever." She turned to her oldest daughter. "Marina, please bring the pain medication."

Tanya held a spoonful of medicine to Anechka's lips. "Drink this, dear. You're Mama's good girl."

She turned to Marina. "I think I'll work in the greenhouse today. Maybe I can get the cucumbers planted. You can stay in the house and take care of Anechka."

"Mama," Marina protested, "do the cucumbers have to be planted today? Can't we wait until Papa is at home?"

"I wish we could, but it's March already. It's high time to plant them." Tanya rose stiffly from her chair and shuffled to the coat hook. "Keep your eyes on Anechka and call me if you need anything."

"But, Mama, it's too much work for you. Maybe you should stay in the house, and I can go to the greenhouse."

"No, dear. I'll be fine. It will be good for me to get some fresh air and move around a little."

Once out in the greenhouse, Tanya allowed her tears to flow. Yes, the cucumbers needed to be planted, but the real reason she wanted to go to the greenhouse was to be alone. Tears slid down her face as she poured out her heart to God.

Tanya's thoughts traveled over the past months. Ever since her surgery a year and a half ago, her health had been a struggle, and recently there had been increasing pain in her spine. Now, after many tests, the dreaded results had come back. The cancer had returned—and it had spread.

Why is God allowing this to happen? Why didn't the doctors find it earlier?

Tanya's thoughts continued to travel as she filled pot after pot with the rich, black soil. *What will happen to my children if I die?* She was tired of fighting. It would be wonderful to be pain-free in heaven—and to see her precious baby Solomia!

But the thought of leaving her daughters behind was almost more than she could bear. If only Valentine would repent and be a true Christian! That would make it so much easier. She shuddered at the thought of her daughters living alone with their short-tempered papa. Who would be their mediator? Who would teach them to forgive their papa? Tanya groaned. The pain in her heart was as sharp as the pain in her spine.

But the doctors still seemed hopeful. They told Tanya that with surgery to remove the cancer-filled lymph nodes and then chemo treatment, they could fight the cancer. They wanted her to do it as soon as possible. Her suitcase was already packed.

The silence of the greenhouse was interrupted by the ringing of her phone. Tanya brushed the dirt from her fingers and picked it up. It was a friend who always had a word of encouragement. "I'll be stopping by to drop something off," she said. "I'll be there shortly."

When the barking of the dogs announced her friend's arrival, Tanya strode outside to meet her. When she returned to the greenhouse minutes later, tears of joy shone in her eyes. "Lord," she prayed brokenly, "your love is without limits. Thank you for showing your love through friends who care."

Her heart felt overwhelmed with gratitude and unworthiness at the gift of love her friend had dropped off. This and other money the church was providing would help pay the hospital bill. Brothers and sisters in the States were also donating money.

As she pondered her blessings, she seemed to hear a quiet voice saying, "If I can supply the financial needs for your surgery and your chemo treatment, don't you think I can also take care of your children? You are part of my family. I will care for you."

Sweet peace washed over her soul. Yes, God's love was limitless. He would provide for her needs and care for her family. No matter what the future held, God was in control and His presence would be near.

The upcoming surgery and the chemo treatments weighed heavily on Tanya's mind, and she asked to be anointed again. The following Sunday, the ministry and a few close friends gathered for the special service. God's presence filled the room as the little group sang and prayed.

"You see how weak I feel and how the road ahead looks dark," Tanya prayed. "Please strengthen my body and my faith. If it is not against your will, please heal me. Whatever comes, help me be faithful to you!"

When Valentine took his turn praying, tears slid down Tanya's cheeks. His prayer did not sound at all like the words he spoke at home sometimes. His prayer was one of broken surrender and love for his wife and family. Which was the real Valentine?

I will not give up on him, she resolved. *Maybe God is speaking to him through my cancer. Maybe this is what it takes for him to come to Christ.*

Tanya felt peace and joy wash over her soul. No matter what lay ahead, God would be there.

chapter 55

Death's Door

2020

The hospital walls closed around Tanya like prison walls. The surgery was over, and pain and utter weakness shackled her to the bed. Even if she had wanted to run away, she couldn't have. Memories of her earlier surgery a year and a half ago flooded back. The utter weakness, pain, and despair were all too familiar.

She had not expected it to be different this time, but the waves of grief and depression surprised her. She thought she had accepted Solomia's death and moved on with life, but now her heart ached so deeply. It was not just the pain of losing her daughter—it was an ongoing pain. The pain of living with abuse and false accusations. The pain of worrying for her daughters.

It was Valentine's accusations that hurt the most. He had accused her of being a poor mother and of using surgery as an excuse to get away from her work at home. He had refused to come with her to the hospital. The last words she had heard him say still rang in her ears—bitter, accusing words.

The days crawled by, and Tanya could finally go home. Although nearly three weeks had passed, she still felt weak and fragile. Because of COVID-19 restrictions, no visitors had been allowed in the hospital, and the three weeks had felt like three months.

During her hospitalization, spring had warmed its way into the country, melting the mounds of snow and leaving the ground bare and muddy.

All day long, Tanya burned with fever. She felt too weak to get out of bed, and when a sister from church stopped by, she was almost too tired to talk with her.

By evening, she was sure she was dying. Her fever soared, and the sheets on her bed became soaked with sweat. Tanya realized that, except for a miracle, she would likely not make it through the night.

"Marina, bring Bogdonna and Anechka to me," she whispered. Quietly the girls entered her room. Tanya could tell by the girls' serious expressions that they sensed the seriousness of the moment. Only little Anechka was carefree and happy.

"Girls, I think I'm dying." Tanya was surprised at the peace she felt as she broke the news to her daughters. "I don't know if I will still be here when you wake up tomorrow morning. I feel so sick."

Marina reached for her mama's hand, her lips trembling as she held back the sobs.

Tanya was not done. "I just want to tell you, my dear daughters, how much I love you. You have been a wonderful gift of God to me. I wish

I could stay here and be the mother you need."

Tanya closed her eyes, and for a moment the only sound in the room was Bogdonna's sniffles. This was harder—much harder—than she had imagined. Ever since the cancer diagnosis a year and a half ago, she had been trying to prepare herself for the final goodbye. But now that it was here, it was hard.

"*Ouwee*, Mama?" Anechka's big blue eyes filled with concern as she stared at her mother.

Tanya reached for her and held her close. "Yes, dear. Mama's not feeling well."

Turning to her older daughters, she continued, "Forgive me for the times I've failed you, for the times I was impatient and not the mother you deserved." She wiped her eyes. "I wish we would not have to part, but I will be waiting for you in heaven."

A weight lifted from Tanya's shoulders as she gave her daughters her final words of love and admonition. Goodbyes, she knew, were a painful but necessary part of grieving. It was for her daughters' sake, as much as her own, that she bid them farewell.

Marina offered to stay up with her, but Tanya urged them to go to bed. She did not dread the thought of dying alone. It would be better than having her daughters watch her struggle with every breath. "I'll call you if I need something," she whispered. "Right now I just need to rest."

Valentine's snoring was proof that he was beside her, but it brought little comfort. They lay next to each other, but a huge gulf separated them.

Perhaps death was the best option. Valentine had told her more than once that life would be easier without her. Her heart ached with the memory of those words. She wondered how he would respond when he awoke and found her dead. Would he care?

Death's Door

Every breath was agony. Every bone and muscle ached, and her head throbbed. Suddenly a wave of peace washed over her. Her fever lifted, and she felt like she could sink into deep rest. Perhaps the angels had come. She looked at the clock. It was two o'clock.

Sunlight streamed through the curtains when Tanya awoke. She looked at the rumpled covers beside her. She had not even heard Valentine get up. She could hear the muffled voices of the girls in the next room. *How could I have slept so long?* She felt rested and peaceful and alive. It was a startling feeling. The bedsheets were still damp from her feverish sweating during the night, but her head did not throb and she felt cool and refreshed.

Marina knocked lightly on the door and entered the room. "How are you doing, Mama?"

Tanya propped herself up on the bed and smiled. "I feel much better than I did last night! I believe I might make it after all!"

"Praise the Lord! That's wonderful! I was worried about you. Babushka called this morning and wanted to talk to you. I told her you were resting and would call her back."

"Sure, I can do that. I think I can actually talk today." Tanya lay back on her pillow. "Could you please bring me a drink of compote or tea?"

After Valentine and the girls had left for church, Tanya picked up her phone. She planned to call in and listen to the service later, but now she wanted to return Valya's call.

"Oh, Tanya! How are you doing?" Valya greeted her.

Tanya smiled. Valya was always so intense. "Better than yesterday!" she replied.

Before she could say more, Valya butted in. "Oh, Tanya, I have been so worried about you. All day yesterday I thought about you and prayed for you. Last night I lay in bed worrying about you. I couldn't sleep, and finally, at two o'clock, I got out of bed and knelt and prayed and cried and cried. My heart was so burdened for you!"

"Oh, Mama!" Tanya exclaimed. "God heard your prayers. Yesterday I was so sick I thought I was dying. But at two o'clock last night, something changed. My fever left, and I was able to sleep. God answered your prayers!"

As spring arrived in full force, the countryside was garbed in blossoming trees, cheery tulips, and freshly turned rich soil. But the beauty carried a haunting air of sadness. While nature was bursting with life, it seemed to be slipping away from Tanya.

She wanted to hang onto it, to savor these days with her family, but chemo was wringing her body ruthlessly, leaving her gasping for breath and aching for healing. As it ate away at her kidneys, Tanya wondered if she would die from kidney failure.

The doctors had prescribed IVs to help wash her kidneys, so Alona often came over after a chemo treatment to give her the IV. Tanya could not have asked for a better nurse. Tanya hated to make a busy mother even busier, but Alona never complained. Her presence radiated cheer and hope, and Tanya always felt better emotionally after Alona's visits.

Life with chemo treatments was a roller coaster. After the treatments, Tanya would dip so low that she thought she was going to die. But then, after a few days, her strength would rally, and she would feel better again. Sometimes she even felt well enough to go to church or out to the garden.

One Sunday when the pastor opened the service for testimonies or confessions, Tanya got to her feet. She hoped the others would not mind her sharing her heart again. All week something had been bothering her, and she needed to share it with the others. "That verse about giving up our family for Christ's sake has been speaking to me. I fight the thought of leaving my family behind if God calls me home. I don't want to die! But I think God is telling me to let go of my family and trust them to Him. I want to be willing to do that. Please pray for me!"

"Unless something changes, I don't think we can give you any more chemo treatments." The doctor peered over his glasses at Tanya. "Your kidneys cannot handle it. I don't think you will survive one more round of chemo."

The doctor's words sounded like a death sentence, but Tanya hardly cared. She hated the treatments and wondered how she would ever survive six of them. Now she was suddenly finished after only three.

"Do you have any idea what I can expect?" Tanya asked hesitantly. "How long do you think it…?" She could not bring herself to say the dreaded words. Who likes to think or talk about death? She was not afraid of heaven; it was the path to get there that scared her. Would it be long and painful? Or would the angels come quickly?

The doctor's face was sober. "I really can't tell you what to expect. Perhaps the three treatments you received will be enough to knock back the cancer. Maybe it will even go into remission. You might have six months or a year. Maybe longer." He cleared his throat and handed the stack of medical papers to Tanya. "Maybe after a break from chemo, you will want to return in several months for more treatments."

Tanya nodded. The message was clear. Her days were numbered.

"We thank God for His goodness in giving our dear sister Tanya thirty-nine years of life." Connie's voice trembled. "This birthday is extra special because there were times this past year that we wondered if we would see this day. Let's go around the circle and take turns sharing a word of encouragement or telling how Tanya has blessed us."

As Tanya looked around the circle of friends who had gathered to celebrate her birthday, her heart was full. They were all here, her dear sisters from church, everyone from the babushkas to the youth girls.

As Tanya listened to one sister after another share words of encouragement or fond memories, her heart felt as though it would overflow. She had never realized how her life with all its weaknesses and failures could be an inspiration to others. Tears shone in the eyes of many as they gave Tanya their birthday wishes and thanked her for her faithfulness.

"May I have a turn to talk?" Tanya wondered. "I don't feel worthy of everything you said tonight. God alone knows how often I stumble and how I struggle. But I am thankful for your encouragement. You are my family, and I thank God for you. You are all so precious to me."

She paused as tears came to her eyes. "I don't know how many more birthdays I will be able to celebrate. But God has been faithful in the past, and I know He will not fail me in the future."

Together they sang some of Tanya's favorite songs, then they shared sweet fellowship as they enjoyed the refreshments.

"This was my best birthday yet," Tanya remarked as the last of the ladies left. "God is so kind to me."

chapter 56

The Missionary in the Hospital

2020-2021

By fall, Tanya was undergoing a new round of chemo treatments. While these treatments were milder than the ones she had taken earlier, the downside was that she had to stay in the hospital for ten days at a time. The two weeks at home between the treatments never seemed long enough.

"I don't think I'm in the hospital to find healing," Tanya told a friend on the phone one day. "I think God has put me here to encourage other hurting people." As long as Tanya was able to share God's love with others, life was worth living. In fact, she sometimes wondered if God had allowed her to have cancer specifically so she could share hope with others in the hospital.

"Tell me more about your family," a nurse asked one evening. "You said you have three daughters?"

Tanya nodded. "Yes, the youngest one is turning three next Wednesday. I'm so glad I get to be with her on her birthday! Last year I was feeling too sick to celebrate, and the year before that I was in the hospital waiting for surgery. It will be special to be at home this time."

"Wow, your treatments are timed just right! Do you plan to do anything special?"

"I don't know. Perhaps Valentine will grill some shashlyk. That's always a treat. We might invite a few friends over."

"I have a little girl too," Zoya said. "She just turned four."

Tanya enjoyed the visits with this nurse. Often during break time when the other nurses sat in the nurses' lounge, Zoya brought her cup of tea into Tanya's room and visited with her. Tanya sensed that she was seeking something more in life.

"How's your family today?" one of Tanya's roommates asked one day after hearing her talk to them on the phone. "Are they doing okay?"

Tanya laughed. "Oh, they seem fine, but I'm eager to get back home!"

"We might not let you go!" one of the other roommates said. "We don't want you to leave."

"I will miss you too; that's for sure!" Tanya replied, swallowing hard. All the women in her room were so open and kind. The hours passed quickly as the women shared life experiences and stories. Often they asked her to read to them from the Bible or the *Seed of Truth*.

The ten days passed quickly, and almost before Tanya knew it, she was free to go home. She gathered her belongings and looked around the room. "Goodbye, my friends and fellow cancer warriors!" she said to the other women. "I'm going to miss you!"

"And we'll miss you too!" Baba Mila said. She climbed out of bed and shuffled over to Tanya, wrapping her in a tight hug. "Tanya, you have been like sunshine in our hospital room. You brought healing to my spirit." She wiped tears from her eyes.

"Perhaps we'll meet again if we're both coming back for another treatment," another one said. "I hope we'll be in the same room again the next time!"

"You have my phone number," said the third. "Let's keep in touch."

Tanya nodded, her eyes brimming. "God be with you all!" She shouldered her bags and trudged down the corridor. It tugged to leave these dear, hurting women. She wished she could somehow ease their pain.

She was going down the steps when she heard someone call her name. "Tanya! Wait!" She turned and saw Nurse Zoya running after her.

"Please wait. I have something for you." Zoya was puffing when she reached Tanya. "I just want to thank you for the inspiration you have been to me." She gave Tanya a quick hug. "Something about your positive spirit attracted me. I just want to say thank you."

"Give God the glory," Tanya quickly replied. "I enjoyed learning to know you too. This world would be a better place if all nurses were as friendly and compassionate as you are!"

Zoya shook her head. "It's my job. I have to do it. But sometimes the hopelessness gets to me. When I see so many suffering people every day, I feel depressed." She bit her lip and looked away. "But I always felt more alive after visiting with you. Your joy and positive spirit encouraged me." She held out a gift bag. "Here's a little birthday gift for your daughter. I knew you couldn't go shopping for her birthday, so I bought her one." She smiled. "I want her birthday to be a special day for both of you."

Tanya found it hard to speak. "Thank you!" she whispered. "May God reward you for your kindness."

Tanya sat at the bus stop, waiting for a ride back to the village. She had been in town for blood tests, and the results were discouraging.

But that was not the only thing she was discouraged about. She and Valentine had gotten into an argument that morning, and she still felt bad about it. As usual, it was about money. She had only told him the truth, but now she wondered if she should have remained quiet. Why could they never have a good discussion? It seemed every time they tried to talk, they ended up arguing.

Tanya was so immersed in her own grief that when someone took a seat next to her, she barely noticed. Until the stench hit her.

As Tanya gagged violently, she glanced at the woman sitting next to her. Her bloodshot eyes, stringy hair, and dirty clothes created a most repulsive picture.

Tanya turned her face away, resisting the urge to move to another seat. She knew the woman beside her had a soul and deserved to be treated with respect, even if she was repulsive. But what could she say to help her? Her own hope was waning. What could she offer to this poor soul?

Tanya rummaged through her purse and pulled out a tract. It was one she had read before, but right now she needed it for her own good. Tears trickled down her cheeks as she read the title: "Where Is God When Life Hurts?" As she read the inspiring words, the burden of her heart eased, and she felt God's presence.

Just then a bus pulled in, and a few passengers got off. Tanya grabbed her purse and started toward the bus. Then she glanced at the woman still sitting there and held out the tract she had been reading. "Here's something for you to read," she said. "It has encouraged me through my hard times. Maybe it can do the same for you."

Tanya hurried into the bus and dropped into an empty seat. As the bus pulled away, she looked back at the woman still sitting at the bus stop. She was wiping her eyes.

A lump filled Tanya's throat. *But for the grace of God, that could be me.*

All through the winter, Tanya continued chemo treatments, and for a while the tumors were kept in check. But as the winter wore on, Tanya's cough worsened, and severe back pain plagued her. She tried hard to be strong and to not give in to the depression and despair that hung over her like a cloud.

She hated to see the way her sickness was affecting her family. Little Anechka was hard to manage at times, and she found herself too weak to discipline her. This made her feel like a failure as a mother.

Bogdonna's education was also suffering. From her latest report card, Tanya knew her daughter's grades were dropping. The girls tried to keep up with schoolwork even when they stayed at home, but it was just not the same.

The cancer was taking its toll on Valentine as well. He hated to see Tanya suffering, but he didn't know how to express his grief and loss. As her condition worsened, he became more demanding and critical. Some days it seemed like no one in the family could do anything right. The stress level ran high, and Tanya wondered if her death would simplify life for the whole family.

As the winter days crept closer to spring, Tanya could feel her strength waning. She tried hard to hide her pain, but being cheerful was hard when every breath hurt. One day the pain was so sharp that it leaked from her eyes.

Little Anechka noticed. "Mama, why are you crying? Does it hurt so much?"

Tanya nodded, trying to smile. She wanted to be brave for her daughter's sake.

"Let's pray and ask Jesus to help you. I know He can!" Anechka smiled trustingly at her mother. "Come, Papa. Let's pray for Mama!"

Anechka knelt by the couch and looked expectantly at her parents. Tanya winced as pain shot through her, but she knelt beside her little daughter. Valentine joined them, and together they prayed. As Tanya listened to her daughter's heartfelt prayer, she breathed her own prayer: *O God, may my daughter always have such a strong faith in you!*

After Anechka's prayer, Valentine prayed. Tanya allowed the tears to flow as she listened. *He really wants to do what is right!* Her heart ached for him. He was sick too—just in a different way. He did not want to be caught in the vices of sin any more than she wanted to be sick with cancer. But he seemed powerless to change.

O God! Have mercy on him and heal him! she cried in her heart. *We need a miracle!*

When they rose from prayer, Tanya's faith had been strengthened. She still had pain—lots of it—but she also had grace. And she knew she could count on God's grace to lead her and her family safely home.

One Sunday Tanya was feeling well enough to join her family at church. When the time opened for people to share, she and her family went forward to sing. They could not sing like a choir, but they sang from their hearts—and that's what mattered.

> *Amazing grace, how sweet the sound*
> *That saved a wretch like me!*
> *I once was lost, but now I'm found.*
> *Was blind, but now I see.*

This song had always been one of Tanya's favorites. It was truly the grace of God that had saved her—a drunkard's daughter and a lost sinner. And it was the grace of God that was keeping her going now.

Through many dangers, toils, and snares
I have already come.
'Tis grace has brought me safe thus far,
And grace will lead me home.[1]

Tanya's voice trembled as they sang. *Dangers, toils, and snares.* There had been many of them, but God had been faithful. And grace would lead her home. It would be there for her children as well. Perhaps someday they could stand in a family circle in glory and sing about God's amazing grace.

---

[1] "Amazing Grace," by John Newton (1772).

chapter 57

"I Will Lift Up My Eyes"

2021

"Here's your jar of milk," Connie said as she stepped inside.

Tanya turned from where she stood at the kitchen sink, peeling red beets for borsch. "Oh, thank you."

"How have you been feeling?" Connie asked, setting the jar on the table. "I keep thinking about you."

"About the same," Tanya said. She sat down on a chair and motioned for Connie to do the same. She enjoyed these weekly chats when Connie was on her milk route. "I don't have much energy, but I can help around the house. I often wish I could do more outside work. My mind tells me I could do it, but my body says otherwise."

Connie nodded. "That would be tough! You must take care of yourself. But I have a question. Next weekend Wayne needs to preach in

Chernivtsi. Some of our family would like to go along and spend a few days in the Carpathian Mountains. I've heard you say you would like to go to the mountains with your family. Would you be up to going with us?"

Tanya could hardly believe her ears. For years she had dreamed of going to the Carpathians with her family. But that dream had died along with so many others when cancer began to ravage her body. To think of going on a family trip was almost too good to be true. But then she thought of her husband. Would he agree to this? "Oh, that would be wonderful!" she said. "But I don't know what Valentine will say."

Connie nodded. "I understand. Wayne will talk to him about it. We first wanted to make sure you were willing to try it. Do you think you could handle such a trip?"

Tanya thought for a moment. "If Valentine can be persuaded, I will go. It won't be easy, but I think it will be worth it."

The next Saturday when the Hurshes' Sprinter pulled up to the Kosenko home, everyone was ready to go. "Where are we going to put all our stuff?" Valentine asked in surprise when he saw the loaded van. "Are you sure you have room for us?"

"Oh, yes! If you're willing to sit tight," Wayne laughed. "You and Tanya can sit in the front with me, and the girls can join the rest of my family in the back."

Before leaving, they paused for prayer. Tanya could feel God's presence, but the road to Chernivtsi was bumpy as always.

The excitement in the back of the van ran high. Little Anechka was thrilled to be going on a trip, and she bounced happily from one person's lap to the next.

The bumps in the road jarred Tanya, causing her bones to ache, but the sounds of laughter and enjoyment reminded her why she was taking this trip. She was doing it for her children. She wanted them to have good memories.

It was after midnight when the van bounced up to the Chernivtsi church house. Tanya's legs shook as she got out of the van. The trip had been almost too much for her.

The next morning at church, Tanya was happy to see friends she had not seen for a long time. Many of the church people's faces were familiar. She had learned to know them when the two churches met halfway every year for an Easter Monday picnic, but this was her first time at the Chernivtsi church.

After lunch with some friends, they again piled into the Sprinter. Rain poured from the dark clouds, hiding some of the scenic beauty as the van wound its way up the mountain roads. Pavel, an acquaintance who knew the mountains well, drove ahead of them, guiding them up the mountain.

Deeper and deeper into the glory of the mountains they drove. Finally the road ended at a rushing river. Several logs lay across the river, leading to a steep trail going on up the mountain.

"Where are we staying?" Bogdonna asked dubiously.

"I think it's in one of the houses up there," someone said, pointing to several little huts farther up the trail.

Pavel parked his vehicle and came over to the van window. "Here we are! Welcome to the Carpathians!"

There was an excited scramble as everyone tumbled out. The rain had ended, and the sun broke through the clouds as if to welcome them.

Pavel and his father grabbed some of the suitcases and began the trek across the bridge and up the slippery path. The rest followed. Tanya dared not look too closely at the water that swirled beneath her as she inched her way across the bridge.

Several times she stopped to catch her breath. She noticed she was not the only one who ran out of breath as they climbed. Only the two mountaineers and a few of the young boys made it to the house without stopping.

"It's beautiful, isn't it?" Anya asked as she paused beside Tanya. She set down her suitcase and looked out over the mountains. Low clouds hung below them like lace, covering the valley below. Above them floated more clouds, with a few rays of sunlight filtering through.

"It's lovely!" Tanya answered. She took a deep breath as she gazed at the scene before them. The river wound its way through the rich green valley, and here and there little houses dotted the mountainside. "The air feels so fresh—so clean!" she exclaimed.

"Do you think you can make it up to the house?" Anya asked. She nodded toward the little cottage still a hundred meters away.

"Yes, I'll be fine. But it's a workout."

By the time they reached the little house, Pavel had already gotten a fire going in the stove. Tanya huddled next to it, soaking in the warmth. The damp mountain air had chilled her to the bone.

The little house built on the side of the mountain was tiny, but Pavel assured them it was large enough to raise a family of five children. "You're welcome to use the summer kitchen too," he added, showing them the little room next to the house. A tiny wood stove took up a large portion of it. Two single beds were squeezed against the wall.

"I built this house with my own hands and raised my children here," Pavel's father said. "I would still live here if my children would let me, but they took me to the city with them." He stroked the beams fondly. "There's no better place to live than in the mountains."

"Papa, maybe you could play a song or two for them," Pavel suggested.

The little old man reached down into his sock and pulled out a flute. With a face wreathed in delight, he played several mountain folk songs. The music seemed to bounce off the mountain walls and fill the air with magic.

Tanya watched with interest. It seemed they had stepped back in time. Something about the wizened old man triggered memories of her great-grandpa Prokip. Although he had died when she was just a child, he had always held a special place in her heart.

"Well, we really should be going," Pavel said. "We'd like to get back home before dark." He handed the key to Wayne. "Enjoy your stay here. Maybe you'll like it so much that you'll want to buy the place. It's for sale, you know."

As soon as the hosts were out of earshot, Bogdonna burst out, "I thought we would be in a nice house! This place is tiny, and there are no conveniences!"

"At least it's clean," Tanya replied.

"And the view outside is lovely!" someone else chimed in. "I think we'll have a good time."

Darkness was setting in as Valentine built a fire and began grilling sausages. By the time supper was ready, the fire in the stove had taken some of the dampness out of the house.

Excitement and happiness surged through the air as the two families crowded into the living room and made plans for the rest of their stay. Before retiring for the night, they knelt together in prayer. As Tanya looked around the circle of loved ones, her heart swelled with gratitude.

Somehow little Anechka missed the excitement and novelty of the cabin experience. The only time she had ever slept away from home was in the hospital. For her, this was no picnic. "Take me home!" she cried. "I want to sleep in my own bed!"

Valentine tried to explain that this would be their home for only a few days, but she was still terrified. "Take me home to my bed!" she screamed again and again. Tanya also tried to comfort her, but she kept screaming in fright. Finally her crying subsided, and she drifted off to sleep.

During the night, a storm came up. The wind whirled around the summer kitchen, and the rain pounded on the windows. "What kind of adventure is this supposed to be?" Valentine muttered. "Pretty soon we'll get washed down to the river! Maybe Anechka is right; we should have stayed at home."

The sky was still heavy with rain when they awoke the next morning, but a night's rest and the light of morning had refreshed the travelers. By noon, the rain had ended and fluffy white clouds dotted the sky.

"Would you like for me to stay here with you?" Connie asked Tanya as the others prepared to go for a drive to enjoy more of the majestic mountains. "I don't mind staying with you."

"Don't worry about me," Tanya assured her. "I'll be fine by myself. I'll be glad for some peace and quiet. And I can wash the dishes. I don't feel like I can contribute much on this trip, but that is one thing I can do."

"We can work on the dishes together," Connie protested.

"Honestly, it will make me feel good if I can do them," Tanya replied.

Tanya watched a bit longingly as everyone else hiked down the steep path, back across the shaky bridge, and to the van. The rain had turned the path into a slide, and Tanya couldn't help but chuckle as she saw them slipping and sliding in the mud.

Going with them was not an option. After the hard ascent the day before, Tanya was content to stay put. She dipped water from the filled bucket at the well and put a kettle on the stove to heat. She was glad she could at least do the dishes.

After the dishes were done, she settled on the bed with her Bible. Through the window, she had a good view of the mountains. She flipped through her Bible until she found the Psalm she was looking for: "I will lift up mine eyes unto the hills, from whence cometh my help. My help cometh from the Lord, which made heaven and earth."[1] She turned her gaze back to the mountain. "Yes, Lord, I feel your presence. I lift my eyes up to you, the Creator of all this glory."

Deep in her heart, Tanya sensed that she was nearing the end of her battle with cancer. The splendor of the mountains stirred a longing for the glories of heaven.

By the time the others returned from their explorations, Tanya's soul was refreshed. That evening while the others braved the cold mountain air and sat around the fire watching Valentine grill supper, Anya joined Tanya in the summer kitchen.

"I am so glad we could go on this trip," Tanya said. "It would have been easier to stay at home. This trip might even shorten my life by a few days, but that's all right. I'm glad we came." She straightened her shoulders and smiled. "I want my children to remember more than just hospitals, pain, and suffering."

Leaving for home the next day seemed symbolic to Tanya. She was nearing the valley of death, but she looked forward with courage. The Maker of the majestic mountains would be with her as she walked through the valley. She was not alone.

---

[1] Psalm 121:1-2

chapter 58

Trials and Temptations

2021

The trips to the hospital for treatment caused more pain than relief, so Tanya finally gave up the fight. No longer did she pray for healing; she only interceded for patience to be faithful to the end.

The summer produced an abundance of fresh fruits and vegetables, and from her seat on the couch, Tanya managed the canning. She knew the day was nearing when Marina would have to do it all on her own, and Tanya determined to do everything she could to prepare her for that day.

Some days the pain was so strong that Tanya never left her room. While the injections of pain reliever took the edge off her pain, it left her nauseated and tired.

When Tanya's fortieth birthday neared, the sisters from church planned a birthday party for her. It was kind of them, but it was the last thing Tanya felt like doing.

"Please forgive me," she said, "but I'm just not up to it. I'm in too much pain to be sociable." The ladies were kind and understanding, but Tanya felt bad.

On the day of her birthday, Connie stopped by with a big box. "Happy fortieth birthday, dear Tanya! We want you to know how special you are to us, so we prepared forty gifts for you."

"You didn't have to!" Tanya protested. "I really don't need anything!"

"We wanted to do this! The gifts are small and practical, hopefully things you and your family can enjoy and use. Open one each day and make your birthday last as long as possible."

After Connie left, Tanya and the girls clustered around the box, feeling the packages and trying to guess what was in them.

"Are you really allowed to open only one gift a day?" Marina wondered.

"They are your birthday gifts; you should be able to open them whenever you want!" Bogdonna added.

"I'll open them whenever I need a bit of extra encouragement," Tanya said. "It might be more than one a day, but I don't think it matters."

Before a week had passed, all the gifts were opened. Most of them were practical ones that the whole family could enjoy. There were boxes of tea, a pack of Jell-O, a package of cookies, a candle, and many others.

Near the bottom of the box, Tanya found a package that made her cry. It was a photo album full of photos from the ten years Tanya had been attending church. As she paged through the album, she walked back memory's lane: her baptism, a family picture when Bogdonna was a little girl, school days when she was a teacher. Many were photos she had never seen before. Not only were they a gift to her, they would also keep the memories alive for her daughters.

"I would like to go to church today," Tanya said hesitantly as the family ate breakfast one Sunday morning. "Would one of you push me in the wheelchair?"

"But are you sure you are up to it?" Marina asked.

Tanya shook her head. "Barely, but I need to get out. I want to see my church family and be at the house of prayer once more. I probably won't be able to stay for the whole service, but I want to be there for a while."

"I'll push you, Mama," Bogdonna said, her ever brave smile on her face. "It was so kind of the church to give us a wheelchair."

Since the church services were now being held at the remodeled printshop, it was within walking distance of the Kosenko home. But Tanya's days of walking were over. Although she could still take a few steps around the house, walking the half mile to church was not an option.

As Bogdonna pushed the wheelchair down the road, Tanya smiled despite her pain. Marina held Anechka's hand and walked next to the wheelchair, while Valentine walked ahead of them.

Bogdonna pushed the chair carefully, trying to avoid the bumps on the road. Even so, Tanya winced in pain, but she continued smiling bravely.

Joy surged within Tanya's heart as they neared the church house. Several weeks had passed since she had been to church. How good it would be to see everyone again!

Tanya noticed a strange hush as Bogdonna pushed the wheelchair to a corner at the back of the church. "Tanya, it's so good to see you!" said one sister as she squeezed her hand. "How have you been?"

"About the same," Tanya replied. "I should probably not have forced myself to come to church today, but I wanted to see everyone again!"

"We're happy to have you here."

Love and sympathy pooled in the eyes of the sisters as they paused by the wheelchair to speak a word to Tanya. Many of them had not seen her for several weeks, and in that time, Tanya's health had gone from bad to worse. Tanya was relieved when the service began.

"Let's sing 'What a Friend We Have in Jesus,'" announced the song leader.

> *Have we trials and temptations?*
> *Is there sorrow anywhere?*
> *We should never be discouraged.*
> *Take it to the Lord in prayer.*[1]

As the congregation stood to sing, Tanya bowed her head and let the salty tears trickle. Right now it seemed her whole life was nothing but trials and temptations. Discouragement hung over her like a cloud, threatening to hide the rays of sunshine.

Tanya was so deep in thought that she barely noticed when the congregation finished singing and a visiting brother took his place behind the pulpit.

"Are trials from God? Or are they from the devil? How should we feel about trials that come into our life?"

Tanya leaned forward in her wheelchair, eager to hear how the speaker would answer the questions. It was almost as if he had been reading her mind.

"Turn with me to James 1. 'My brethren, count it all joy when ye fall into divers temptations…Blessed is the man that endureth temptation: for when he is tried, he shall receive the crown of life, which the Lord hath promised to them that love Him.' Brothers and sisters, if you are experiencing a trial, take courage. Trials give us a choice. How will we respond?"

---

[1] Written by Joseph Scriven in 1855.

The words fell on Tanya like a refreshing rain on parched ground. But by the time the children returned from their Sunday school classes, pain burned in her muscles, making it nearly impossible to concentrate on the service.

"Mama, it's too bad we have to go home now," Bogdonna said as she pushed the wheelchair toward home. "You didn't even hear the main message."

"It's all right," Tanya said. "It was worth going to hear the devotions and singing. And God sent the visiting brother to preach exactly what I needed to hear."

Late one evening, Tanya stirred as she heard footsteps on the porch. She glanced at the clock; it was too early for the others to be coming home from prayer meeting. Someone rapped gently on the door and then opened it several centimeters. "Knock, knock. May I come in?"

Tanya recognized the voice of her friend. "Yes, Anya, come in." She patted the couch beside her. "Come in and make yourself at home."

Anya slipped off her shoes and sat on the couch next to Tanya. "I was at prayer meeting this evening, and all the sisters in our group prayed for you. When it was time for the topic, I just couldn't stop thinking about you. I knew you were here alone, so I decided to come sit with you."

"Thank you, dear. It does get a little lonely being here alone. But I am glad for the quiet."

"How are you?" Anya asked. "I keep thinking of you."

"Like usual." The smile on Tanya's face was tired. "I'm not getting better, but neither am I much worse. The pain is constant."

The minutes slipped by as they visited.

"What were the prayer requests tonight?" Tanya wondered. "I often pray when I lie awake at night and can't sleep. It's about the only thing I can do for others these days."

Anya nodded, too choked up to say much. "We need your prayers."

The two friends chatted about many things, but finally Tanya brought up a topic that was weighing on her mind. It had been bothering her for quite a while, but she dreaded bringing it up.

"I keep thinking about what will happen when school starts. I really want Marina to be able to go to school. She is so close to graduating."

Anya nodded, knowing full well that if it had not been for Tanya's sickness, Marina would have graduated long before now.

"And I'm worried about Anechka," Tanya continued, shifting the pillows behind her back. "I don't know if I will still be here when school starts. I don't like to think of Anechka staying at home alone with Valentine every day while the girls are at school." Tanya's voice trailed off, and a shadow crossed her face. "You're not teaching this year, are you? Would you consider…?" She paused, unable to continue. She hated to ask for favors.

"Do you think Anechka would be happy staying with me?" Anya offered hesitantly.

"Would you mind?" Tanya asked, her eyes brimming with relief. "It would mean so much to me if I knew she'll be taken care of. You have a way with her. She likes you."

Anya nodded. "I'd be glad to look after her. I love Anechka dearly." Her voice faltered. "But I can't take your place."

The two sat in silence for a moment, each deep in thought. "You don't know what a load you've taken off my shoulders," Tanya said. "It means so much to know that Anechka will be taken care of after…after I'm gone."

chapter 59

The Pilot

2021

"Marina!" The urgency in Tanya's voice woke Marina from her sleep in the next room. "Marina! Come here, please!"

Marina rubbed the sleep from her eyes and hurried to her mother's bedroom. "Yes, Mama?" She stepped to her mother's side, putting her hand gently on her mother's shoulder. "Is it time for a shot?"

Tanya nodded miserably. "I tried to do it myself, but I couldn't keep my balance."

Marina helped her mother to her feet. While Tanya leaned against the cupboard for support, Marina gave her a shot in her hip.

"My legs are so heavy," Tanya groaned. "They hurt!"

Marina blinked back tears as she helped Tanya back into bed. "Your legs are more swollen than ever, Mama, aren't they?"

Tanya nodded. The dread in her heart felt as heavy as her legs. *My kidneys must be giving out.* She had noticed it a week ago already. Every day her legs felt heavier, and she felt weaker. "Marina," Tanya's voice was just a whisper, "I think it's time for me to go to the hospital."

"No, Mama," Marina protested. "Can't you stay here?"

Tanya shook her head. "Maybe the doctors can help me get rid of the fluid in my legs. Maybe they can find a better pain reliever."

Marina squeezed her mother's hand. "Let's see what Papa says when he comes in for breakfast."

―――

"Tanya." Valentine stepped to the side of the bed and sat down.

Tanya nodded but did not lift her head.

"Marina said you wanted to talk to me?"

Again Tanya nodded. "I would like to go to the hospital." Her voice was barely above a whisper. "Could you please call someone to take me?"

"Do you think they can help you?" he asked.

Tanya shrugged her shoulders. "Maybe they can at least get rid of the fluid in my legs. I can't even walk by myself anymore."

"Are you sure it's the thing to do?" Valentine could see that Tanya was not doing well, but he felt so helpless. "They might keep you in the hospital." He hesitated for a moment. "The girls likely wouldn't be allowed to visit you, and I'm really busy right now. You'd be by yourself." He did not intend to sound unkind. He only wanted to help her think it through.

"I thought about that, but I still want to go. I can't stand it here any longer."

He looked at her questioningly. What had she meant by that? "You mean you can't stand the pain?"

"The pain, the stress, everything. I just need to go. You don't need me here. I don't want the little girls to see me suffer."

Valentine nodded, at a loss for words. What could he say? It would be foolish to tell her they needed her at home when his actions said otherwise. Perhaps she was right. Maybe it would be best for Bogdonna and Anechka to not have to watch their mother suffer.

Several hours later, the arrangements were made. Tanya was packing her suitcase when the phone rang. She sighed when she saw it was Alla, a sister in the church. Although Tanya loved her dearly, she didn't feel like talking. Taking a deep breath, she answered the phone, willing her voice to sound strong.

"Hello, Tanya." Alla's voice sounded excited. "How are you today?"

It was a question Tanya had learned to dread. What could she say? She did not like to dwell on the negative, but neither could she deny the truth. "About the same," she replied.

"You're not planning on going anywhere, are you?" Alla seemed to burst with eagerness. Without waiting for Tanya to respond, she plunged on. "Oh, Tanya, I had a dream last night. I dreamed you were the pilot of a large airplane."

Tanya could not keep back a smile. "Me, a pilot? I've never even been on an airplane!"

"Yes, you were the pilot," Alla rushed on. "You were flying the plane toward heaven."

A lump formed in Tanya's throat.

"And you know what, Tanya?" Alla cleared her throat. "Your whole family was on that plane. Our whole congregation was on it. You were flying our church to heaven!"

After the phone call ended, Tanya sat dazed. Could it be that she was like a pilot, leading her family and her church to heaven? A thrill of excitement surged through her. *I'm packing my bags not just to go to the hospital—but to heaven.* She smiled as she folded her favorite blanket

The Pilot

and added it to the pile. *I will need these things for only a little while.* The calmness of her heart surprised her.

She was preparing for her final flight. And someday, by God's grace, they would all be together in heaven.

chapter 60

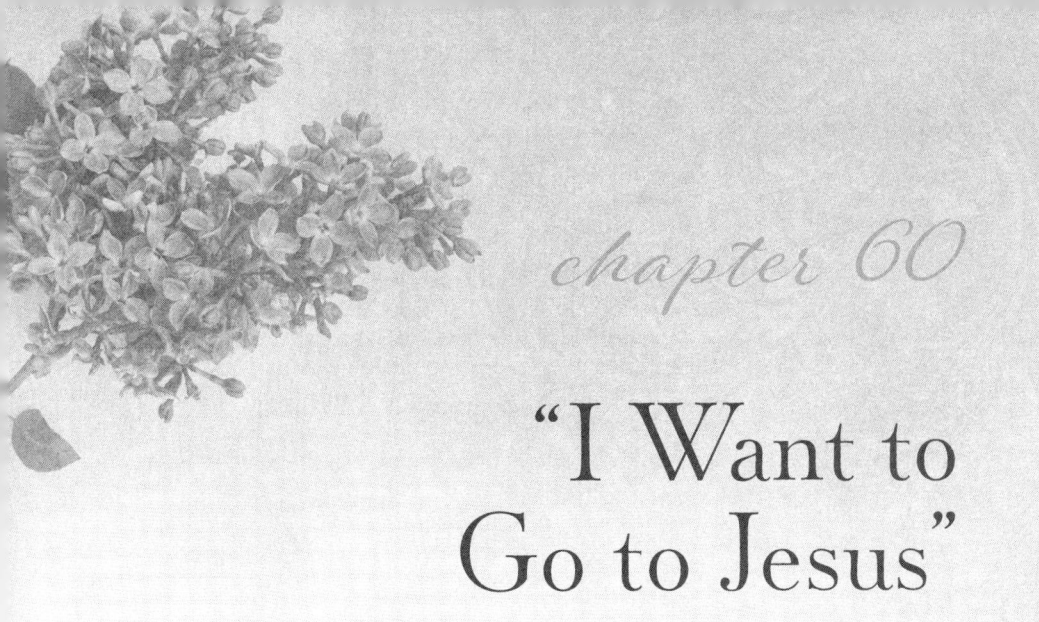

"I Want to Go to Jesus"

2021

Thin rays of sunshine filtered through the clouds, bringing a dim light into the hospital room where Tanya sat. The first night in the hospital had passed. Tanya had drifted in and out of sleep, never able to rest soundly. She looked up when Marina returned from the hospital café with a cup of hot tea.

"Here's some tea, Mama." Marina carefully poured half of the steaming liquid into Tanya's cup. While they sipped their morning tea, they discussed their day.

"I'll stay here until the doctor checks in on you. But I should probably go home to make lunch for Papa and the girls," Marina said.

Tanya nodded.

"Do you mind staying here alone?" Marina wondered. "Or would you like someone to come? I plan to come back for the night."

Tanya shrugged. "I don't know. I can probably stay here alone. I hate to be a bother." She bit her lip and looked out the window.

"Last night at church, Anya asked if there's anything she can do to help. Shall I ask her to come?"

Tanya's lips curved into a faint smile. "I would be glad if she wants to come."

"Okay, I'll tell her. I think she really wants to come. And it will be good for you."

That afternoon Tanya greeted her visitor with a smile. Despite her earlier words, it felt good to have someone to talk to.

"Marina and I have it all figured out," Anya said. "She will try to be here at night and until midmorning, then I will be with you during the afternoon."

"How's Volodia?"

"You mean the man who was admitted last night from your village?" the nurse asked. "He's doing all right. He asked about you and wondered how you were doing."

After the nurse left, Tanya turned to Anya, who was there for the afternoon. "Could you please get a wheelchair for me?"

Anya looked surprised. Tanya had not left her hospital room for a week. She had refused when Marina had offered to take her on a stroll down the hospital hall.

Tanya moaned softly as Anya lifted her heavy legs onto the foot prop. "Take me to Volodia's room," she requested.

Following the nurse's directions, they headed for Volodia's room in the opposite wing of the hospital. The small room was crowded with five ailing men, leaving little room for the wheelchair.

"Tanya!" Volodia said in surprise when he saw who the visitor was. "I've been thinking about you ever since I heard that you were also in this hospital. I wanted to come and visit you."

"Dyed Volodia, it's good to see you." Tanya's voice was strong as she talked to her old village friend. "How are you doing? I was sorry to hear that you are sick."

Volodia explained his ailments, then looked keenly at Tanya. "How are you doing? Are you getting better?"

"No." A sad smile played on her lips. "I'm not getting better, but I am getting ready."

"Ready for what?" Volodia asked.

"For eternity."

Volodia looked at her questioningly, not sure how to respond.

"My time is almost over," Tanya explained. "I'm getting ready for heaven. Soon I'll be leaving all this behind. God has a better home prepared for me. None of us know when we will die. The main thing is that we are ready. If we have asked the Lord to forgive our sins and are living in obedience to Him, we don't need to be afraid of dying."

The two chatted a little longer, and then Tanya was ready to go back to her room. She had exhausted her strength and could talk no longer.

"Tanya, how long do you think they will keep you here?" Anya asked one day.

Tanya shook her head sadly. "I don't know. The doctor said there's nothing more he can do for me, but I don't want to go home. I just want to go to heaven."

"Why don't you want to go home?" Anya probed.

"I can't handle the stress and the noise," Tanya replied. "And I don't want my little girls to see me like this."

The next morning Anya again brought up the subject. "Tanya dear, I have a suggestion. Would you consider coming to my house? You could stay with me, and Marina and I could take care of you. It would be quieter than here at the hospital, and you would be closer to your family."

"But I don't want to be a bother." Tears filled Tanya's eyes and her voice was hushed. "I just want to go to Jesus!"

"I know," Anya said, stroking her back. "But you're not a bother. I want you to come. I would count it a privilege."

Tanya's eyes filled with tears. "Thank you so much. I am willing to come."

The move to Anya's house was not easy. The ride from the hospital jarred Tanya's cancer-eaten bones, and she was in great pain. For hours, nothing could numb her pain. "Lord, I cannot bear this pain!" she cried. "It hurts so much; I'm losing my mind. Won't you please come for me?"

Each breath became a prayer as Tanya begged God for mercy and relief from the pain. But the sky was dark. And in that deep darkness, God felt far away.

Gradually, as time passed, her pain lessened and she could rest.

Over the next few days, Tanya slowly became weaker. She was thankful for Anya and Marina's care for her, but the pain and discomfort made her long for heaven.

Tanya's eyes lit up every time Bogdonna and Anechka came to visit her. She was so glad to see them, but there was also a sadness. She knew her time with them was limited.

One great pain in Tanya's heart remained unresolved: *Where is Valentine? Why doesn't he come to see me? I know he can't handle the pain. But please, God, have him come. I want to see him.*

chapter 61

Faithful to the End

September 11, 2021

The barking of the dog announced someone's arrival. When Anya went to the door, there stood Bogdonna and Anechka.

"We came to see Mama," Bogdonna said. She held a bouquet of roses. Anechka, her eyes shining in anticipation, clutched a piece of chocolate.

"Come in!" Anya welcomed. "I'm so glad you came. Your mama will be happy to see you!" She lowered her voice. "She is getting weaker and might not talk. But she can still hear, so talk to her."

Bogdonna nodded soberly.

"Tanya, you have visitors!" Anya announced. "Bogdonna and Anechka have come to see you!"

With effort, Tanya lifted her head and reached for her daughters. She wrapped Anechka in a brief hug and squeezed Bogdonna's hand.

Then she dropped her head back on her pillow.

"Mama, I brought some flowers for you!" Bogdonna said, holding out the roses.

Tanya nodded.

"And here's a chocolate for you!" Anechka set the candy on the stand beside her mother.

For a moment the girls stood awkwardly, watching their mother. Was this really their mama? Bogdonna sat beside Tanya and caressed her back.

"Bogdonna, are you eager for school?" Anya asked. "Who will be in your class?"

With a bit of coaching, Bogdonna talked about her new teacher, her classmates, and other interesting tidbits. Although Tanya did not talk, she nodded her head and smiled at times. It was easy to see that she was listening and could understand what they were saying.

Bogdonna and Anechka smiled bravely as they left. But inwardly, their hearts were torn. Would Mama keep getting worse? Would she die?

Later that afternoon, Tanya's friend Leah stopped in. She sat at Tanya's side and encouraged her. "Sister Tanya, God cares about you. He has not left you." Gently she held Tanya's hand. "He loves you. Can you feel His love?"

Slowly but confidently, Tanya nodded her head. Even in the midst of the darkness, Tanya could still feel God's love and presence.

"Mama, won't you please try my borsch?" Marina pleaded. "Try it and then tell me if it tastes all right. Oksana told me how to make it."

Tanya gave a slight shake of her head.

Marina looked at Anya and explained. "Mama always made the

borsch. Even when she didn't feel well, she made the borsch. I've hardly ever done it." Her voice trembled.

When the phone rang, Marina answered, her face still troubled.

"How's your mama?" a church sister asked.

Marina's shoulders sagged as she searched for an answer. "She's getting closer and closer to the goal." Her lip quivered.

A few minutes later the phone rang again. "Papa says I need to go home and help him," Marina said after the call had ended. "I'll come back for the night." She carried the untouched bowl of borsch to the kitchen, then returned to her mother's side.

"Mama, I am going home, but I'll be back tonight." She squeezed her mother's hand.

There was no response, only the shallow, ragged breathing.

As Marina left, Anya followed her out to the entrance. "Marina," she said in a hushed tone, "do you know what dress your mama wants to be buried in? We need to make sure her clothes are ready."

"You're right. I don't think it will be much longer." Marina's hands trembled as she tied her shoes. She straightened and smiled bravely. "Mama wants to be buried in her baptismal dress. I'll see if I can find it."

"Please do. Bring it along when you come tonight. And, Marina, I really think your papa should come too."

Marina shrugged her shoulders. "I know he should, but he won't want to." She bit her lip and turned away. "He never even asks how Mama is doing. He won't want to come."

"Not even if he knows it's his last chance to see her?" Anya asked.

"Maybe. I'll try to persuade him."

After Marina left, Anya sat on the floor beside Tanya's couch, holding her hand. The lump in her throat grew, and tears clouded her eyes. How long would it be until Tanya was released from her body of pain?

Anya reached for a songbook. She didn't know if Tanya could hear her, but she sang song after song. Later in the afternoon, her mother Connie arrived, and they kept singing. They were singing "Safe in the Arms of Jesus" when the dog again announced someone's arrival.

Anya opened the door. There stood Marina—and Valentine. Sorrow was written across his face. It had not been easy for him to come. He followed Marina to the living room.

"Tanya, I have come to see you." His voice was husky and tinged with pain. He knelt by his wife and lifted her limp hand into his strong, work-stained one. "Tanya, my dear, can you hear me?"

The form that had been lying so still for hours suddenly stirred. Tanya opened her eyes in wonder. "Valentine!" The voice that had been silent for so long now spoke audibly.

"Yes, dear, it's me." Valentine squeezed her hand. "How are you doing? Do you have a lot of pain?"

Tanya shook her head and tried to speak, but no words came.

For nearly half an hour Valentine knelt by her side. He asked her for forgiveness and assured her of his love.

Tanya listened, wide awake, her eyes fixed on the man with whom she had shared so much of her life.

"I must go," Valentine finally said reluctantly. "The little girls are at home alone. Shall we pray before I leave?"

Marina dropped to her knees beside her papa.

"I want to stand." The clear, audible voice startled Valentine and Marina. Tanya was straining to sit up.

"But, Mama, you can't stand!" Marina protested.

"I want to stand!" Tanya repeated, more urgently this time.

"Here, Mama, let me help you sit up. You can't stand, but maybe you can sit up." Tenderly Marina and Valentine pulled Tanya to her favorite sitting position. Valentine then prayed, committing his wife to the Lord and begging for God's presence.

Before he left, he squeezed Tanya's hand and told her goodbye. The only answer was a slight nod. Then Valentine was gone, swallowed into the darkness of the night.

After Valentine left, Anya and Connie joined Marina around Tanya's bed, where she sat with her head bowed on a pillow in front of her, seemingly asleep. They listened as Marina told of her mother's amazing response to her father's visit.

"Oh, I think it's time for a morphine shot," Marina said, glancing at the clock. She broke the vial of morphine and was filling the syringe when Anya spoke.

"Marina," she called softly, "I don't think she will need that shot." Her voice broke as she reached for Tanya's hand. "Tanya, my friend, can you hear me?"

There was no response. Tanya's hand hung heavy and lifeless. The angels had come and carried her away.

"Mama!" Marina rushed to her side and quickly felt for a pulse. There was none. "Mama! Oh, Mama!"

A sacred hush and a holy triumph filled the room. Tanya had been faithful to the end. She had made it home.

Epilogue

The redeeming grace that shone from Tanya's life is reflected in her daughters today. Marina is studying in college and planning her wedding to Jonathan Mast. Bogdonna attends school and keeps house for her papa and little sister. Anechka brings sunshine wherever she goes.

Valentine continues to bring his little family to church every Sunday. Despite his addictions and the grief of losing his wife, he is searching for God and striving to do what is right. Pray that God's grace would continue to transform his life.

Author's Note

Tanya and I became close friends when we taught school together from 2012 to 2014. As we lived life together, I heard stories from her past and began dreaming of someday writing her life story. I pictured the two of us as wrinkled babushkas, sitting on the porch, looking back over the years and discussing the stories we wanted to include in the book.

God, however, had other plans. Never did I imagine that her story would end so early, or that it would include cancer and so much suffering and pain. I had shared my idea of writing a book with Tanya earlier, so when cancer came, I brought it up again. She agreed it was time to begin.

As the cancer ravaged her body and the future looked bleaker, we began spending more time talking about the past. This book was not built on formal interviews, but on years of living as close friends. Tanya was as much a part of my life as I was of hers. When she died, a part of me died too.

Walking with Tanya through her cancer journey was a cherished gift, but one wrapped in so many layers of pain. Her life and death have impacted my life forever. In the days of grief that followed her death, I found writing her story and caring for her little girl to be painfully healing.

Tanya's legacy lives on. Many of those who knew her remember the testimonies she shared. They remember her faith, her courage, and God's grace that showed through her weakness.

Tanya's desire was to give God the glory for His work in her life. She often recited the words from her favorite poem, "Pain Is Never Wasted."

> *Pain is never without gain,*
> *Hearts are never hurt in vain.*
> *Every tear you ever cry,*
> *God will use to beautify.*

Today, through this book, Tanya still testifies that God is gracious and faithful.

Farewell, My Friend

I did not hear the angels' wings or whispered words, "Let's go."
I only felt their presence sweet, for they were there, I know.
You left so quietly, dear friend. A breath and you were gone.
But mem'ries of the times we shared forever will live on.
It hurt my heart to see you lie in death so very still,
But greater far the anguished cry when you lay weak and ill.
Your agony had shattered all my trust in God's great care.
But as you suffered, wrapped in pain, each breath became a prayer.
Although I could not feel God's love, His tenderness, and grace,
You testified that He was there as death stared in your face.

Because of you, I choose to trust and hold the Father's hand,
Although my heart is wounded deep and I can't understand
Why God allowed such suffering; why He allowed such pain,
But this I know that our great loss is now your rightful gain.
I choose to follow in your steps and trust the Father's heart.
I'll look to Him in hour of need and trust He'll grace impart.
And, Tanya dear, my precious friend, though parted now we be,
I promise, by the grace of God, to serve Him faithfully.
And someday soon we'll meet again, on heaven's golden shore,
And there together we will praise our Savior evermore.

With love,
Anya

About the Author

Anya Hursh lives in a quaint village house in Ukraine, the country she has called home for most of her life. She spends her days wrestling with words, teaching English classes, and investing in the lives of the people around her. She writes to process life and to record God's faithfulness. She loves beauty, safety, and peace, and has learned that these things can be found even among the shards and shrapnel of a war-torn country.

Home is her happy place, but she also finds fulfillment in serving in parts of the country where the needs—and sometimes the dangers—are great. She feels rich to have friendships that span decades of ages and oceans of water. Stop by her cottage for a visit and a cup of tea, or email her at redeeming.grace.ua@gmail.com. You can also write to her in care of Christian Aid Ministries, P.O. Box 360, Berlin, Ohio 44610.

About Christian Aid Ministries

*C*hristian Aid Ministries was founded in 1981 as a nonprofit, tax-exempt 501(c)(3) organization. Its primary purpose is to provide a trustworthy and efficient channel for Amish, Mennonite, and other conservative Anabaptist groups and individuals to minister to physical and spiritual needs around the world. This is in response to the command to "Do good unto all men, especially unto them who are of the household of faith" (Galatians 6:10).

CAM supporters provide millions of pounds of food, clothing, Bibles, medicines, and other aid each year. Supporters' funds also help victims of disasters in the U.S. and abroad, put up Gospel billboards in the U.S., and provide Biblical teaching and self-help resources. CAM's main purposes for providing aid are to help and encourage God's people and bring the Gospel to a lost and dying world.

The Way to God and Peace

We live in a world contaminated by sin. Sin is anything that goes against God's holy standards. When we do not follow the guidelines that God our Creator gave us, we are guilty of sin. Sin separates us from God, the source of life.

Since the time when the first man and woman, Adam and Eve, sinned in the Garden of Eden, sin has been universal. The Bible says that we all have "sinned and come short of the glory of God" (Romans 3:23). It also says that the natural consequence for that sin is eternal death, or punishment in an eternal hell: "Then when lust hath conceived, it bringeth forth sin: and sin, when it is finished, bringeth forth death" (James 1:15).

But we do not have to suffer eternal death in hell. God provided forgiveness for our sins through the death of His only Son, Jesus Christ. Because Jesus was perfect and without sin, He could die in our place. "For God so loved the world that he gave his only begotten Son, that whosoever believeth in him should not perish, but have everlasting life" (John 3:16).

A sacrifice is something given to benefit someone else. It costs the giver greatly. Jesus was God's sacrifice. Jesus' death takes away the penalty of sin for all those who accept this sacrifice and truly repent of their sins. To repent of sins means to be truly sorry for and turn away from the things we have done that have violated God's standards (Acts 2:38; 3:19).

Jesus died, but He did not remain dead. After three days, God's Spirit miraculously raised Him to life again. God's Spirit does something similar in us. When we receive Jesus as our sacrifice and repent of our sins, our hearts are changed. We become spiritually alive! We develop new desires and attitudes (2 Corinthians 5:17). We begin to make choices that please God (1 John 3:9). If we do fail and commit sins, we can ask God for forgiveness. "If we confess our sins, he is faithful and just to forgive us our sins, and to cleanse us from all unrighteousness" (1 John 1:9).

Once our hearts have been changed, we want to continue growing spiritually. We will be happy to let Jesus be the Master of our lives and will want to become more like Him. To do this, we must meditate on God's Word and commune with God in prayer. We will testify to others of this change by being baptized and sharing the good news of God's victory over sin and death. Fellowship with a faithful group of believers will strengthen our walk with God (1 John 1:7).